FOR EVERY SEASON

Daily Devotions *by Greg Laurie*

ALLEN DAVID
PUBLISHERS Dana Point, California

FOR EVERY SEASON

ISBN 0-9762400-0-9

Printed in the United States of America.

Published by: Allen David Publishers—Dana Point, California
Coordination: FM Management, Ltd.
Cover photo: Peter Barrett for Masterfile ©2004
Copyediting: Karla Pedrow
Design: Highgate Cross+Cathey, Ltd.

Now when they saw the boldness of Peter and John, and perceived that they

were uneducated and untrained men, they marveled. And they realized that

they had been with Jesus. (Acts 4:13)

Monday

KEEPING PACE

"I strain to reach the end of the race and receive the prize. ..."
(Philippians 3:14 NLT)

I heard about one man who made some New Year's resolutions. In 2001 he said, "I will not get upset when Sam and Charlie make jokes about my baldness." In 2002 it was, "I won't get annoyed when Charlie and Sam kid me about my hairpiece." Then in 2003, "I will not lose my temper when Charlie and Sam laugh at me for wearing a girdle." In 2004, "I will not speak anymore to Charlie and Sam." As the years passed, he changed his resolutions.

We adjust our resolutions as time passes because we are unable to keep them. But we don't need a New Year's resolution. We need a spiritual solution, and it is found in the pages of Scripture. In Philippians 3, the apostle Paul helps us understand what our priorities should be. On more than one occasion, he used athletic metaphors to describe the Christian life. In this passage, he compares it to running a race. But we need to understand that it is not a fifty-yard dash. It is a long-distance run. That is why we must pace ourselves.

It is not all that significant if you have held first place in a race for nine out of ten laps. What matters is the tenth lap. Whoever crosses the finish line first is the winner. The problem is that a lot of people have a yo-yo relationship with God: up and down. Either they are experiencing the ultimate spiritual high or they are down in the dumps. We need spiritual consistency. And we need God's help to stay with it. If we want to win in the race of life, then we need to learn to pace ourselves.

Tuesday

PLAYING BY THE RULES

"Remember that in a race everyone runs, but only one person gets the prize. You also must run in such a way that you will win." (1 Corinthians 9:24 NLT)

If you participate in an athletic event, you must play by the rules. You can't make your own. You can't say, "If I hit the ball eight feet, then that is a home run. Here are my rules." That is not the way it works. You must play by the rules. Even if you hit the ball out of the park, you still must cross and touch every single base. If you miss one base, that home run doesn't count, and you are disqualified.

For example, if you want to compete in track and field in the Olympics, then you must play by the rules. One rule is that athletes are prohibited from using drugs like steroids to enhance their performance. We remember the 1988 Olympic games in which Carl Lewis won the gold medal because Ben Johnson was disqualified for steroid use. Johnson didn't play by the rules.

In the same way, this race of life we are running has a rulebook. It is called the Bible. It is not for us to pick and choose what parts of the Bible we like. You can't say, "I like certain truths in the Bible. I like the part about God's love and forgiveness. But this part about denying yourself and taking up the cross ... that must not be in the original language. I don't believe it." You can't do that. If you are going to run this race, and run to win, then you must play the rules that God has given to you in Scripture. We must play by the rules, or we will be disqualified.

EXCESS BAGGAGE

"Let us strip off every weight that slows us down, especially the sin that so easily hinders our progress. And let us run with endurance the race that God has set before us." (Hebrews 12:1 NLT)

I am the kind of a person who likes to drag a lot of stuff with me when I travel. I have been traveling for many years, yet I still overpack. I want to bring everything I own. But excess baggage makes traveling more complicated.

In the same way, when you are running the race of life, you need to run light. Sometimes we drag along a lot of excess weight. But notice that the Bible tells us to "strip off every weight that slows us down, especially the sin that so easily hinders our progress." Sin is sin, and there are certain non-negotiables to which we must hold fast. Then there might be something that is a weight in your life that may not necessarily be a weight in another's life. By that I mean, there may be something you are doing that is impeding your spiritual progress. Periodically, I need to take stock of my life as a Christian and look at the things I am doing with my time. I need to ask myself the question, "Is it a wing or a weight? Is it speeding me on my way spiritually, or is it slowing me down? Is it increasing my spiritual appetite, or is it dulling it?"

How often we are so busy doing a lot of things that aren't really all that important, but they seem important at the time. We need to ask ourselves if we need to do all of those things. Are they slowing you down? Lay aside the weight and the sin that hinders your progress.

Thursday

OBSTACLES IN THE RACE

"You ran well. Who hindered you from obeying the truth?" (Galatians 5:7)

T he Bible tells the story of the great patriarch, Abraham, who was called by the Lord to leave his homeland and his family. God would lead him to a land where he had never been. Abraham wanted to take everyone along, but the problem was that many of his family members were unbelievers. They were dragging Abraham down spiritually. Most notable among them was his nephew, Lot. God told Abraham to part company with Lot, but it took him awhile to obey. As long as Lot was hanging around, God's blessing was not upon Abraham in the way it could have been. Finally, Abraham obeyed the Lord, and he and Lot parted ways. Then God's blessing came upon Abraham once again.

As you are running your race as a Christian, you may find yourself being hindered by someone. Is there someone in your life like Lot who is slowing you down? After spending time with certain people, do you feel spiritually drained? Perhaps you've thought, "That person brought out the worst in me. They didn't help me in any way." While we want to minister to people and reach them with the gospel, we must be careful not to do so at the expense of our own spiritual lives. There might be someone who is slowing you down in the race of life.

Is someone dragging you down spiritually? Is someone hindering you from doing what God has called you to do? You need to ask yourself, "Is this person a wing or a weight? Is he or she speeding me on my way or slowing me down?" Running the race is not just running toward what is right. It is also running away from what is wrong.

THE RIGHT MOTIVE FOR RUNNING

"Yet indeed I also count all things loss for the excellence of the knowledge of Christ Jesus my Lord. . . . " (Philippians 3:8)

Back when I was in high school, I ran track and field. Whenever a pretty girl was watching, I always ran faster. I wanted to impress her.

If you are a Christian because someone else is or because you want to impress someone, then I have news for you: you are not going to make it in the race of life. You must run this race for the Lord himself. That is what will give you the strength to keep going.

The apostle Paul made clear his motive for running this race when he said, "That I may know Him and the power of his resurrection, and the fellowship of His sufferings ... " (Philippians 3:9). Notice that Paul didn't say, "That I may know *about* Him." We know about a lot of things today. We know about certain celebrities. You may have read articles that describe these people. You may know a lot about them. But you really don't know them.

In the same way, you can say, "I know all about Jesus. I know all about the Bible." But Paul didn't say He wanted to know *about* Jesus. He said he want to know Him. There is a difference. You need to know about Him, but you also need to know Him. And that comes through a relationship with Jesus Christ.

Hebrews 12 says, "Let us run with endurance the race that is set before us, looking unto Jesus, the author and finisher of our faith ... " (verses 1–2). That is the right motive for running. That is what will help you finish the race with flying colors.

Weekend

Don't Look Back

"But this one thing I do, forgetting those things which are behind and reaching forward to those things which are ahead, I press toward the goal. ... "
(Philippians 3:13–14)

If you want to run the race of life successfully, then don't look back. If you ever have run a race and looked over your shoulder to see what your competitor was doing, then you know that looking back can break your stride and ultimately cause you to lose the race.

Paul, along the same lines, says in Philippians 3:13, "Forgetting those things which are behind. ... " If you are going to walk with the Lord, then you must forget the things that are behind. Here, the word, "forget," doesn't mean a failure to remember as much as it means no longer being influenced or affected by the past.

Here is what you need to do as you enter into a new year: Forget the things that are behind. While you may not be able erase them from your memory, you don't need to let them influence you. Sometimes we dredge up the things God has forgiven and forgotten. The Lord says, "I will remember their sins no more" (Jeremiah 31:34). Yet many times we will bring past sins up, forgetting the fact that our God has a big eraser. Why should we choose to remember what God has chosen to forget? If God has forgiven my sins and forgotten them, then I need to leave them behind, learn from my mistakes, not do the same thing again, and move forward.

In addition to forgetting our sins, we should also forget our victories. Certainly, we are to thank God for them. But we need to remember that it is a new year with new opportunities.

Monday

STRAINING TOWARD THE GOAL

"I press toward the goal for the prize of the upward call of God in Christ Jesus."
(Philippians 3:14)

The word used for "press" in Philippians 3:14 carries in the meaning of "strong exertion." Every muscle of the runner is burning. He can see the ribbon. He has only a few more feet to go in the race. He must press on.

It is the same in our lives as Christians. There are times when it just gets hard. But it is then that we learn what it means to walk by faith and not by feeling. You can't live on an emotional high as a Christian. You must pace yourself in this race you are running. You can't expect that every time you go to church, you will have some great emotional encounter with God. Sometimes you will. Sometimes you won't. Growing up and learning to walk by faith are part of spiritual maturity.

When you first made a commitment to Christ, you discovered the joy and wonderful peace that comes from being forgiven. But you must realize that this is a walk by faith. You must press on even when it gets hard.

Maybe, as you have been running, you have found yourself in a place where you are dragging burdens, sins, or other things along. Maybe you find that you don't even know why you are running the race anymore. Maybe you have become discouraged. Look up and remember that it is Jesus whom you are running for. Two thousand years ago, He loved you so much that He went to the cross and died there. He shed His blood for you. Then He rose again from the dead. Because He did that for you, you can live for Him today. He will give you the strength.

Tuesday

INSIDE OUT

"You try to look like upright people outwardly, but inside your hearts are filled with hypocrisy and lawlessness." (Matthew 23:28 NLT)

People make changes in their lives for many reasons. Often it is when they face a crisis in life. It might be a heart attack. It might be the loss of a spouse through death or divorce. It might some other crisis that hits them, and they begin to evaluate their priorities and take stock of their lives. They determine to make changes.

But often the same people who vow to change end up going back to their old ways. We often hear of celebrities being admitted to drug rehabilitation centers. We hear about the great changes they have made. They tell their stories on television and write books about it. But then a few months later, we read that they have gone back to their old ways. Why? Because they have made moral changes in their lives, but they haven't gotten to the root of their problem, which is the absence of God in their lives.

Jesus warned the Pharisees, "First wash the inside of the cup, and then the outside will become clean, too" (Matthew 23:26 NLT). Jesus was telling them they were missing it when they only concentrate on the outward. They must first take care of the inward.

The clear mandate given to the church from the lips of Jesus himself was to go into this world and preach the gospel, because when people truly find Him, it will change their lifestyle. If, as believers, we allow other things to detract us from this calling, then we are also missing it. As Jesus said, "First wash the inside, ... and then the outside will become clean, too." That is where we must focus our efforts.

TRUE CONVERSION

"And when people escape from the wicked ways of the world by learning about our Lord and Savior Jesus Christ and then get tangled up with sin and become its slave again, they are worse off than before." (2 Peter 2:20 NLT)

Sometimes we hear about well-known people who claim to have made a commitment to Jesus Christ. Often, it is around election time. When they address Christians, they speak of their great faith in God. After the elections, we seldom hear about it again.

Then there are people who say they are believers, but a month or two later, they go back to their old ways again. They say, "I tried Christianity, but it didn't work for me." But in reality, they never really found Christ.

Others will turn to God when they hit hard times. Awhile later, you see them going back to their old ways, and you wonder what happened. I would suggest that many of these people never were converted at all. They went through the motions, but Jesus Christ never became a part of their lives. Often, they end up worse than before.

When Jesus Christ truly comes into our lives, He takes up residence. And He doesn't just do a basic housecleaning; He does a thorough one. There is real change. But when a house has only been swept, that is, when someone has made only moral changes, he or she is still vulnerable to the Enemy. This is why we must recognize the futility of simply turning over a new leaf or making a few New Year's resolutions. We must realize the problem is deeper than our moral sins. We must get to the heart of the matter and have Jesus Christ take residence in our lives and change us from the inside out.

Thursday

BALANCE

"Now concerning spiritual gifts, brethren, I do not want you to be ignorant."
(1 Corinthians 12:1)

Through the years, I have made my periodic trips to the gym to get back in shape. On one such occasion after I joined a local gym, a trainer took me on a tour to show me the various machines and how they worked. (Some of them are a little difficult to figure out these days!) One thing the trainer mentioned especially caught my attention. He explained that it is important to work out every part of your body so you have a balanced physique. To fail to do so, he said, causes imbalance. A person needs cardiovascular exercises as well as strength training.

As the trainer began to describe the importance of balance and how the entire body needed exercise and needed to be trained for good overall performance, I began to think about the body of Christ. We, too, need overall balance. And in our own personal lives as Christians, the key is balance.

In Romans 12, we find that God has distributed gifts of the Holy Spirit into the lives of believers for the benefit of the whole church. Because of the abuse of some, many have recoiled from these wonderful gifts that God has given. Some have seen the excesses and those who have gone too far in one direction with these gifts, and they think, "I don't want anything to do with that kind of activity."

However, you can go too far in the other direction as well. The gifts of the Spirit are real, and they are available for Christians today. Not only should we be using them in our lives, but we also should be seeking the gift or gifts He has placed in our lives.

Friday

THE "BEST" GIFTS

"Having then gifts differing according to the grace that is given to us, let us use them. ... " (1 Corinthians 12:6)

What are the best spiritual gifts for a believer to have? It all depends. If I am having a difficult time sharing my faith with someone, and you come along and have been gifted as an evangelist, then that is the best gift at that particular moment. But then let's say I am trying to understand the meaning of a particular passage of Scripture, and God has given you the gift of teaching. For you to come along could be a great benefit to me. Then again, let's say that I am undertaking a complex project, and I need help. What I really need is someone with the gift of helps or administrations. Or, let's say that I'm lying in a hospital bed, and I'm discouraged. I don't really need a Bible study. I don't need someone to come and help me organize my life. I need someone with the gift of exhortation or encouragement. I need someone to come and help me see that God is still in control of my life. Each one of these gifts is important, as God has distributed them.

We make a big mistake when we think some gifts are of greater importance than others. They all have their place, and God has given them as He has chosen. Therefore, we need to pray, "Lord, what are my gifts? Help me to discover them. Help me to develop them. Help me to use them."

One day when you stand before God, you will be held accountable for what He called you to do. And one day, He will reward you for how faithful you were with what He gave you.

Weekend

THE POWER OF IMPARTATION

"But now you are free from the power of sin and have become slaves of God. Now you do those things that lead to holiness and result in eternal life."
(Romans 6:22 NLT)

Are you happy with the way that you are right now? Are there things in your life you would like to see dramatically altered? Perhaps like many other people, you make bold resolutions whenever a new year rolls around. You make plans regarding what changes you want to make in the coming year. But it's not long until you have gone back on those great resolutions.

In the same way, as Christians we are often defeated in day-to-day living because we don't really realize how many resources God has placed in our spiritual account. A lot of times we say, "God help me. God, give me this. God, give me that." Meanwhile, God is saying, "Will you please go check your account? I have deposited more than you could ever use. Check it out."

Can you imagine a soldier fighting a battle with no ammunition, while he was sitting on a bunker filled with thousands and thousands of rounds of ammo, more than he could use in a thousand wars? He has more than he needs right under him, but he is trying to fight the battle without it.

Our defeat in our battle with sin and temptation lay largely in our ignorance of the facts. There is in Jesus Christ the power to live a new life and to no longer be under sin's control. That power is not in imitation, because you can imitate Jesus all you want and try to be like Him. The power comes from impartation. God has done something for you, and now it is for you to appropriate that divine provision.

Monday

THE KEY TO HOLINESS

"Well then, should we keep on sinning so that God can show us more and more kindness and forgiveness? Of course not! Since we have died to sin, how can we continue to live in it?" (Romans 6:1–2 NLT)

S adly, there are many believers today who live with a misconception that they must do something to earn God's approval. When they have had a good week and have been reading their Bibles or doing certain good deeds for the Lord, they feel that God will be pleased. But when they have had a hard week, when they have fallen, when they have sinned, they think God is not pleased with them. Sometimes they believe they shouldn't even go to church or read the Bible. "Why bother?" they think. "God is not pleased with me. I don't have His favor. It would be hypocritical for me to do that." All the while, they don't realize they have God's uncon-ditional favor and love regardless of what they do. But that is not a license to sin. It is an incentive to respond to Him in love.

If, as believers, we can truly get hold of what this means, if we can understand that it is not a license to live as we please, then it should be an incentive for us to serve the Lord, love Him, and show gratitude toward the One who loves us uncon-ditionally, knowing us for what we are. An understanding of this truth can revolutionize our lives.

In some people's estimation, holy living, which is keeping rules and regulations, will bring salvation. But holy living, which we are not capable of to start with, will not bring salva-tion. However, salvation will produce holy living. If you are truly saved, it will result in changes in your lifestyle.

Tuesday

THE PROBLEM WITH PRIDE

"If we say that we have no sin, we deceive ourselves, and the truth is not in us."
(1 John 1:8)

I had to laugh when I heard the story of two men who approached the great British preacher, C. H. Spurgeon, one day and told him, "Spurgeon, we have reached sinless perfection."

"Really?" he asked.

"Yes," they said, "We are absolutely perfect."

Spurgeon was holding a pitcher of water at the time, and he poured it on their heads. When they began to react like any other sinners would, he found out just how perfect they were.

You see, the people who walk around claiming to have reached sinless perfection are victims of one of the most powerful yet subtle sins: pride. None of us will reach sinless perfection—not in this life. Granted, before we were Christians, we were under the control and power of sin. We went along with whatever our sinful natures dictated. But something dramatic happened when we received Christ. We were changed. The Bible says that we became new creations in Christ. Old things passed away and all things became new (see 2 Corinthians 5:17). That is not to say we still don't struggle with sin and temptation. The Scripture clearly teaches that we will sin and that we will have lapses.

Although the Bible tells me I will sin, there is a difference between sinning and being sorry for it, and sinning habitually, persistently, and continually. If someone claims to be a Christian and yet continues in sin, my question is whether that person has ever been truly converted. Some people wonder whether such a Christian ever could lose his or her salvation. I would suggest that another question should be asked instead: Did he or she ever experience salvation to begin with?

TRUE CONVERSION

" 'Yes, I am going to send you to the Gentiles, to open their eyes so they may turn from darkness to light, and from the power of Satan to God. Then they will receive forgiveness for their sins and be given a place among God's people, who are set apart by faith in me.' " (Acts 26:17–18 NLT)

When the apostle Paul stood before King Agrippa and explained what God had called him to do in proclaiming the gospel, he broke it down into one of the most clear presentations I have found anywhere in the Bible. Paul said that God had called him to proclaim this message, which was to open the eyes of his listeners that they might turn from darkness to light, from the power of Satan to God, and that they might receive the forgiveness of sin and an inheritance among those who are sanctified. Here, we see three steps: One, your eyes are opened. Two, you turn from darkness to light. Three, you turn from the power of Satan to God. As a result, you are forgiven and receive adoption and an inheritance among God's people.

Many people have taken step one, but they have never made it to step two. They have had their eyes opened and have seen there is a God and there is a devil. They have also seen there is a choice to be made. They have seen that Jesus Christ is the answer to their problems and that they need to trust in Him and turn from their sin. They intellectually agree with these things. But they haven't taken step two, which is turning from darkness to light and from the power of Satan to God. And until you have taken that step, you are not truly converted.

Thursday

BECOMING NEW

"Therefore, if anyone is in Christ, he is a new creation; old things have passed away; behold, all things have become new." (2 Corinthians 5:17)

The Scripture is full of descriptions of the believer's new spiritual life. God promises He will give us a new heart. In Ezekiel 36:26, God says that He will "give you a new heart and put a new spirit within you; [He] will take the heart of stone out of your flesh and give you a heart of flesh."

God also will give us a new song. The psalmist wrote, "He has put a new song in my mouth—praise to our God ... " (Psalm 40:3).

The Bible also promises there will be a new self. Ephesians 4:22–24 says, "That you put off, concerning your former conduct, the old man which grows corrupt according to the deceitful lusts, and be renewed in the spirit of your mind, and that you put on the new man which was created according to God, in true righteousness and holiness."

As believers, our spiritual lives are new, but we still have the capacity to sin. And though we have the capacity of sin, the tyranny and penalty of sin in our lives has been broken. However, sin's potential has not been fully removed, because we have two natures within that are constantly at battle: a new nature and an old nature. As you know, it's very easy to sin. It comes naturally to us. But the new nature doesn't come naturally; it comes supernaturally. These two natures are battling, and each day, you determine which nature you are going to build up. Which will prevail? The one you build up the most. Every time you obey God and resist sin, you are building the new nature.

WHEN OPPORTUNITY KNOCKS

"So Elijah went and found Elisha son of Shaphat plowing a field with a team of oxen. … Elijah went over to him and threw his cloak across his shoulders and walked away again." (1 Kings 19:19 NLT)

What was Elisha doing when Elijah called him into the Lord's service? Was he walking around saying, "I wonder if God ever will do anything in my life?" No. He was busy. He was plowing a field.

You will find this pattern throughout Scripture. The people God uses are people who are faithful with what He has put before them. The people God uses in big things are people who are faithful in little things. A lot of people of think that, one day, they would like to perhaps dedicate their lives to Christian service. They say, "I would like to go to another country and maybe become a missionary." That is great, but how about serving the Lord where you are right now? Do you think that some mystical thing will happen the moment you step onto foreign soil? Seize the opportunities around you today.

If you want to go to a foreign land where people speak a different language, I know of such a place. The people indigenous to this region are small of stature and hard to understand. They try your patience. They are called kids, and the mission field is called Sunday School.

When we are busy looking for distant opportunities, we might miss the ones that are right in front of us. Are you serving the Lord right now with what He has called you to do? If so, be faithful in that. Hang in there. Do it well. Do it as unto the Lord. He sees you, and He will one day reward you openly.

Weekend

THE COST OF COMMITMENT

*"So Elisha turned back from him, and took a yoke of oxen and slaughtered them.
... Then he arose and followed Elijah, and became his servant." (1 Kings 19:21)*

When Elijah threw his mantle, or his outer garment, on Elisha, it was a symbolic gesture that said, "I'm passing on my calling to you." From the account we find in 1 Kings 19, we discover a few things about Elisha. First, we know that he was a relatively wealthy man and came from an affluent home. How do we know that? Because the Bible says that he had twelve yoke of oxen. Back in those days, owning one pair of oxen meant that you were pretty well off. To have twelve would mean that you had a considerable acreage. So, for Elisha to follow Elijah was not an easy life.

Elijah's invitation was not to a leisurely life on easy street. Elijah's life was a hard one. He had many enemies. He had people that hated him, most notably, Queen Jezebel. For Elisha to follow Elijah would mean that he would have the same enemies. The same people that hated Elijah would now hate him.

Many people are surprised to find that the Christian life is not a playground, but a battleground. The day that you decide to follow Jesus Christ, you begin to face opposition from the devil. He doesn't want you to grow spiritually. He doesn't to you to move forward. So, he will use every trick up his sleeve to try and pull you back.

We must recognize that to follow Christ means there is a price to pay. We may lose some friends. We may have to give up a few things. It may be difficult at times. But certainly, it is worth it.

Monday

A PASSION FOR THE LOST

*"My heart is filled with bitter sorrow and unending grief for my people,
my Jewish brothers and sisters. I would be willing to be forever cursed—
cut off from Christ!—if that would save them." (Romans 9:2–3 NLT)*

The apostle Paul had something essential for effective evangelism: a God-given burden for those who did not know Jesus Christ. In his case, the burden was for his own people, the Jews. He cared. It burned inside him.

General William Booth, founder of the Salvation Army, once said that his desire, had it been possible, would be to dangle his evangelism trainees over hell for twenty-four hours. That way, they could see the reality that awaits those who do not know Jesus Christ.

That wouldn't have been necessary for Paul, who spoke of his love and burning passion for unbelievers. I think it is there for us in Scripture so that we don't become so obsessed with our own struggles and spiritual growth that we forget about people who need to know Christ. I think Paul makes an amazing statement in Romans 9 when he says, in essence, "If it were possible, I would give up my hope of eternal life so that others who do not know could come to faith" (NLT) That's a pretty dramatic statement.

As believers, you and I have a responsibility to those outside the church—those outside the faith. If God's love is really working in our lives, it should motivate us to do something for Him. Do you have a God-given burden for those who do not know Jesus Christ? If you don't, do you want one? If you pray that God will give you this burden, then be careful. The results could be life-changing. You just may be surprised at how quickly He answers you.

Tuesday

MOVED TO ACTION

"And they said to me, 'The survivors who are left from the captivity in the province are there in great distress and reproach. The wall of Jerusalem is also broken down, and its gates are burned with fire.' So it was, when I heard these words, that I sat down and wept, and mourned for many days; I was fasting and praying before the God of heaven." (Nehemiah 1:3–4)

Alexander McLaren said, "You tell me the depth of a Christian's compassion, and I will tell you the measure of his usefulness." How deep does your compassion go? God is looking for such people.

How does it affect you, knowing there are many people who do not know Christ, knowing they are basically on their way to a certain judgment? Does it move you? Until you are moved in the depths of your soul, you will not be moved to take any action.

Nehemiah was a man in a position of great influence and power as he served under the king. He was not a preacher or priest or scribe. He was what we might call a layman today. But Nehemiah loved God. One day, someone told him about the plight of the Jews and how the city of Jerusalem was now lying in ruins. Nehemiah began to weep and pray and say, "Lord, what can I do about this problem?" After his weeping came working. After his despair came determination. The devastation of Jerusalem touched him, and he wanted to do something about it. So he prayed and he devised a plan. Then that plan began to unfold.

These are two essential ingredients for effectively sharing our faith. It must start with a God-given burden, leading us to prayer. And then we need to go out and do something.

WHO WILL GO?

"Also I heard the voice of the Lord, saying: 'Whom shall I send, and who will go for Us?' Then I said, 'Here am I! Send me.'" (Isaiah 6:8)

God said in the presence of Isaiah, "Whom shall I send, and who will go for Us?" In a sense, God is still asking this question. *Whom shall I send? Who will go for us?* Will you go? Will you stand in the gap?

If God's Holy Spirit were to search among us today, I wonder if He would find men or women willing to stand in the gap. Willing to pray. Willing to be available. Willing to reach out to those that do not know Him.

A lot of Christians will say, "I'm too timid. I'm afraid of this and that." But I think a lot of Christians don't really have a burden for those who don't know the Lord. I think if that burden is burning with enough passion, a believer will work through the obstacles. That is not to say there aren't things we should learn so we can share our faith more effectively. But it is to say that if the burden is really there, a believer will go out and do something with it. The bottom line is that sharing our faith isn't really a big deal to many of us. This is why it is so important that we have a God-given burden for unbelievers.

I would rather make every mistake to be made in sharing my faith than to never do anything. At least I will hopefully learn something from my mistakes. But when we do nothing for fear of being rejected or for fear we will not meet with resounding success, we are really missing what God has called us to do.

Thursday

THE MESSAGE PROCLAIMED

"And how shall they hear without a preacher? And how shall they preach unless they are sent? As it is written: 'How beautiful are the feet of those who preach the gospel of peace, who bring glad tidings of good things!'" (Romans 10:14–15)

From the original Greek, we could translate the final question in Romans 10:14 as, "How shall they hear without one preaching?" The Phillips translation puts it this way, "How can they hear unless someone proclaims Him?" Therefore, we see the emphasis is not on a preacher, but on preaching.

We may think the work of evangelism is only for those who are called to be evangelists. Granted, there are people in the church whom God has raised up to be evangelists, and certainly evangelism is not limited to those who preach to hundreds or thousands at a time. I have seen many individual believers who obviously have this gift.

While it is true that some are called to be evangelists, it is also true that every Christian is called to evangelize. Many times, however, we avoid sharing our faith, deciding instead to just live it out, be a good witness, and leave the preaching to others. Yet in I Corinthians I:2I, it says, "For since, in the wisdom of God, the world through wisdom did not know God, it pleased God through the foolishness of the message preached to save those who believe." This does not mean we need to scream and yell and wave a Bible to get the point across. What it does mean is that we are to recognize the primary way God has chosen to reach the lost is through the proclamation of the gospel—by people. God has chosen the agency of His proclaimed Word to bring people to salvation.

PEOPLE REACHING PEOPLE

*"Yet faith comes from listening to this message of good news—
the Good News about Christ." (Romans 10:17 NLT)*

I t is worth noting that no person in the New Testament
came to faith apart from the agency of a human being.
Have you ever stopped and thought about that? We can
find example after example.

There was the Ethiopian (see Acts 8:26–39). There are
many ways that God could have reached this man from a
distant country. He could have sent an angel to meet him.
Instead, the Lord sent an angel to Philip and told him to go.
So Philip went and proclaimed the gospel to that man, and
he believed.

Then there was the Philippian jailer (see Acts 16:27–34).
God could have reached him in many ways. Instead, He
allowed Paul and Silas to be incarcerated and to ultimately
proclaim the gospel, bringing that man and his family to faith.

We can think of Cornelius, a man who was searching
for God (see Acts 10). An angel spoke to him and told him
he needed to meet a man named Simon Peter. The angel
explained where to find him. Interesting. The angel could
have given him the gospel. But God chose to use Simon Peter.

What about Saul? While it is true that he was converted
through an encounter with Christ on the Damascus Road,
his conversion was sandwiched between experiences with two
people who influenced him. First, it was the witness of Stephen
that softened Saul's heart and made it receptive to the seed of
the Word when he was confronted by Jesus Christ. Afterward,
God sent Ananias to follow up on Saul and pray for him to
receive the power of the Holy Spirit. So you see, God used
people. And He wants to use you.

Weekend

GOD'S DYNAMITE

*"For Christ didn't send me to baptize, but to preach the Good News—
and not with clever speeches and high-sounding ideas, for fear that
the cross of Christ would lose its power." (1 Corinthians 1:17 NLT)*

There is explosive power in the message of the gospel,
because Paul says, "It is the power of God at work,
saving everyone who believes . . ." (Romans 1:16). The
word "power" that Paul used in this verse originates from the
Greek word, dunamis. It is the same word Jesus used in Acts
1:8: " 'But when the Holy Spirit has come upon you, you will
receive power [dunamis] and will tell people about me everywhere' ... " (NLT). The English words "dynamic," "dynamo,"
and "dynamite" also have been translated from this word,
dunamis. Paul was saying that the very message of the gospel
is the dynamite of God. It is the dynamic of God.

We often underestimate the raw power of the gospel in
reaching even the most hardened heart. We think we need
to add to it, gloss it over, or even complicate it. But there is
distinct power in the simple message of the life, words, death,
and resurrection of Jesus Christ. Don't underestimate its
appeal. Don't be ashamed of its simplicity. Don't add to it or
take away from it. Just proclaim it, and then stand back and
watch what God will do. As Paul said, "I know very well how
foolish the message of the cross sounds to those who are on
the road to destruction. But we who are being saved recognize
this message as the very power of God" (1 Corinthians 1:18).

The gospel is a simple message, one that we in the church
have heard time and time again. But we should never underestimate its power.

Monday

PROCLAIMING CHRIST

"But we preach Christ crucified. ..." (1 Corinthians 1:23)

Today, people are standing up and being counted for many things. In fact, I am amazed at the perverse, even horrendous things people will speak up for and what some are even willing to die for. Yet here we are with the life-changing message of the gospel, and often we hide in shame or are embarrassed by what we have to say. But it is time for us to stand up and be counted as well. Jesus said, "For whoever is ashamed of Me and My words in this adulterous and sinful generation, of him the Son of Man also will be ashamed when He comes in the glory of His Father with the holy angels" (Mark 8:38).

In the first-century, the thought of Jesus dying on the cross was scandalous to the Jews. The Greeks, who prided themselves on their cultural and intellectual attainments, thought it was nonsense. But the apostle Paul said, "We preach Christ crucified, to the Jews a stumbling block and to the Greeks foolishness, but to those who are called, both Jews and Greeks, Christ the power of God and the wisdom of God." (I Corinthians 1:23–24).

Are you ashamed of the simple message of the gospel? I hope you're not ashamed of the gospel of Christ, because God's righteousness is revealed in it. You see, we have our own sense of righteousness and our own sense of what is right and wrong. But God's righteousness is a lot different than ours. It is only at the cross that the righteous requirements of the law and of God are satisfied. It is impossible to fulfill them apart from the cross. So it is through the gospel that the righteousness of God is revealed.

Tuesday

STRIKING AT THE ROOT

"For I decided to concentrate only on Jesus Christ and his death on the cross."
(*1 Corinthians 2:2 NLT*)

Over the years, I have received many letters in which I am invited to get involved with a certain cause or to join a boycott or a march. I admire people who get out there and want to stand up for what is right, and I think that we as Christians need to make our presence known in this culture and society. But I personally have chosen to strike at the root of the problem, which is sin. I have chosen to seek to help this society by preaching the gospel, because I have found that a change in one's lifestyle does not bring about salvation. But true salvation will always bring about a change in one's lifestyle.

When the apostle Paul went to Rome, there were many social ills that he could have addressed. Instead, he chose to strike at the root of the problem. Rome was a city filled with slaves, yet Paul would not center his preaching on slavery. Rome was a city of rampant immorality, but Paul's message did not center on moral reform. Rome was a city of financial corruption, but Paul would not center his preaching on the problems of the day. His message was simple. He struck at the root. He gave them the gospel.

I can work to bring reform and morality to my culture and society. I can even work to help get laws passed that would slow down the spread of sin and corruption. But if I can lead others to Christ, then their morals and their lifestyles will ultimately change. Not only will they have the hope of heaven, but they will also be different people in our society and culture.

By Faith

"For we walk by faith, not by sight." (1 Corinthians 5:7 NLT)

It is no coincidence that the phrase, "walk by faith," is used in Scripture. Notice that Scripture doesn't tell us to *sprint* by faith; it tells us to *walk* by faith. To walk speaks of continual, regulated motion. The Bible says Enoch walked with God. Many believers have their bursts of energy. For a few months, they run. Then they collapse for awhile. They need to learn what it is to walk with God.

Of course, we like things fast. We have microwave dinners, e-mail, cell phones, and instant messaging. We have so much technology to make our lives a little easier and, most importantly, faster. Then, when we come to the Christian life, we say, "All right, what's the angle? What's the shortcut?" Here it is: "The just shall live by faith" (Romans 1:17). It's a day-by-day process.

We are always looking for the angle, for the inside track. But it's very simple. The Bible declares that the just shall live by faith. Not by feeling. Not by emotion. Not by fear. Not by worries. By faith.

I know sometimes that it seems like nothing is happening in terms of our spiritual growth. There are times when we don't really feel like we are changing, because as we look at ourselves every day, we don't necessarily see any changes. But as we are walking by faith day by day, month by month, and year by year, we are being transformed.

Colossians 2:6 tells us, "As you therefore have received Christ Jesus the Lord, so walk in Him, rooted and built up in Him and established in the faith, as you have been taught, abounding in it with thanksgiving." That's it. The just shall live by faith.

Thursday

CONTEMPLATING THE CROSS

"How we thank God, who gives us victory over sin and death through Jesus Christ our Lord!" (1 Corinthians 15:57 NLT)

I heard about a man who was trying to start his own religion, but it wasn't going very well so far. He decided to approach the French statesman, Charles-Maurice de Talleyrand, and ask him what he should do to gain converts. The statesman told him, "I recommend that you get yourself crucified, die, and then rise again on the third day."

Jesus' death on the cross and resurrection on the third day is the cornerstone of the Christian faith. It is what sets our faith as Christians apart from the faith of all others. Yet many view Christ's crucifixion as a rude interruption of what was an otherwise successful ministry. But the cross was at the forefront of the mind of Jesus Christ from the very beginning. This is where He knew He was headed, and He spoke of it often. The Bible even tells us that before He even came to this earth, a decision was made that He would ultimately go to the cross. Scripture calls Him "the Lamb slain from the foundation of the world" (Revelation 13:8 NLT).

It was at the cross that the righteous demands of God were satisfied. It was at the cross that God and humanity were reconciled once again. It was at the cross that a decisive blow was dealt against Satan and his minions. It was at the cross that our very salvation was purchased. Therefore, we cannot talk about the cross too much or contemplate it too often.

WANTED: NEW BELIEVERS

"And the Lord added to the church daily those who were being saved."
(Acts 2:47)

I love new believers. They are the lifeblood of the church. When I have the privilege of speaking to other pastors, I tell them that if they don't have a constant flow of new believers coming into their congregations, they will become spiritually dead. We can either evangelize or fossilize. Show me a church in which new believers are not coming in, and I'll show you a church that is stagnating. Show me a church that has new believers coming in on a regular basis, and I'll show you a church that has vibrancy and life.

Granted, new believers need older believers to stabilize them. New believers' hearts are full of zeal, but they don't understand the ground rules yet. They need older believers to teach them. Still, older believers also need new believers. They need their zeal. They need their passion. They need their excitement to remind them of what they have forgotten.

Sadly, it is usually the new believers who want to do the most when they know the least. When we ask people to help out with something at Harvest Christian Fellowship, so often we have new believers who come and say they want to help: "I will do whatever you need. I would like to sign up for six ministries." While we are very appreciative of their willingness to serve, we want them to have a good foundation first so they can be properly trained and equipped to do what God has called them to do.

On the other hand, there are older believers who have known the Lord for years, maybe even decades, who don't give a passing thought to helping out at church. It should be just the opposite.

Weekend

THROUGH THE STORM

" 'So take courage! For I believe God. It will be just as he said.' "
(Acts 27:25 NLT)

Sometimes we may think that when we're in the will of
God, it will be smooth sailing. But many times it is just
the opposite. Doors slam in our faces. Obstacles appear
in our paths and storms arise that threaten to drive us off
course. That is why we need to remember there is a devil who
wants to stop us from doing what God wants us to do.

As the apostle Paul was on his way to do the will of God, he
hit some tough times. An incredible storm arose that caused
the people in his boat to despair of their lives. But there was
no obstacle big enough to stop Paul. He always seemed to rise
above his circumstances. As he went through the storm, he
knew God had shown him what to do, and he would let nothing
deter him from that course.

Often when a hard time hits, when a crisis hits, when a
tragedy hits, we want out. We ask God for an airlift out of our
problems. But many times God's wants us to learn in the midst
of them. Romans 8:35–37 says, "Who shall separate us from
the love of Christ? Shall trouble or hardship or persecution
or famine or nakedness or danger or sword? ... No, in all
these things we are more than conquerors through him who
loved us." Notice the phrase, "in all these things" (NLT). It isn't
saying we won't face some of these things. But it says that *in them*
we are more than conquerors.

If you are seeking to obey the Lord, expect opposition.
Expect obstacles. Expect difficulties. But also expect God
to see you through.

Monday

NEVER ALONE

" 'For last night an angel of the God to whom I belong and whom I serve stood beside me, and he said, "Don't be afraid, Paul, for you will surely stand trial before Caesar! What's more, God in his goodness has granted safety to everyone sailing with you." ' " (Acts 27:23–24 NLT)

Time and time again God reminded Paul of His presence, no doubt when he needed it the most. God knows what we need, and He knows when we need it. He knew when Paul could use that extra assurance. When he was in that prison cell in Jerusalem, the Lord appeared to him and told him to be courageous (see Acts 23:11). Then from prison in Rome, he wrote to Timothy, "But the Lord stood with me and gave me strength ..." (2 Timothy 4:16 nlt). In some special way, God reassured Paul of His presence. Acts 27 tells us that the Lord sent an angel to reassure him.

You can take heart in the face of danger or uncertainty because of your awareness of God's presence with you. When your heart sinks, when it seems as though your life falling apart, you must remember the Lord is there with you. You are not alone. No, there are not always easy answers. But we can be sure of this: He will be with us through the storm.

God was standing by Paul's side, and God is with us in our storms as well. He may not necessarily send an angel. We may not necessarily hear an audible voice. But if we pay attention, we can hear the still, small voice of God. And certainly, He will speak to us through His Word. Then we, like Paul, can reassure others that the Lord is in control.

Tuesday

Unwavering Faith

"And the Lord will deliver me from every evil work and preserve me for His heavenly kingdom. To Him be glory forever and ever. Amen!" (2 Timothy 4:18)

One of the things that amazes me about the apostle Paul is how he always seemed to rise to the top of every situation and seized every opportunity to preach the gospel. We read in the Book Acts that when Paul and Silas were thrown in prison, they began to sing praises to God at midnight. An earthquake struck, the walls fell, and the next thing you know, the very jailer that was responsible for chaining them up and whipping them asked, "What must I do to be saved?"

Then, when Paul was brought before the various dignitaries of Rome, he became master of every situation. For example, when he was before Felix, he reasoned with him regarding righteousness, self-control, and the judgment to come. When he stood before Festus and Herod Agrippa II, he said, "Why should it be thought incredible by you that God raises the dead?" He posed the question to Herod Agrippa II, "Do you believe the prophets? I know that you do believe." He was a prisoner on a ship, and in a short time, the crew, the captain, the soldiers, and the Roman centurion were taking orders from Paul—and everyone was listening to him!

Paul was bold. He didn't seem to be afraid of anything. He never seemed to get down. His life wasn't always easy. In fact, it was very difficult. But the words he penned to the believers at Philippi seemed to always hold true: "I have learned in whatever state I am, to be content" (Philippians 4:11). He was fully convinced of the faithfulness of God and was sustained by that conviction.

FROM ORDINARY
TO EXTRAORDINARY

"The eyes of the Lord search the whole earth in order to strengthen those whose hearts are fully committed to him." (2 Chronicles 16:9 NLT)

A conversation took place many years ago between D.L. Moody, before he became the great evangelist, and another man. The man said to Moody, "You know, the world has yet to see what God can do with and through the man who is totally committed to Him." Those words went deep into Moody's heart, and he prayed, "Lord, I want to be that man." He sure came close.

The Book of Acts is a story of ordinary men and women who did extraordinary things because they allowed God to have His way in their lives. In the same way, God wants to use you to turn your world upside down for Christ. It starts with your saying, "Lord, I want to make a difference. I don't want this world to turn me around. I want to turn it around. Use me."

The world has yet to see what God can do with and through the man or woman who is totally committed to Him. Will God find such people today? I wonder if you would say, like Moody, "I want to be that person." If you will, then your life can make a difference. It will be exciting in the days ahead to see what God will do through and with you. But He wants you to be available to Him.

One of these days, your life will come to an end. What will you say of your life? What will others say? How great it would be to say, like Paul, "I have fought a good fight, I have finished the race, and I have remained faithful" (2 Timothy 4:7). What will you say?

Thursday

WHEN GOD SEEMS DISTANT

John the Baptist, who was now in prison, heard about all the things the Messiah was doing. So he sent his disciples to ask Jesus, "Are you really the Messiah we've been waiting for, or should we keep looking for someone else?" (Matthew 11:2–3 NLT)

Have you ever had something happen in your life that caused you to say, "Where is God?" None less than the greatest prophet who ever lived, John the Baptist, faced this struggle.

John had put it all on the line for Jesus Christ. He had baptized Him in the Jordan River. He pointed his own disciples to Jesus, whom he believed was the Messiah. John had clearly pledged his complete loyalty to Jesus. Yet a strange series of events took place after that. One moment, he was out preaching to the multitudes and baptizing people. The next moment, he was in prison. The great John the Baptist began to entertain some doubt. So he sent his disciples to Jesus with this question, "Are you really the Messiah we've been waiting for, or should we keep looking for someone else?"

Jesus' disciples and John commonly believed that Jesus would establish His kingdom then and there. But they failed to recognize that before Christ would establish His kingdom, He would first come to suffer and die for the sins of humanity. John misunderstood the prophesies of Scripture, and therefore felt that Jesus was not doing what He was supposed to do.

Sometimes we, too, misunderstand God and His Word when He doesn't do what we think He should do or when He doesn't work as quickly as we would like Him to. But even when we cannot understand God's ways, His methods, or His timing, He still asks us to trust Him. And He is trustworthy.

Friday

Dealing with
Discouragement

"Why are you cast down, O my soul? And why are you disquieted within me?
Hope in God; for I shall yet praise Him, the help of my
countenance and my God." (Psalm 42:11)

It is not unusual for even the most spiritual people to have
their days of doubt. Moses, on one occasion at least, was
overwhelmed by his circumstances. After he had listened
to the constant complaining of the children of Israel, he basi
cally told the Lord, "I'm fed up. Just kill me. I don't want to
deal with this another day."

Elijah, after his contest with the prophets of Baal on Mt.
Carmel, heard that Jezebel had put a contract out on his life.
He was so overwhelmed by his circumstances, so discouraged,
so uncertain, and so filled with doubt that he said to God,
"Take my life."

Even the great apostle Paul had moments when he was
discouraged. He wrote to the church at Corinth, "We were
burdened beyond measure, above strength, so that we
despaired even of life" (2 Corinthians 1:8).

Jeremiah, the great prophet, faced it as well. He was ridiculed and harassed for giving out the Word of God. Because
he was tired of the pressure he was facing, it made him want to
stop giving out God's Word altogether. He said, "The word of
the Lord was made to me a reproach and a derision daily. Then
I said, 'I will not make mention of Him, nor speak anymore in
His name' " (Jeremiah 20:8–9).

You are not the only one who has ever faced doubt or uncertainty or has been perplexed as to why God did not work in a
certain way. We may be in the midst of God's working and can't
see the big picture as He can.

Weekend

In His Time

"Then Jesus said to them plainly, 'Lazarus is dead. And I am glad for your sakes that I was not there, that you may believe. Nevertheless let us go to him.'"
(John 11:14–15)

Martha, Mary, and their brother, Lazarus, were close friends of Jesus. He often would spend time in their home in Bethany. When Lazarus became sick, Martha and Mary sent word to Jesus. No doubt they thought that Jesus would drop whatever He was doing and rush back to Bethany. But Jesus intentionally delayed His arrival.

In fact, Jesus didn't show up until much later. By the time He hit town, not only had Lazarus died, but he had been dead four days. Martha walked up and said, "Lord, if You had been here, my brother would not have died." Loose paraphrase: "Jesus, you blew it. You had the perfect situation here. You could have healed him, but you didn't show up."

Jesus told her, "Your brother will rise again."

Martha replied, "I know that he will rise again in the resurrection at the last day."

Jesus said, "I am the resurrection and the life. He who believes in Me, though he may die, he shall live. And whoever lives and believes in Me shall never die. Do you believe this?" Martha didn't quite get it, so Jesus said, "Lazarus, come forth!" and her brother came out of the tomb. Martha wanted a healing. Jesus wanted a resurrection.

Sometimes we limit God. Sometimes we think God must work on our schedules. But God will not be bound by time. God will not be bound by our schedules. God will work when He chooses and with whom He chooses. Therefore, there will be times when our circumstances don't make sense. Even then, we need to trust Him.

Monday

FROM HIS PERSPECTIVE

"But Jesus looked at them and said to them, 'With men this is impossible, but with God all things are possible.'" (Matthew 19:26)

I heard the story of an elderly minister who liked to visit people in hospitals. He often would take along a little, embroidered bookmark that he carried in his Bible. On the back of the bookmark were a group of tangled threads with no apparent pattern. He would hand this bookmark, with the back facing up, to those who were hurting or upset and say, "Look at that and tell me what it says."

As they looked at all the tangled threads, they would say, "I have no idea what it says. It doesn't seem to say anything."

Then he said, "Now, turn it over." As they would flip that bookmark over, they saw the words, "God is love." The minister would say, "Many times as we look at what God is doing, we just see tangled threads with no rhyme or reason. But from God's perspective, He is dealing with us in love, and He knows what He is doing."

The next time you think it is all over for you, just remember how things turned out for Joseph. Just remember how things turned out for Daniel. No doubt things looked pretty dim when he was in the den of lions. It looked hopeless as well for Shadrach, Meshach, and Abednego when they were thrown into the fiery furnace. Things looked pretty grim for Peter when he was in prison. And things looked bleak for Martha and Mary when their brother died.

You see, things can look bad at one moment, but then God will step in and turn events around. Then suddenly you'll look back and say, "Now I understand what God was doing."

Tuesday

WHEN WE DOUBT

"Now we see things imperfectly as in a poor mirror, but then we will see everything with perfect clarity. . . ." (1 Corinthians 13:12 NLT)

Oswald Chambers said, "Doubt is not always a sign that a man is wrong. It may be a sign that he is thinking." There is a difference between doubt and unbelief. Doubt is a matter of the mind. Unbelief is a matter of the heart. Doubt is when we cannot understand what God is doing and why He is doing it. Unbelief is when we refuse to believe God's Word and do what He tells us to do. We must not confuse the two.

Remember the discouraged disciples on the Emmaus road? In their minds, Jesus had failed in His mission and had been crucified. Jesus joined them on that road and began to speak with them. In the end, they said, "Didn't our hearts feel strangely warm as he talked with us on the road and explained the Scriptures to us?" (Luke 24:32 NLT). God dealt with their doubt through His Word. And God will deal with your doubt through His Word. When you are facing doubt, that is not the time to close the Bible. That is the time to open it and let God speak to you.

Maybe you have been doubting God's ways in your life. Maybe you have been asking "why" a lot lately. Maybe His timing doesn't seem to make any sense. The Bible says, "All that I know now is partial and incomplete, but then I will know everything completely, just as God knows me now" (1 Corinthians 13:12 NLT). It all will be resolved in that final day when we stand before God. God doesn't ask us to understand everything. He asks us to trust Him and follow Him.

BEYOND EXCUSES

"And this is the condemnation, that the light has come into the world, and men loved darkness rather than light, because their deeds were evil." (John 3:19)

The Pharisees of Jesus' day were not simply doubting the work of God; their hearts were filled with unbelief. They did not reject Jesus and His Messiahship for lack of evidence, because He had fulfilled so many Old Testament prophesies. They did not reject Jesus because His lifestyle was inconsistent with His preaching, because He was absolutely perfect. Even Pilate, as he was preparing to condemn Him, said of Jesus, "I find no fault in Him." Judas Iscariot, His betrayer, said, "Truly I have betrayed innocent blood."

These religious leaders rejected Jesus because He interfered with the way they had chosen to live. He was a threat to their lifestyle and to their religious system. In spite of all their rhetoric and claims of interest in spiritual things, they were not really searching for the truth. Nor were they searching for the Messiah. Otherwise, they would have embraced Jesus.

You see, the Pharisees' rejection of Jesus Christ was but a reflection of every person who intentionally rejects Him. People do not reject Jesus Christ because they have examined the evidence and concluded He is not the Messiah. Most people that I talk to who say they are not Christians never have read the Bible. They haven't even read the Gospel of John from beginning to end. They never have carefully examined the claims of Christ. People don't reject Jesus Christ because of the hypocrisy of some inconsistent people. People reject Jesus Christ because He is a threat to their lifestyle. They don't want to change. They want things left as they are, because they hate the light and their deeds will be exposed.

Thursday

THE ULTIMATE SIGN

Then some of the scribes and Pharisees answered, "Teacher, we want to see a sign from You." (Matthew 12:38)

Would miracles make more people believe? Would unbelievers become believers if they were to see a bona fide miracle? The scribes and Pharisees' demand for a sign prompted Jesus to give them some of His most solemn and searching words:

"An evil and adulterous generation seeks after a sign, and no sign will be given to it except the sign of the prophet Jonah. . . . The men of Ninevah will rise in the judgment with this generation and condemn it, because they repented at the preaching of Jonah; and indeed a greater than Jonah is here." (Matthew 12:39, 41)

A casual reading of Jesus' response seems almost harsh. After all, here were some individuals who were simply asking for a miracle. He had performed many of them. What's one more? Perhaps that miracle could have brought them to faith. Why didn't He grant their request?

The answer is that Jesus always looks at the motives behind what people say and do. He is far more interested in what is going on in our hearts than what is coming out of our mouths. As He looked in their hearts, no doubt He saw the real reason behind their request: They wanted to destroy Jesus. Matthew 12:14 tells us that the Pharisees "took counsel against Him, how they might destroy Him."

Jesus died on the cross for them and for all of humanity, and rose again from the dead, because we all were separated from God by sin. That is the message Jesus essentially was giving to the Pharisees. That is the message He essentially is giving to us. It is the greatest sign of all. It is the ultimate sign.

A Matter of the Heart

"And you will seek Me and find Me, when you search for Me with all your heart."
(Jeremiah 29:13)

It is fascinating to note how Jesus dealt with different people. He never dealt with any two individuals in precisely the same way. He would look beyond the outward veneer and see their hearts. When a person was really seeking and a miracle was in order, Jesus did one. There are numerous miracles He did for hurting, searching people, like blind Bartimaeus, or the woman whose child was sick, or the woman who spent everything on doctors and needed a miracle, or the ten lepers who came to Him, looking for His touch.

But when people came to Jesus with the wrong motives, it was a different story. In fact, on some occasions, He did not even reveal Himself to them. For example, John 2:23 tells us that when Jesus was in Jerusalem for the Passover, many people believed in Him when they saw the signs He did. But it goes on to say, "Jesus did not commit Himself to the, because He knew all men, and had no need that anyone should testify of man, for He knew what was in man" (vv. 24–25). Here were these people who believed after they saw Jesus' miracles, but He would not commit Himself to them. That really seems strange, doesn't it? But let's consider what the word "commit" means. It means, "to entrust someone with something." Jesus would not entrust these people with His truth. If they were true seekers, Jesus would have revealed Himself to them.

These people who saw His miracles weren't seeking with their whole hearts. They were merely excited about the miracle Jesus had done on that particular day. Therefore, Jesus would not commit Himself to them.

Weekend

PREACHING THE CROSS

For Jews request a sign, and Greeks seek after wisdom; but we preach
Christ crucified, to the Jews a stumbling block and to the Greeks foolishness,
but to those who are called, both Jews and Greeks, Christ the power
of God and the wisdom of God. (1 Corinthians 1:22-24)

W e may look with some envy on first-century believers who seemed to have miracles as part of their daily lives. Certainly, there were dramatic miracles that took place during their time. We read of great things happening, such as the man at the gate Beautiful who received the ability to walk. Peter was released from prison by an angel. A woman was raised from the dead. We can look back on that time with some fondness and say, "Those were the good old days."

Realistically, though, I think we should recognize that the Book of Acts is a record of what God did over a 30-year period. As we read it, it almost appears as though miracles happened every 12 minutes. But the truth is that it's a record of miracles that took place over a long period of time.

Some Christians may think that if they could perform a sign or miracle for the unbelievers they know, then they would believe. But here is the sign they need to know about: what Jesus accomplished on the cross. It is the preaching of the cross that will make the difference. "We preach Christ crucified," Paul said. That is our message. That is what we have to say. Paul said, "For I determined not to know anything among you except Jesus Christ and Him crucified" (1 Corinthians 2:2)

Though I believe in miracles and hope to see more in my lifetime, one thing will never change: the simple message we must proclaim.

Monday

WALKING WITH WISDOM

"Many will say to Me in that day, 'Lord, Lord, have we not prophesied in Your name, cast out demons in Your name, and done many wonders in Your name?' And then I will declare to them, 'I never knew you; depart from Me, you who practice lawlessness!'" (Matthew 7:22–23)

Today we have people who seek experience for the sake of experience, wanting to have what they think is a touch from God. We have self-proclaimed prophets who give their messages and proclaim their visions, but are rarely held accountable for the outcome.

We must be careful. On one hand, we don't want to limit God through unbelief, because we want Him to do His miracles in our lives. On the other hand, we simply cannot believe everyone and everything.

I believe in miracles. I believe in the supernatural. I believe God can heal. But we cannot seek experience at any cost. Experience must always be subservient to truth. It must always be ordered under what is right. We cannot say something is true because we have experienced it. Rather, we should know something is true because it is found in Scripture and it verifies our experience.

In the Book of Acts, we never read about a miracle that was announced ahead of time. When God used Peter to heal the man at the gate Beautiful, we don't read that it was advertised beforehand: "Be at the gate Beautiful today. Miracles! Signs! Wonders! Don't miss it!" They never announced miracles in advance, because their focus was not on miracles. Their focus was on proclaiming the Word of God. They left miracles up to the Holy Spirit.

We must be especially careful in these last days, because not all miracles come from God. Remember, Satan is a great imitator.

Tuesday

TIME WELL SPENT

Those who are wise shall shine like the brightness of the firmament, and those who turn many to righteousness like the stars forever and ever. (Daniel 12:3)

I heard the other day that the average American will have spent fifteen years in front of the television during his or her lifetime. Can you imagine fifteen years of sitting in front of that box, clicking away? What a waste of life.

On the other hand, the Bible speaks of many rewards in heaven for the person who faithfully serves the Lord during his or her lifetime, and even speaks of crowns that will be given. In fact, I think we might be shocked when the awards are presented in heaven. We may expect them to go to all the big names that we know. But just imagine if most of the awards were given to someone named Maude Firkenbinder. You hadn't heard about her. She never pastored a church. She never recorded Christian music. She never wrote a book. But she used the gifts that God gave her. Maybe God called her to be a person of prayer. Maybe she labored in obscurity somewhere. But God saw her faithfulness and rewarded her openly.

When you get to heaven, what will you have to show for your life on this earth? Every man will be tried. Every woman will be tried. All of your accomplishments will be evaluated when you stand before Christ. It is not so much a judgment for sin, but a judgment of time that was spent in a worthless way. Did you have more passion or excitement for your career or for a sport or for your possessions than you had for the things of God? It will all come to nothing. Wasted hours. Wasted days. Wasted years.

MAKE THE RIGHT CHOICE

Simon Peter answered, "You are the Messiah, the Son of the living God."
(Matthew 16:16 NLT)

As we look over the pages of history, it's interesting to read the statements that have been made about Christ. Pontius Pilate said, "I find no fault in Him." Napoleon said, "I know men, and Jesus was no mere man." Strauss, the German rationalist, said, "Jesus was the highest model of religion." The French atheist, Renan, said, "He was the greatest among the sons of men." Theodore Parker said, "Jesus Christ was a youth with God in His heart." Robert Owen said, "He is the irreproachable one." Yet all of these titles and descriptions fall short of identifying Jesus for who He really was: the Son of God, God in human form, the Messiah.

Many today would describe Jesus as a great moral teacher. But in his book, *Mere Christianity*, C. S. Lewis responds to such a statement by saying that if this were the case, then Jesus was either a lunatic or a devil. He goes on to say, "Let us not come with any patronizing nonsense about His being a great human teacher. He has not left that open to us. He did not intend to."

We don't have the option of saying that Jesus was a great moral teacher. How could He merely be a teacher and say the things He said with His exclusive claims of divinity? And what about saying He was the only way to God the Father? Certainly that would be wrong if it were not true.

So, Jesus really leaves us only two choices: to either accept Him, believing that He is indeed God the Son, or to reject Him. But to say He was a great man or a religious man is simply not an option.

Thursday

UNLIKELY CONVERSIONS

"Today, if you will hear His voice, do not harden your hearts." (Hebrews 4:7)

An attorney was trying to deliver an important paper to a man who was determined to avoid him. The man reasoned that the attorney had some type of subpoena, so he went out of his way to dodge him. Fourteen years passed, and the man found himself in the hospital, dying of cancer. Through a strange series of events, the attorney was admitted to the hospital and was assigned to the same room as the dying man. The man turned to the attorney and said, "Well, you never got me. I've escaped you all this time, and now it doesn't matter. You can even serve your subpoena. I don't care."

The lawyer replied, "Subpoena? I was trying to give you a document that proved you had inherited $45 million dollars!"

Many people go out of their way to avoid Christians and the opportunity to have a relationship with Jesus Christ. All the while, their hearts grow harder, and they risk becoming calloused to the point of no return. We don't know when that point will come in their lives. Maybe you even know someone who seems as though they have reached it.

We can take heart when we look at the conversion of Saul of Tarsus. It was so radical and unexpected that when it happened, first-century Christians thought he was attempting to infiltrate their ranks and persecute the church even further. They didn't believe that God could save someone as wicked and hostile toward the church as Saul. But we know that Saul became Paul the Apostle.

If you know someone who seems so far gone and permanently hardened toward the gospel, keep praying. You never know. That person just might be the next Paul.

UNDEFEATED

"And I also say to you that you are Peter, and on this rock I will build My church, and the gates of Hades shall not prevail against it." (Matthew 16:18 NLT)

Through the years, there have been those who have set themselves against the church and have tried to destroy it. The Roman emperor, Diocletian, set up a stone pillar on which these words were inscribed: "For having exterminated the name Christian from the earth." I wonder how he would feel if he could see the monument today. It didn't work.

There have been those who have tried to stop the work of God. Communist countries, for example, have tried. One Roman leader made a coffin to symbolize his intention, in his words, to "bury the Galilean" by killing His followers. But he soon learned that he could not put Jesus in that coffin. Finally, he ended up believing in the One that he tried to destroy. Nothing and no one has ever been able to stop the church, because Jesus established it, and He said, "The gates of hell shall not prevail against it."

Now, the devil will not cooperate with our attempt to get the gospel out. He will oppose it with everything that he has. "The gates of hell" refers to the forces of the devil, and when Jesus says the gates of hell shall not prevail against the church, He is not saying that these forces will not try to attack us. Rather, what He is saying, primarily, is that as we move forward as soldiers in His army, the devil's opposition will not prevail. The truth of the matter is that he will lose in the end.

We may lose a battle here and there. But clearly, we will win the war in the end.

Weekend

A Life Worth Living

"I have come that they may have life, and that they may have it more abundantly." (John 10:10)

Sometimes people think Christians live the most boring lives imaginable. But nothing could be further from the truth. The fact of the matter is that a happy life is a holy life—a life that is lived for God. Jesus not only promised us life beyond the grave, but He certainly promised us a dimension of life on this earth that is worth living when He said, "I have come that they might have life and have it more abundantly."

There are two ways we can live our lives: the right way and the wrong way. There are two paths we can take: the narrow path that leads to life or the broad way that leads to destruction. There are two foundations we can build on: the rock or sinking sand. The result is that we can either live a happy and holy life or a miserable and unholy life.

When most people think of a life dedicated to God, they envision something full of misery and rules and regulations. The picture that most unbelievers have of a Christian is one of gloom and boredom.

But when you know God and you realize that the Bible is not a mere book, but God's living Word to each of us, it takes on a whole new meaning. When you realize that prayer is not just going through some ritual, but it is communicating with the all- powerful, all-knowing, all-loving God who is interested in you, that means a lot. That is something that the world does not have. There is nothing like it out there. When you truly come to know God, you realize the Christian life is the greatest life there is.

Monday

THE REAL THING

"But none of these things move me; nor do I count my life dear to myself, so that I may finish my race with joy, and the ministry which I received from the Lord Jesus, to testify to the gospel of the grace of God." (Acts 20:24)

Imagine that you have just come out of a wonderful restaurant and had a great meal. You are thinking, "That was great." Then you happen to glance over at the gutter, where you notice a discarded burrito from a fast-food restaurant. Are you going to say, "All right! A burrito!" and pick it up? Of course not. You will not eat that thing, because you are satisfied. You have just experienced the real thing. You don't want a cheap imitation.

In the same way, when you know the Lord and have been experiencing a real relationship with Him and then the devil comes along and offers you some cheap imitation, you will see it for what it is. When you see who Jesus is, then you see what the world is. But if you are only looking at this world and not spending enough time with the Lord, you will have a diminished view of God and an exalted view of this world—when it should be the other way around.

Everything you need in life is found in a relationship with God. You can discover that the easy way or the hard way. Are you finishing your race with joy? Or, are you going outside of your relationship with the Lord, trying to find some happiness that this world might offer? I can tell you right now that it will be a dead-end street. It will never satisfy you, because once you have had the real thing, cheap imitations will never suffice.

Tuesday

A MAN OF SORROWS

Then Jesus brought them to an olive grove called Gethsemane, and he said, "Sit here while I go on ahead to pray." He took Peter and Zebedee's two sons, James and John, and he began to be filled with anguish and deep distress. (Matthew 26:36–37 NLT)

If I had the opportunity to know my entire future from today on, I think I would pass. I would rather not know. But Jesus, being God, knew everything about His future down to the smallest detail. As He agonized in the Garden of Gethsemane, He knew that in just a few short hours, He would be nailed to a Roman cross and crucified. He knew that He would be humiliated. He would be beaten. He would go through a horrendous whipping. He knew the great anguish that was ahead.

The Bible tells us Jesus was "a man of sorrows, acquainted with bitterest grief" (Isaiah 53:3 NLT). The Bible also says in Hebrews, "This High Priest of ours understands our weaknesses, for he faced all of the same temptations we do, yet he did not sin. So let us come boldly to the throne of our gracious God. There we will receive his mercy, and we will find grace to help us when we need it" (4:15 NLT).

In other words, God knows what you're going through. You have a High Priest—that is, Jesus—who has faced the challenges you presently face. Jesus was in this horrendous, difficult time, experiencing deep loneliness and abandonment by His friends. Yet He went through it.

The next time you face difficulty, the next time you face hardship, the next time you feel misunderstood and abandoned, remember that Jesus already has experienced those things. You have someone who understands you, sympathizes with you, and is there to strengthen you.

HIS WILL, NOT MINE

*He went on a little farther and fell face down on the ground, praying,
"My Father! If it is possible, let this cup of suffering be taken away from me.
Yet I want your will, not mine." (Matthew 26:39 NLT)*

There are some people who teach that we should never pray, "Not my will, but Yours be done," because it supposedly voids what you have just prayed for. What nonsense. If Jesus prayed this, certainly we should follow His example. He gave us the same pattern in the Lord's Prayer when He said, "May your Kingdom come soon. May your will be done here on earth, just as it is in heaven" (Matthew 6:10 NLT). I never need to be afraid to say, "Lord, Your will be done."

Then there are those who say that we should only pray for something once; otherwise, we are demonstrating a lack of faith. Yet Jesus taught His disciples, "Keep on asking, and you will be given what you ask for. Keep on looking, and you will find. Keep on knocking, and the door will be opened" (Luke 11:9 NLT). We give up far too easily sometimes.

We won't always know the will of God in every situation. Then there are times when we will know the will of God, but we won't like it. Finally, there are times when we will know the will of God, but we don't understand it.

I like what the late D. L. Moody said, "Spread out your petition before God, and then say, 'Thy will, not mine, be done.'" Moody concluded, "The sweetest lesson I have learned in God's school is to let the Lord choose for me." Have you found that to be true? We must never be afraid to trust an unknown future to a known God.

Thursday

THE REASON FOR REJECTION

Inside, the leading priests and the entire high council were trying to find witnesses who would lie about Jesus, so they could put him to death. (Matthew 26:59 NLT)

We might wonder how the religious leaders of Jesus' day could be so heartless as to take Him and put Him to such a quick death. Where was their compassion? Where was their sense of fairness? Even if they didn't accept Him as the Messiah, what was behind this hatred toward Him? Why their desire for such a quick execution?

We could take the same question and apply it to the broader one of why people reject Jesus Christ without ever taking time to consider His claims. Why do people reject the revelation of Scripture, while in most cases, they have never taken the time to read it for themselves? Why is that people refuse to give at least a fair hearing to the message of the gospel? Jesus said, "Their judgment is based on this fact: The light from heaven came into the world, but they loved the darkness more than the light, for their actions were evil" (John 3:19 NLT).

Someone may say, "The reason I am not a Christian is because I disagree with this or I have problems with that." According to Jesus, the real reason is that their deeds are evil. They don't want to come into the light, where their deeds will be exposed. Everything else is nothing more than an excuse people hide behind.

I am not saying that people do not have legitimate questions to ask. I am not saying people do not grapple with some of these truths. What I am saying is that when people are true seekers of God and they are presented with the answers to their questions, they will believe.

BAD COMPANY

Peter said, "I swear by God, I don't know the man."
And immediately the rooster crowed. (Matthew 26:74 NLT)

Peter's denial of Jesus did not happen over a period of seconds or minutes, but over a period of hours. An hour had passed from the time the first person said, "You were one of those with Jesus the Galilean," to the time Peter made his second denial. He had ample opportunity to hightail it out of there, but he remained in this situation. It just reminds us of the fact that no person is safe from temptation except the one who flees from it. Peter, having been warned by Jesus himself, of all people, should have avoided any place where he could be weakened. He definitely should have steered clear of all roosters. I would have said, "Are there any roosters here? Because I'm leaving if there are. The Lord mentioned a rooster."

Greater men and women of God than most of us certainly have been compromised by lowering their standards and allowing themselves to be drawn into sin. People like Solomon. Samson. David. They all found out the hard way. Are we better than they were? Are we more spiritual than they were? I don't think so.

If someone like Simon Peter was capable of falling, then surely we are. First Corinthians 15:13 tells us, " 'Bad company corrupts good character' " (NLT). Peter was around people who were dragging him down spiritually. Are you in a similar situation today? Have you entered into relationships where people are dragging you down? Maybe it's a romance. Maybe it's a close friendship. Are you finding yourself compromising your principles to fit in and not offend anyone? Perhaps you need to reconsider who your friends are. Perhaps you need to make some immediate changes.

Weekend

Like Sheep

Once you were wandering like lost sheep. But now you have turned to your Shepherd, the Guardian of your souls. (1 Peter 2:25 NLT)

On more than one occasion, the Bible compares Christians to sheep. I don't know if I'm really happy about that, because sheep are not the most intelligent animals on earth.

It would have been nice if God had compared us to dolphins. Now there's an intelligent animal. I once had the opportunity to talk to a man who trained dolphins. I asked him, "Are dolphins really as intelligent as they seem?" He said, "In some ways, yes, and in some ways, no. They are very intelligent in many ways, because a dolphin can read a symbol and understand what it means." That is amazing to me.

But Jesus didn't compare us to dolphins. He compared us to sheep. And sheep are some of the stupidest animals around. They are easily spooked. They are vulnerable. They have no defense mechanisms to speak of. They can't run very fast. They are in constant need of care and attention. They have a horrible tendency to follow each other, even to their own death. It has been documented that if one sheep walks off a cliff, the others will follow.

The Bible says, "All of us have strayed away like sheep. We have left God's paths to follow our own" (Isaiah 53:6 NLT). Think about how many people have bought into the same lies, generation after generation. They fall into the same junk, the same addictions, and the same traps again and again.

We are like sheep. That is a fact. The question is, are you going to be a smart sheep or a dumb one? Smart sheep stay close to the Shepherd, and that is where we all need to be.

Monday

CRUCIFIED WITH CHRIST

Then Jesus said to His disciples, "If anyone desires to come after Me, let him deny himself, and take up his cross, and follow Me." (Matthew 16:24)

When Jesus referred to taking up the cross, I'm sure the meaning wasn't lost on the disciples. The cross, as the people would know in this time and culture, was a hated and despised symbol. It was the symbol of a very cruel death. The Romans crucified many people on the roads leading into their cities as a warning to any man or woman who would dare defy the powers of Rome. The cross was meant to humiliate. It was meant to torture. Ultimately, it was meant to kill.

Today, the cross is shrouded in religiosity. It has become a symbol of many things, from a religious icon to an ornate piece of jewelry. It is not necessarily a bad thing to wear a cross, but I think we have lost the meaning of it. Imagine wearing a little replica of an electric chair around your neck, studded in diamonds, or maybe a little hangman's noose. Wearing jewelry like that would be rather morbid, because those are symbols of death and pain. But that is what the cross symbolized. So when Jesus told the disciples, "If you want to follow me, you must take up your cross," they would readily understand what He was speaking of.

The cross speaks of dying to self, of putting God's will before our own. If this sounds like a horrible, negative life-style, consider Paul's words: "I have been crucified with Christ; it is no longer I who live, but Christ lives in me" (Galatians 2:20). It's through death that we find life. May God help us to see that His trade-in deal is the best there is.

Tuesday

WALKING WITH JESUS

After that, He appeared in another form to two of them as they walked and went into the country. (Mark 16:22)

I think it's interesting to note those to whom Jesus chose to appear after His resurrection. We don't read about Him appearing to Caiaphas or Caesar. Now if it had been me, the first person I would have appeared to would have been Pilate: "Yo, Pilate! Remember me? Can't keep a good man down, can you?" Or, I would have appeared to Caiaphas, the high priest who, for the most part, orchestrated the crucifixion. But it is interesting how Jesus appeared to two disciples on the road to Emmaus and joined them on their journey. We don't know who they were, and they are not mentioned again in the Bible.

The Bible tells us that Jesus appeared in another form to them as they went into the country. In other words, He was going incognito. They didn't know that it was Jesus. The last sight they had of the Lord was His beaten and bloodied body. Surely they wanted to get that image out of their minds.

There they were, walking along, and Jesus was walking with them. It's a reminder to us that at all times, even when we don't realize it, Jesus is walking with us. Isaiah 43:2 promises, "When you pass through the waters, I will be with you; and through the rivers, they shall not overflow you. When you walk through the fire, you shall not be burned, nor shall the flame scorch you."

Maybe when you are in church, you feel close to God. But wherever you go, you can know that Jesus is with you there too. When you are going through hard times, even when you cannot feel Him, Jesus is there.

TRUE DISCIPLES

"These who have turned the world upside down have come here too." (Acts 17:6)

The Christian life is more than just saying a prayer or walking down an aisle and getting "fire insurance" as it were. The Christian life is meant to be dynamic. It is meant to be exciting. It is meant to have a radical effect on the way that you live and your outlook on life, because Jesus Christ not only wants to be your Savior. He wants to be your Lord. He not only wants to be your friend, but He also wants to be your God.

But I'm afraid that many today are living a substandard Christian experience. That term is really an oxymoron in many ways, because if it is a Christian experience, then it shouldn't be substandard. In a sense, that isn't even a technically correct term.

You really can't be a substandard Christian. Yet there are many who are failing to receive all that God has for them. How did a handful of ordinary people living in the first century turn their world, as they knew it, upside down? They did it without television, without radio, without mega-churches, and without all the resources that we think are so important today in reaching the goal of world evangelism.

How is it that they were able to do it? I think you could sum it up in one word: disciple. They were disciples of Jesus Christ—not fair weather followers, but true disciples. They weren't living an anemic, watered-down, ineffective version of the Christian life. They were living the Christian life as it was meant to be lived—as Christ Himself offered it and as the early disciples apprehended it. If we want to impact our culture today, then we, too, must be disciples.

Thursday

DISCIPLESHIP'S IMPORTANT DISTINCTION

"Go therefore and make disciples of all the nations, baptizing them in the name of the Father and of the Son and of the Holy Spirit. ..." (Matthew 28:19)

What does it mean to be a disciple? Certainly we need to know the answer to that question. After all, Jesus told us to "Go therefore and make disciples of all nations. ..." But how can we make disciples if we are not disciples ourselves? Are the qualifications of discipleship different from those of simply coming to faith? I believe the answer is yes.

First, Jesus tells us that if we want to be His disciples, we must deny ourselves. This is a foundational issue. We have a choice in life: we can either live for ourselves or we can deny ourselves. We can either ignore the cross, or we can take it up and follow Him.

The great barrier to being a disciple of Jesus Christ is summed up in one word: self. Self-obsession is not something unique to our generation, although the Bible does say that in the last days, people would be lovers of themselves and lovers of pleasure more than lovers of God (see 2 Timothy 3:1–5). Certainly we are living in a time of great self-obsession, especially in the United States. Yet we can trace its roots all the way back to the Garden of Eden. When Satan came to Eve, he essentially appealed to her selfish nature.

That is why Jesus said, "If anyone desires to come after Me, let him deny himself ... " (Matt. 16:24). Jesus didn't say, "Love yourself." He didn't say, "Have a positive self image." He said, "Deny yourself." That is what we need to do, because that is what gets in the way.

MAKING DISCIPLES

Therefore, go and make disciples of all the nations, baptizing them in the name of the Father and the Son and the Holy Spirit. Teach these new disciples to obey all the commands I have given you. And be sure of this: I am with you always, even to the end of the age." (Matthew 26:19–20 NLT)

In Matthew 26:19–20, we find the "marching orders" from Jesus that we know as the Great Commission. There are two things we should remember about it. First, these words are a command. That is why we call it the Great Commission and not the Great Suggestion. Jesus did not say, "Look, if you are in the mood, if it works into your busy schedule, as a personal favor to Me, would you consider going into the world and making disciples?" No. In the original language, this is a command.

Second, these words were not only given to the original eleven disciples. Nor were they exclusively for pastors, evangelists, and missionaries. They are for every follower of Jesus Christ. If we are His disciples, then we are commanded to go and make disciples of others. It doesn't necessarily mean we need to cross the sea. But certainly a good start would be crossing the street to talk to a neighbor.

What does it mean to make disciples? Jesus said, "Teach these new disciples to obey all the commands I have given you." Simply put, it means that you demonstrate discipleship for them by the way that you live. And of course, you verbally communicate God's Word.

I want to challenge you today to become a disciple of Jesus Christ—not just a fair-weather follower or simply a church-going person. Would you be His disciple? If so, your life will never be the same.

Weekend

ON THE MOUNTAINTOP

About eight days later Jesus took Peter, James, and John to a mountain to pray.
And as he was praying, the appearance of his face changed, and his clothing
became dazzling white. (Luke 9:28–29 NLT)

The transfiguration of Jesus was a significant event.
It was the halfway point on a very difficult journey.
From here, Jesus went backward from the cradle and
forward to the cross. Jesus apparently believed the time was
right for the disciples, specifically Peter, James, and John,
to have a greater glimpse of His glory.

Jesus singled these three out on a number of occasions.
When Jesus raised a child from the dead, He took Peter, James,
and John. Later, at the Garden of Gethsemane, there were
Peter, James, and John. Perhaps they were the super-spiritual
disciples, the spiritual elite. Or maybe they just needed special
attention. Whatever the reason, Jesus took these three with
Him, and He was transfigured before their eyes. His garments
became as white as light. His face shone like the sun. Moses and
Elijah's presence there with Him only added to the drama of
this wonderful day.

Peter couldn't contain Himself any longer and exclaimed,
"Master, this is wonderful! We will make three shrines—one
for you, one for Moses, and one for Elijah." Essentially he was
saying, "Let's stay here. This is the right idea. You glorified.
You shining. Let's just camp out here."

Believers today have a tendency to do this as well. As
this world grows darker, we are inclined to withdraw into
a Christian subculture instead of realizing there is a world
in need around us. God wants us to reach the world with
the gospel. But to do so, we need to come down from our
mountaintops and live this Christian life in the real world.

Monday

SPIRITUAL SLUMBER

*Then it happened, as they were parting from Him, that Peter said to Jesus,
"Master, it is good for us to be here; and let us make three tabernacles:
one for You, one for Moses, and one for Elijah"
—not knowing what he said. (Luke 9:33)*

Why did Peter say what he said during such a significant event as the Transfiguration? The Gospels give us two reasons: One, he didn't know what to say, and two, he was "heavy with sleep." This was a bad time to fall asleep. Imagine what else Peter might have seen had he been fully awake and watchful.

This, of course, would not be the last time that Peter, along with James and John, would fall asleep on the watch. In the Garden of Gethsemane, Jesus told them, "Watch and pray. ... " Then He went a few feet away and began to pray. When He came back, they were all sleeping. They were missing out on a significant event in the life of the Lord.

I wonder how much we miss out on because of our spiritual slumber. How many times are we spiritually slumbering when God wants to speak to us through His Word? Because we are too preoccupied with other things, we don't have the discipline to pick up the Bible and open it. How many times are we spiritually slumbering instead of going to church and being fed from the Word of God? How many times are we spiritually slumbering when the Lord would want us to speak up for Him? We're asleep on the watch.

Like the disciples, we, too, can miss out on what God wants to do in and through us. We need to be awake. We need to be alert. We need to be paying attention.

Tuesday

TABLOID MENTALITY

Now I urge you, brethren, note those who cause divisions and offenses, contrary to the doctrine which you learned, and avoid them. (Romans 16:17)

It seems as though we are living in a day of tabloid mentality. I have never seen a culture and society so obsessed with gossip, innuendos, and rumors. Just turn on the TV and you'll find all kinds of programs that probe into the personal lives of others.

This tabloid mentality has even entered the news media, where reporters hunt for that juicy piece of gossip. The tragedy is that if someone is charged with a crime today, we try him or her in the media before they ever have had the opportunity to enter a court of law where evidence is presented and where they face their accusers.

Sadly, this kind of thinking can even enter the church. When we hear something about someone else, immediately our ears perk up. But what does the Bible tell us? It says that love believes the best of every person. It doesn't say that love believes the worst. This means when someone says something about a Christian brother or sister, you should immediately have some disbelief in your heart. The reason is that you are to believe the best of that individual. We must be very careful, because many times we accept rumor as truth. Then to make matters worse, we start repeating what we've heard without checking the facts.

One of the things the Bible says that God hates is the one who sows discord among others (see Proverbs 6:16–19). This is the person who spreads rumors, who spreads innuendos, and who slanders others. God hates this.

Don't be someone who spreads rumors. Don't be someone who gossips. It's wrong. It's sinful. And it displeases God.

Wednesday

CARING ENOUGH
TO CONFRONT

*Dear brothers and sisters, if another Christian is overcome by some sin,
you who are godly should gently and humbly help that person back onto
the right path. And be careful not to fall into the same temptation yourself.*
(Galatians 6:1 NLT)

You would think that, after observing the behavior of
some people, they have a verse in their Bible that says,
"Brothers and sisters, if someone is caught in a sin, go
and tell as many people as possible. And then ultimately go and
try to drive that person away." But this is not what Scripture
tells us to do.

In Matthew 18, Jesus gave us the steps we should take when
it appears someone has fallen into sin (and I emphasize the
word *appears*). First, we must know all the facts. When you hear
something about someone, instead of talking about it, determine to go to that person and say, "I heard this about you. Is it
true?" Hopefully, you can get the issue resolved immediately.

But to fail to go to someone when you know a sin is being
committed is to actually cause that individual, and the church
as a whole, the greatest harm. Scripture says, "A little leaven
leavens the whole lump (Galatians 5:9 NLT). In most cases, you
will find that believers rarely approach a sinning believer or
allegedly sinning believer. Instead of seeking to help a person
who possibly may have never sinned at all, they end up slan-
dering that individual. This is wrong. If you have ever had
this happen to you, then you know how painful it can be.

Remember, the devil wants to turn believers against each
other. He will attack us from the outside, but many times,
when that does not work, he seeks to infiltrate our ranks and
divide us.

Thursday

WHY FORGIVE?

Then Peter came to him and asked, "Lord, how often should I forgive someone who sins against me? Seven times?" (Matthew 18:21 NLT)

Talk about a person who had been wronged. Joseph's brothers had done all kinds of horrible things to him. They betrayed him, their own flesh and blood, and sold him into slavery. But through an amazing course of events that were directed by the hand of God, Joseph became the second most powerful man in the world at that time in history. One day, his brothers were brought before him—the very ones who had betrayed him. With one word, they could have become headless brothers. It could have been payback time for Joseph. But I love what he said: "Don't be afraid of me. Am I God, to judge and punish you? As far as I am concerned, God turned into good what you meant for evil. He brought me to the high position I have today so I could save the lives of many people" (Genesis 50:19–20 NLT).

Did Joseph's brothers deserve to be forgiven? No. But if we resort to that kind of thinking, we must ask ourselves, "Do we deserve to be forgiven by God?" No. So we should forgive as God has forgiven us.

There is no point in burying the hatchet if you're determined to mark the site. Let it go. Forgive. Forget. Put it behind you. Move forward. If you refuse to forgive people who have wronged you, then you will become a bitter person. The problem with bitterness is that it infects those around you (see Hebrews 12:14–15 NLT).

If someone has sinned against you, you must learn to forgive. I know it is not an easy thing to do. But when you forgive someone, you release a prisoner—yourself.

LORD OF ALL

> *"So likewise, whoever of you does not forsake all that he has cannot be My disciple." (Luke 14:33)*

It was George Bernard Shaw who said, "There are two sources of unhappiness in life. One is not getting what you want. The other is getting it." This statement reminds me of the rich young ruler who came to Jesus seeking answers. Here was a man who, of all men, should have been content and fulfilled. He had great influence and affluence. Yet in spite of all his accomplishments, there was something missing in his life. He asked, "Good Teacher, what good thing shall I do that I may have eternal life?"

Jesus told him, "If you want to enter into life, keep the commandments." Jesus was not implying that by keeping the Ten Commandments one would be saved. Rather, Jesus held the Ten Commandments up as a mirror to this man to show him his sin.

The ruler replied, "All these things I have kept from my youth. What do I still lack?"

I think Jesus probably smiled at this. He saw what this man was really all about. So He took it up a notch and said, "If you want to be perfect, go, sell what you have and give to the poor, and you will have treasure in heaven; and come, follow Me."

Jesus knew the problem with this young ruler was that possessions had possessed his soul. But Jesus just as easily could have said something completely different to someone else. What is really holding someone back from Christ and from further spiritual progress can vary from person to person.

We would do well to come before Jesus and ask, "Lord, is there anything in my life that is getting in the way of my relationship with You?"

Weekend

THE REWARDS
OF RIGHT CHOICES

Then Peter said, "See, we have left all and followed You." (Luke 18:28)

Peter had been listening in on the conversation between the rich, young ruler and Jesus. It revealed, beyond a shadow of a doubt, that possessions had possessed this young ruler's soul. He could not do what Jesus had asked, and as a result, he went away sorrowful.

Peter, after seeing what this ruler couldn't give up, pointed out, "See, we have left all and followed You" (Luke 18:28). In other words, "What's in it for us?" Now, what did Peter actually leave? He left a few broken-down nets and a fishing boat, but he left something. Granted, it wasn't a lot. But he left it behind.

Jesus answered, "Assuredly, I say to you, there is no one who has left house or parents or brothers or wife or children, for the sake of the kingdom of God, who shall not receive many times more in this present time, and in the age to come eternal life" (verses 29–30). Jesus was saying, "It will be made up to you, Peter."

This promise holds true today. Whatever you have given up for Jesus, it will be made up to you. Maybe you have lost a friendship here and there. Maybe you gave up a certain life-style. Maybe you have made changes in your life, and so you should have. But God will make it up to you. I think, when you look back, it will only become clearer to you that you made the right choice in following Him. You will realize that not only has God made it up to you in this life, but also that He will make it up to you in eternity when you hear Him say, "Well done, good and faithful servant."

Monday

POWERED BY HIS SPIRIT

Don't act thoughtlessly, but try to understand what the Lord wants you to do. Don't be drunk with wine, because that will ruin your life. Instead, let the Holy Spirit fill and control you." (Ephesians 5:17–18 NLT)

When we think of being filled with the Spirit, we often relate it to an emotional experience or a feeling of euphoria. But in reality, the word, "filled," could be translated, "controlled by." It is a word that speaks of what happens when the wind fills the sails of a boat and guides it along. So God is saying that we are to let His Spirit fill us and control our lives.

Another interesting thing about this word is that in the original language, it is in a tense that speaks of something that should be done continually. So you could translate this sentence, "Be constantly filled with the Spirit." This is not a one time event. Instead, it is something that takes place over and over again, just as we repeatedly fill the gas tanks in our cars to keep them running. God wants to refill us with His Spirit. It is a great thing to say each day, "Lord, fill me with your Spirit. Lord, fill me once again." You may have emotional experiences. You may not have emotional experiences. But that has very little to do with the reality of being filled with and controlled by the Spirit.

One other thing about this phrase from Ephesians 5:18 is that it's a command, not a suggestion. The Scripture is not saying, "If it works with your schedule, if you don't mind, would you please consider maybe letting the Holy Spirit fill and control you?" Rather, God is saying that He commands us, He orders us, to be filled with the Holy Spirit.

Tuesday

THANKFUL IN EVERYTHING

In everything give thanks; for this is the will of God in Christ Jesus for you.
(1 Thessalonians 5:18)

In her wonderful book, The Hiding Place, Corrie ten Boom relates an amazing story about the importance of being thankful. Corrie and her sister Betsy were held in a concentration camp known as Ravensbruk, where they lived in barracks that were plagued with lice. Lice were everywhere—in their hair and on their bodies. One day, Betsy said to her, "Corrie, we need to give thanks to God for the lice."

Corrie said, "Betsy, you have gone too far this time. I am not going to thank God for lice."

Betsy said, "Oh, but Corrie, the Bible tells us, 'In everything give thanks.' "

Still, Corrie did not want to thank God for the lice. As it turns out, Corrie and Betsy were trying to reach the other women in their barracks with the message of the gospel, and they had been holding Bible studies. Corrie found out later that because of the lice, the guards would not go into those barracks, and therefore, they were able to have their Bible studies. As a result, they led many of the women to the Lord. So it turns out that God can even use lice.

If the Bible said, "In some things give thanks," I would say, "No problem there!" But it says, "In everything give thanks." That is not an easy thing to do.

This verse doesn't say we should give thanks for everything as much it says in everything. There are some things that happen, and I'm not glad they happened. But I am glad that, in spite of the tragedies, God is still on the throne, and He is still in control of all circumstances that surround my life.

To Know His Will

*I beseech you therefore, brethren, by the mercies of God, that you present your
bodies a living sacrifice, holy, acceptable to God, which is your reasonable
service. And do not be conformed to this world, but be transformed
by the renewing of your mind, that you may prove what is that good
and acceptable and perfect will of God. (Romans 12:1–2.)*

We find in Romans 12:1–2 what we call a conditional
promise. The promise is that you can know what the
perfect will of God is for your life. The conditions
are that you must present yourself to God and that you must
not be conformed to this world. Notice the order. First, you
offer yourself as a living sacrifice, and then you will know the
will of God. We tend to want to know God's will first and then
decide whether we want to give ourselves to it.

It reminds me of when my son Jonathan was little. My wife
would ask him, "Jonathan, are you hungry?"

Often the response was, "What are you cooking?" If it was
vegetables, then he was not hungry at that particular moment.
But if it was ice cream, then he was starving.

In the same way, we will sometimes say, "Lord, what is your
will? Before I am going to surrender to it, I would like to know
what I am getting myself into." But God may tell you something that you don't want to hear. The question is, are you
going to do what He says?

It has been said that the condition of an enlightened mind is
a surrendered heart. If you want to know the will of God, then
you must have a heart that is surrendered. Present yourself to
Him. Then accept His will, no matter what.

Thursday

TASTE AND SEE

"Taste and see that the Lord is good. Oh, the joys of those who trust in him!"
(Psalm 34:8 NLT)

We need to remember that God's will is good. It may not seem like it at times, but it is. His plan for us is good. However, He usually doesn't give us a detailed blueprint. Usually, God reveals His will to us in bits and pieces. He sees the big picture, while we just see a little at a time.

If you had been the father of Joseph, surely like all parents, you would have prayed for the welfare of your child. But when Joseph was sold into slavery by his own brothers, you could have easily said, "God, what are you doing? Why did you allow this?" Yet if God had not allowed this to happen, Joseph never would have been put into that position of influence that enabled him to save the country and his own family.

If you had been the mother of Moses, how your heart would have broken when you saw your own child being taken into the Pharaoh's court! Yet it was all part of God's plan to mold Moses into that leader who would lead Israel out of Egypt and its bondage.

If you had been the mother of Jesus and watched your own son hanging on that cross, how easily you could have said, "Lord, why did you let this happen?" But if Jesus had not died on that cross and taken our sins upon himself, we could not know Him today.

So when you look at the will of God in progress, it may not always make sense. But you must believe that God knows what He is doing. His will is good. Just wait until He finishes what He has begun.

SIBLING RIVALRY

If one part suffers, all the parts suffer with it, and if one part is honored, all the parts are glad. Now all of you together are Christ's body, and each one of you is a separate and necessary part of it. (1 Corinthians 12:26–27 NLT)

I think there may be three big surprises in heaven: One, many of the people we expected to see *won't* be there. Two, many of the people we never expected to see *will* be there. And three, *we* will be there.

Remember the story of the prodigal son? He went out, tarnished the family name, consorted with prostitutes, and threw away his fortune. Then one day, he came to his senses and returned home. His father ran to meet him, smothered him with kisses, and threw a big party. It was a great celebration.

Meanwhile, the prodigal's older brother was out in the field, heard the commotion, and wanted to know what was going on. He was told that his younger brother had returned home. But instead of rejoicing, he was angry and jealous.

This can happen with us. We see God bless someone else in a tangible way, maybe with a promotion at work or another blessing of some kind. Or maybe God puts His hand on a certain individual and begins to use him. In the midst of all this, we say, "Lord, wait a second. I have faithfully served you all of these years. How is it that this Johnny-come-lately pops up, and you are blessing him? It isn't fair. I am much more godly. I am much more committed. And most of all, I am much more humble."

The fact of the matter is that we should rejoice whenever God is being glorified and the gospel is being preached.

Weekend

God's Fellow Workers

Now he who plants and he who waters are one, and each one will receive
his own reward according to his own labor. (1 Corinthians 3:8)

In 1 Samuel 30, we find the story of David leading his men
to a successful battle. As they were returning home, those
who had stayed behind and watched the camp and the
supplies met them. But some of the troublemakers who had
fought in the battle didn't want to give any of the spoils of the
battle to those who stayed by the camp. But I love what David
said: "But as his part is who goes down to the battle, so shall
his part be who stays by the supplies; they shall share alike"
(verse 24).

Whether God has called you to serve Him in such a way that
people see you or whether He has called you to serve Him by
supporting others who are seen, God will bless you and reward
you in that final day.

Maybe you feel as though your life isn't really making a
difference or that what you have to offer God doesn't mean
all that much. You will be in for some surprises in heaven,
because what may not seem very valuable on earth will be of
great value in heaven.

I read a story about a man who found an old, blue-and-
white vase while he was cleaning his attic. He took it to the
auction to sell it, thinking he would probably get, $20, $30, or
maybe even $100 for it. To his utter amazement, the vase sold
for $324,000. It was original, 15th-century art from the Ming
dynasty.

What may not seem that valuable now will be later. Until
then, we need to be faithful with what God has given us to do.

Monday

NOT HOME YET

"But many who seem to be important now will be the least important then, and those who are considered least here will be the greatest then."
(Matthew 19:30 NLT)

A missionary couple who had served for many years in Africa were returning to the United States. Leaving Africa with broken health and no pension, they felt defeated, discouraged, and afraid. As it turned out, President Teddy Roosevelt was traveling on the same ship. Of course, it caused a great commotion as everyone tried to catch a glimpse of the president, who was returning from a hunting expedition. The missionary commented to his wife, "Something is wrong. Why should we, who have given our lives in service to the Lord all these years in Africa, come back and not receive any fanfare or attention? And this man, who has done nothing more than just go on a hunting trip, is the center of attention. It just doesn't seem right."

When the ship arrived, a brass band played and the mayor welcomed the president. The missionary was so discouraged. "It isn't fair," he told his wife. "Why have we not received any attention or adulation for what we have done? God is not treating us fairly."

She said, "Honey, why don't you just go tell that to the Lord?" A little bit later, he was smiling. His wife said, "You look different. What happened?"

He said, "Well, I told the Lord how bitter I was that the president received this tremendous homecoming, while no one greeted us when we returned home. Then it seemed as though the Lord put His hand on my shoulder and said, 'Son, you are not home yet.'"

God sees those things you do for Him, and He will bless you. But remember, we are not home yet.

Tuesday

BE CAREFUL
WHAT YOU ASK FOR

And He gave them their request, but sent leanness into their soul.
(Psalm 106:15)

I sometimes hear people say, "I have been wrestling with God in prayer!" My first thought always is, "I hope you lost." If you have been trying to bend God your way, then that is a problem. Prayer is not trying to move God your way; it is moving yourself His way.

In fact, I'm glad that God hasn't said yes to every prayer I have ever prayed. When I look back on some things I've prayed for, I realize that if the Lord would have allowed them, they could have destroyed me. They were not the right things or the right situations. So, God graciously and lovingly said no.

In John 15:7, Jesus gave an incredible promise regarding answered prayer. He said, "If you abide in Me, and My words abide in you, you will ask what you desire, and it shall be done for you." From the original language, this verse could be translated, "If you maintain a living communion with Me, and My word is at home with you, I command you to ask at once for yourself whatever your heart desires, and it will be yours."

When I read a promise like that, I gravitate immediately toward the part that says I can ask whatever my heart desires and it will be mine. But before that, Jesus said, "If you maintain a living communion with Me, and My word is at home with you. ... " If this is happening in your life, then you are going to want what God wants. If you are maintaining a living communion with God and His words are at home in your heart, then your outlook, desires—and in time, your prayers—will change.

Wednesday

PRIORITIES

And he will give you all you need from day to day if you live for him and make the Kingdom of God your primary concern. (Matthew 6:33 NLT)

A man was out driving in the country during a heavy rainstorm when he came across an old farmer who was surveying the ruins of his barn. He pulled over and to ask the farmer what happened. "Roof fell in," the farmer replied

"What happened with it? Why did it fall in?" asked the stranger.

"It leaked so long, it just finally rotted through," the farmer said.

"Why in the world didn't you fix it before it rotted through?"

"Well, sir," said the farmer, "I just never did seem to get around to it. When the weather was good, there wasn't a need for it. And when it rained, it was just too wet to work on."

Isn't it amazing that when you want to do something, you find the time, no matter how busy you are? But when someone asks you to do something you don't want to do, suddenly there is just no room in the schedule.

This can happen when it comes to the Christian life as well. If we are serving God only when it's convenient, then we are settling for second-best. If we make time for the things of God only when something better doesn't come along first, then we are missing out on what God wants to do in our lives.

How much better it is to make time for the things of God— to put the things of God above everything else. How much better it is to get your priorities right. Instead of making excuses, make time for the Lord. It is not only the simple way to live, but also the best way.

Thursday

THE FIRST AND GREATEST COMMANDMENT

Jesus replied, " 'You must love the Lord your God with all your heart,
all your soul, and all your mind." This is the first and greatest commandment.
A second is equally important: 'Love your neighbor as yourself.' "
(Matthew 22:37–38 NLT)

Some years ago, three hundred whales were found marooned on a beach. Scientists speculated that the whales had been chasing sardines and became trapped in shallow water when the tide went out. Now that's an amazing thing. By chasing little sardines, these gigantic creatures were ultimately led to their doom.

Many people waste their lives chasing sardines, so to speak. They major on the minors and have no clear focus or objective in mind. But God tells us what should be the primary goal of every Christian. If we can get our priorities straight in this area, everything else will come together. In fact, if we can get these two principles operative in our lives, then all the commandments of God will become a natural outflow of our commitment to Him. What are these principles? One, " 'You must love the Lord your God with all your heart, all your soul, and all your mind' " (Matthew 22:37 NLT); and two, " 'Love your neighbor as yourself' " (verse 38 nlt).

When Jesus spoke these words, He was identifying what should be the focus of every person. Essentially, He was saying that love is the basis for all obedience. If you really love God, then you will naturally want to do the things that please Him.

It has been said, "If you aim at nothing, you are bound to hit it." What is your highest priority in life? What are your goals? We all channel our energies and passions and thoughts toward something in life. What is it for you?

How to Love God

Jesus said to him, " 'You shall love the Lord your God with all your heart, with all your soul, and with all your mind.' " (Matthew 22:37)

When Jesus said that we are to love the Lord our God with all our hearts, we need to understand that to the ancient Hebrews, the heart referred to the core of one's personal being (see Proverbs 4:23). So to love the Lord with all our hearts means to love Him with all of our personal being.

Also, the word Jesus used for "soul" in Matthew 22:37 speaks of emotion. It is the same word Jesus used when He cried out in the Garden of Gethsemane, "My soul is exceedingly sorrowful, even to death." So, loving God includes our emotions.

But then, Scripture tells us that we are to love Him with all of our minds. This word, "mind" in the original language corresponds to that which we would usually call "might." It speaks of energy and strength, but also of intellectual commitment and determination.

So you see, to love the Lord includes every part of our lives. We love Him with all of our hearts in the deepest parts of our being. We love Him with all of our souls, with our emotions. But we also love Him with our minds. We love Him with our intellect. We love Him with our ability to reason. We love Him with all of the strength that is in us.

Now it seems as though some people love the Lord with all their minds, but they are afraid to express emotion to Him. There are others who love God, but seem to operate on raw emotion. We need to find the balance. God wants us to love Him with every fiber of our being.

Weekend

THEREFORE, LOVE YOUR NEIGHBOR

Jesus replied, " 'You must love the Lord your God with all your heart, all your soul, and all your mind.' This is the first and greatest commandment. A second is equally important: 'Love your neighbor as yourself.' " (Matthew 22:39 NLT)

W hen Jesus said, "Love your neighbor as yourself," He was not saying that before you can love others, you must first love yourself. That is the common interpretation we often hear, but that is not correct. Jesus is not teaching self-love. Essentially, He is saying that just as you already love yourself, as you already care for yourself and think about yourself, you are to love your neighbor in the same way.

We already love ourselves. As the apostle Paul said, "No one hates his own body but lovingly cares for it ..." (Ephesians 5:29 NLT). And that is true.

Sometimes people say, "I hate myself. I'm so ugly. I'm just so horrible. I just hate myself." Really? If you truly hated yourself, then you would be happy that you were ugly, right? Why is it that people who say they hate themselves spend all their time talking about themselves? "I hate the way that I look," they will say. "I hate this about myself. I hate that about myself." No, the fact of the matter is that all of the attention they shower on their own lives proves they love themselves. The truth is, we *all* love ourselves.

Jesus is saying, "You already love yourself; therefore, love your neighbor." He goes on to say that if you do this, as well as love the Lord with all your heart, all your soul, and all your mind, then all the commandments of God will be fulfilled, because you will naturally do the things that please Him.

Monday

GOD WITH SKIN ON

"So the Word became human and lived here on earth among us. He was full of unfailing love and faithfulness. And we have seen his glory, the glory of the only Son of the Father." (John 1:14 NLT)

I heard the story of a little boy who was frightened one night during a big thunderstorm. Terrified, he called out from his room, "Daddy, I am scared!"

His father, not wanting to get out of bed, called back, "Don't worry, Son. God loves you and will take care of you."

There was a moment of silence. The little boy said, "I know God loves me, but right now, I need somebody who has skin on."

Sometimes, our great and awesome God seems almost untouchable. That is where Jesus comes in. He was God with skin on, walking among us and showing us what God is like I think C. S. Lewis put it well: "The Son of God became a man that men might become sons of God."

God became a man so that you might become God's child. You are not born as a child of God. The Bible says that you need to be born again (John 3:3 NLT). There must come a moment in your life in which you turn from your sins and invite Jesus Christ to come into your life to be your Savior and Lord.

Have you done that yet? Would you like to know with certainty that if you died today, you would go to heaven? You can. He walked among us for a short time on this earth. But you can walk with Him forever. The choice is yours.

Tuesday

WHY JESUS CAME

"I have come that they may have life, and that they may have it more abundantly." (Matthew 20:28)

Ever since childhood, I have always had a great admiration for the historical person known as Jesus. I had seen all of His movies. I thought very highly of Him. As a little boy, I lived with my grandmother for a few years. I would thumb through her big family Bible and look at the pictures of Jesus. She also had a picture of Jesus hanging on the wall. I would stare at it and think, "I wish I could have known that man, Jesus."

The one thing I didn't like about the life of Jesus was how the story ended. I thought it should have been rewritten with a happier ending. The part about Him being crucified wrecked everything. He was on this great roll, healing people and teaching people. But then it all came to an end. Why did they have to put Him on a cross and kill Him?

It wasn't until after I became a Christian that I realized that the crucifixion of Jesus actually was the primary reason that He came to Earth in the first place.

Jesus came to die. He spoke of it frequently and in great detail. His arrest and crucifixion didn't take Him by surprise. Jesus summed it up well when He told His disciples, "For even the Son of Man did not come to be served, but to serve, and to give His life a ransom for many." (Mark 10:45).

You see, Jesus was born to die that we might live. Have you accepted the gift of eternal life that Jesus purchased with His death? If not, you can accept that gift today.

TRUE BELIEVERS

*"Those who have been born into God's family do not sin, because
God's life is in them. So they can't keep on sinning, because
they have been born of God" (1 John 3:9 NLT)*

Of the twelve disciples, we envision Judas Iscariot as
the one with shifty eyes, lurking in the shadows.
While the other disciples wore white, Judas would
have worn black. He was the one you would have immediately
recognized as the bad guy.

But I think Judas Iscariot was the very opposite: a phenom-
enal actor who came across as an upright man, devout in his
faith. As one of the Twelve, Judas had been handpicked by the
Lord Himself, but eventually betrayed Him for a few pieces
of silver.

Judas made the wrong choice to do the wrong thing, even
though he had been exposed to so much truth. With his own
ears, Judas heard Jesus deliver the Sermon on the Mount. With
his own eyes, Judas saw Jesus walk on water. He saw Lazarus
raised from the dead. He saw the multitudes fed with the loaves
and fishes. He saw the blind receive their sight. He saw it all.
He heard it all. Yet he became more hardened in his unbelief.

Judas could go deeper into sin because he really never knew
Jesus. If you are a true Christian and you begin to compromise, you will sense the conviction of the Holy Spirit. But if
you can sin without any remorse, then one must question if you
really know God. The true child of God, though still a sinner,
simply will not live in a pattern of sin.

If you find yourself, as a follower of Christ, immediately
experiencing conviction when you start to sin, then rejoice.
It is a reminder that you belong to the Lord.

Thursday

WHY THE CROSS?

"For the message of the cross is foolishness to those who are perishing, but to us who are being saved it is the power of God." (1 Corinthians 1:18)

A true story was reported about a couple that was visiting a jewelry store. As the jeweler showed them various crosses, the woman commented, "I like these, but do you have any without this little man on them?"

That is what so many people want today: a cross without Jesus. They want a cross without any offense, one that will look cool with their outfits. But if we could travel back in time and see the cross in its original context, we would realize that it was a bloody and vile symbol. It would have been the worst picture imaginable to see someone hanging on a cross.

The Romans chose crucifixion because it was meant to be a slow, torturous way to die. It was designed to humiliate a person. The crucifixions outside Roman cities served as warnings to anyone who would dare oppose the rule of Rome.

If there was any other way, do you think that God would have allowed His Son to suffer like this? If there had been any other way we could have been forgiven, then God surely would have found it. If living a good moral life would get us to heaven, then Jesus never would have died for us. But He did, because there was and is no other way. He had to pay the price for our sin. At the Cross, Jesus purchased the salvation of the world.

If you were ever tempted to doubt God's love for you, even for a moment, then take a long, hard look at the Cross. Nails did not hold Jesus to that cross. His love did.

THE ULTIMATE SACRIFICE

"For God so loved the world that he gave his only Son, so that everyone who believes in him will not perish but have eternal life." (John 3:16 NLT)

I heard a true story about a man who operated a drawbridge. At a certain time every afternoon, he raised the bridge for a ferryboat to go by, and then lowered it in time for a passenger train to cross over. He performed this task precisely, according to the clock.

One day, he brought his son to work so he could watch. As his father raised the bridge, the boy got excited and wanted to take a closer look. His father realized his son was missing and began looking for him. To his horror, his son had come dangerously close to the bridge's gears. Frantic, he wanted to go rescue him, but if he left the controls, he would not be back in time to lower the bridge for the approaching passenger train.

He faced a dilemma. If he lowered the bridge, his son would be killed. If he left it raised, hundreds of others would die. He knew what he had to do. With tears streaming down his face, he watched the passenger train roll by. On board, two women chatted over tea. Others were reading newspapers. All were totally unaware of what had just transpired. The man cried out, "Don't you realize that I just gave my son for you?" But they just continued on their way.

This story is a picture of what happened at the Cross. God gave up His beloved Son so that we might live. But most people don't give it a second thought. How about you? Are you conscious of the ultimate sacrifice God made on your behalf? Will you be sure to thank Him?

Weekend

A PIVOTAL BELIEF

"But the fact is that Christ has been raised from the dead. He has become the first of a great harvest of those who will be raised to life again."
(1 Corinthians 15:20 NLT)

I read about a person who wrote the following to a local newspaper advice columnist: *Dear Uticus, Our preacher said on Easter that Jesus just swooned on the cross and that His disciples nursed Him back to health. What do you think? Sincerely, Bewildered.* The columnist replied, *Dear Bewildered, Beat your preacher with a cat of nine tails with 39 heavy strokes, nail him to a cross, hang him in the sun for six hours, run a spear through his heart, embalm him, put him in an airless tomb for 36 hours, and see what happens. Sincerely, Uticus.*

What sets the Christian faith apart from all other beliefs and religious systems in this world? It might come down to this: If you go to the tombs of any of the prophets on which world religions have been founded, you will find them occupied. But if you go to the tomb of Jesus Christ, you will find it empty, because He is alive. We serve a living Savior.

This is why the resurrection of Jesus is such an important message and also why it has been opposed so much throughout history. The devil knows that the Resurrection spells his defeat. He also knows that if you believe this great truth that Jesus died on the cross for your sins and rose again from the dead, it can change your life.

Not only can it change your life, but putting your faith in Him also means that you will have a new, resurrected body someday. As believers, we have this great hope that we, too, will live again.

Monday

THE TIME TO RUN

> *"Now behold, two of them were traveling that same day to a village called Emmaus, which was seven miles from Jerusalem. And they talked together of all these things which had happened."*
> *(Luke 24:13–14)*

I find, as a Christian, that I need to be reminded of things that I sometimes forget. Have you noticed that you don't always know as much as you think you know? I have found that I often forget what I ought to remember, and I remember what I ought to forget.

In Luke 24 we find the story of two men who had forgotten some things they should have remembered. At one time, they had been passionate followers of Christ, but now their dreams had been destroyed as they watched Him die on a Roman cross. Even as He hung there, they were hoping for a last-minute miracle. But no miracle came. They felt discouraged. Let down. So, they decided to leave town.

Jesus said that He would be crucified and after three days, would rise again. He spoke of it often. But they had forgotten. Now they wanted to put as much distance between them and the cross as possible.

We need to remember that every step away from the cross is a step in the wrong direction. When we are hurting or have failed spiritually, that is not the time to run away from the cross. That is the time to run to it.

Maybe something has happened in your life and you feel as though God has let you down. Maybe some tragedy has occurred. But God has not failed you. He has not forgotten you. Now is the time to run back to the cross. Now is the time to remember His Word and the promises it holds for you.

Tuesday

Empty Net Syndrome

"Simon Peter said, 'I'm going fishing.'
" 'We'll come, too,' they all said. So they went out in the boat,
but they caught nothing all night." (John 21:3 NLT)

It was *déjà vu* time for the disciples. They had been fishing all night on the Sea of Galilee and hadn't caught anything. The Lord had risen. He already had appeared to some of the disciples. There were no clear marching orders, so they thought they would go back to what they knew how to do: fish.

Now it is early in the morning, probably still dark. They see a figure standing on the shore. He calls out, "Friends, have you caught any fish?"

Throughout the Bible, God often asked probing questions when He wanted a confession. In the same way, Jesus was asking His disciples, "Did you catch anything? Have you been successful? Have things gone the way you had hoped they would go? Are you satisfied?"

Why did Jesus want them to admit their failure? So He could bring them to the place where they needed to be.

When they cast the net on the right side of the boat as Jesus told them to, their net became so heavy with fish that they couldn't pull it in. The Lord was teaching the disciples an important lesson: Failure often can be the doorway to real success.

We need to come to that point in our lives as well. We need to come and say, "Lord, I am not satisfied with the way my life is going. I am tired of doing it my way. I want to do it your way." If you will come to God like that, He will extend His forgiveness to you. Then He will take your life and transform it in ways you couldn't imagine.

WHAT LOVE LOOKS LIKE

"My little children, let us not love in word or in tongue, but in deed and in truth."
(1 John 3:18)

Have you ever felt like a spiritual failure? If so, then you're in good company. Even the Apostle Peter felt that way after he denied the Lord.

When Jesus told the disciples they would abandon Him in His hour of need, Peter insisted that *he* never would. But Jesus said that Peter would deny Him three times before the rooster crowed that day. And he did.

Now Peter finds himself in an awkward moment. Jesus was crucified and had risen on the third day. He suddenly appears to them at the Sea of Galilee. Before they knew it, Jesus was cooking breakfast for everyone with the fish He had just helped them catch. Maybe as they ate, Peter was remembering when, not all that long ago, he denied the Lord by the glow of another fire.

Eventually, the Lord breaks the silence. He asks Peter a series of questions, each with the same phrase: "Do you love Me?"

Peter had learned his lesson. Instead of boasting of his love for the Lord, he simply answers, "Yes Lord; You know that I love you" (John 21:15–17). In the original language, the word Peter used for "love" was *phileo*. It could be translated, "have an affection for."

At least Peter was being honest. We can talk all day about how much we love God, but never act on it. Peter eventually proved his love for the Lord. A leader in the early church and the writer of two New Testament epistles, he reportedly was crucified upside-down as a martyr for his faith.

How about you? Is your love for the Lord expressed more by your words than your actions?

Thursday

FORTY DAYS

While he was blessing them, he left them and was taken up to heaven.
They worshiped him and then returned to Jerusalem filled with great joy.
(Luke 24:50–52 NLT)

During the 40 days from His resurrection to His ascension to heaven, Jesus was constantly appearing and vanishing before the disciples. I think He was getting the disciples accustomed to the fact that, even when He was not visible physically, He still would be present and available spiritually.

Before this time, the disciples had expected the Messiah of Israel to come and establish His kingdom, and they would reign with Him. There was no doubt in their minds that Jesus was the Messiah. But when He was crucified, it seemed like a colossal blunder. Now, in the days following the Resurrection, they began to realize that this was the plan all along. They understood that the Scriptures predicted that the Messiah would first suffer and later would come and rule in glory on Earth.

In the meantime, Jesus told them they were to "go and make disciples of all the nations, baptizing them in the name of the Father and the Son and the Holy Spirit," and to "teach these new disciples to obey all the commands I have given you" (Matthew 28:19–20 NLT).

After instructing them to wait in Jerusalem, where they would receive the promise of the Holy Spirit, Jesus led the disciples to Bethany and blessed them. Then, before their eyes, He was taken up to heaven.

The Father's promise, the Son's plans, and the Holy Spirit's power united in making these unlearned disciples the most invincible weapons ever to be held by the hand of God.

The disciples worshiped Him. They witnessed for Him. They would wait for Him until He returned. We should do the same.

WITHOUT CONDITION

Having predestined us to adoption as sons by Jesus Christ to Himself, according to the good pleasure of His will, to the praise of the glory of His grace, by which He made us accepted in the Beloved. (Ephesians 1:5–6)

There are a lot of people who think they should keep the Ten Commandments because they are under the impression that God will punish them if they don't. But the fact is that God loves us, and we keep His commandments because we are aware of this.

We need to know that God accepts us as we are. We don't have to do anything to earn His approval. We don't have to do anything to merit His love. In spite of our shortcomings and in spite of our sins, God loves us.

Some people come from homes in which their fathers never expressed love or showed any affection toward them. Therefore, they take that concept of their earthly fathers and place it on their Heavenly Father. They spend the rest of their lives trying to earn the approval of God, who already has given His approval to them. He loves us as we are. Of course, He doesn't want to leave us that way. He wants to change us so that we become more like Christ. Even then, God loves us when we do well, and He loves us when we fail.

Realizing this should cause us to want to love Him. As 1 John 4:19 says, "We love Him because He first loved us." So instead of wanting to keep God's commandments to earn His love, we should want to keep them *because of* His love for us. We should want to keep His commandments because we know they are right. It all comes down to our motives.

Weekend

NO OTHER GODS

"Do not worship any other gods besides me. Do not make idols of any kind, whether in the shape of birds or animals or fish. You must never worship or bow down to them, for I, the Lord your God, am a jealous God who will not share your affection with any other god! . . ." (Exodus 20:3–5 NLT)

What does it mean when God says, "Do not worship any other gods besides me"? It means that we are not to allow anything or anyone to takes the place of God in our lives. That god could be a career. It could be a possession. It could be a relationship. It could be so many things. But the Bible tells us, "Dear children, keep away from anything that might take God's place in your hearts" (1 John 5:21 NLT).

Scripture also warns us about idols that include objects or carved images. Before we dismiss this as an issue from the Old Testament period, let's consider how many religious icons and images we have in our culture today. While I'm not saying all of these are necessarily wrong, I am saying that we don't need them to worship God. Sometimes people say, "I need these things to remind me of God." But a person who knows God, loves Him, and is living in fellowship with Him does not need an image or a representation of God to worship Him. A dependence on such things indicates the absence of an inner spiritual life. Jesus said, "For God is Spirit, so those who worship him must worship in spirit and in truth" (1 John 4:23–24 NLT).

We don't need images. We don't need icons. We don't need symbols. God tells us, "Do not make idols of any kind." Give Him your undivided love.

Monday

MEAN WHAT YOU SAY

"You shall not take the name of the Lord your God in vain, for the Lord will not hold him guiltless who takes His name in vain." (Exodus 20:7)

One of the most obvious ways of taking the Lord's name in vain is through profanity. Unfortunately, most of us have heard the Lord's name taken in vain in that sense. That always bothers me, because that is my Lord they are speaking of. We might even find ourselves correcting someone. "You shouldn't take the Lord's name in vain," we might say. And right we are.

But did you know that profanity isn't the only way to take His name in vain? The phrase, "in vain," is used to describe something that is empty, idle, insincere, and frivolous. Think about that. To take His name in vain means to use His name in an empty or idle or insincere or frivolous way. As Christians, we often find ourselves tossing up little spiritual clichés such as "God bless you," "Praise the Lord," or "I'll pray for you." There is nothing wrong with these statements, but if we say them, we should mean them. We shouldn't say, "Praise the Lord" or "God bless you" when our hearts are not really in it. When we tell people, "I'll pray for you," then we should pray for them. Otherwise, we shouldn't say these things at all.

Jesus said, "But why do you call Me 'Lord, Lord,' and not do the things which I say?" (Luke 6:46). When we say that He's our Lord, yet we don't do what He tells us to, that is the ultimate way of taking His name in vain. Hypocrisy in the church is far worse than profanity in the street. Let's be careful not to take His name in vain.

Tuesday

REMEMBERING GOD

"Remember to observe the Sabbath day by keeping it holy. Six days a week are set apart for your daily duties and regular work, but the seventh day is a day of rest dedicated to the Lord your God." (Exodus 20:8–9 NLT)

The Ten Commandments can be broken into two sections: the first four deal with our relationship with God, while the second six deal with our relationships with people. The last of the commandments regarding our relationship with God pertains to the Sabbath. The Sabbath day was something that was set aside for the Jewish people, a day in which they were to worship the Lord and rest from their labors. God was, in essence, saying to His people that they were to keep this day as a holy day to Him.

But I also believe that the Sabbath day was pointing to something more than a 24-hour period. In fact, the New Testament tells us, "For all who enter into God's rest will find rest from their labors, just as God rested after creating the world" (Hebrews 4:10 NLT). The rest the Sabbath pointed toward was a rest in a relationship with God in which we recognize that we do not have to do things to earn His approval, but have found it in what Christ has done for us.

In our modern society in which we work so hard for success, few people seem to take time off to remember God and to thank Him for all that He has done for them. We seem to be too busy for God—that is, until a crisis hits and we suddenly find time to ask for His help. Let's be sure we are taking time to honor God and to thank Him for all He has done for us.

THE PROBLEM WITH ANGER

"Do not murder." (Exodus 20:13 NLT)

The sixth commandment obviously forbids the taking of another human life for no justifiable reason. We might say, "Well, I've never murdered anyone. At least I can say I haven't broken this commandment." But in the Sermon on the Mount, Jesus declared,

You have heard that the law of Moses says, "Do not murder. If you commit murder, you are subject to judgment." But I say, if you are angry with someone, you are subject to judgment! If you call someone an idiot, you are in danger of being brought before the high council. And if you curse someone, you are in danger of the fires of hell. (Matthew 5:21–22 NLT)

So, anger in our hearts can be like murdering someone. According to 1 John 3:15, "Anyone who hates another Christian is really a murderer at heart. And you know that murderers don't have eternal life within them" (nlt). The word, "hate," used here means "to habitually despise." It is not speaking of only a passing emotion of the affections, but a deep-rooted loathing. Now we all lose our tempers here and there. But this is speaking of hating, loathing, or despising someone. It is allowing bitterness toward someone to develop over a period of time—to the point that you are seething with anger every time you see that person or hear his or her name.

Spreading lies about someone, gossiping about them, or assassinating their character can be like murder. If you love God, then you will love your neighbor. And if you love your neighbor, you won't do these things to them.

Thursday

A Word to Children

"Honor your father and mother. Then you will live a long, full life in the land the Lord your God will give you." (Exodus 20:12 NLT)

The fifth of the Ten Commandments deals with the family, but in essence establishes the foundation for how we are to treat our fellow human beings. The family provides the strength of our country today. It has been said that a family can survive without a nation, but a nation cannot survive without the family.

In Ephesians 6:1, the apostle Paul says, "Children, obey your parents because you belong to the Lord, for this is the right thing to do" (NLT). Why should children obey their parents? Because it is the right thing to do. God says this is right. That is all you need to know. It is sort of like when you would ask your mom or dad, "Why do I have to do this?"

"Because I said so."

"But I don't understand."

"I know. One day you will understand, but for now it is because I said so."

What is right and wrong is not based on what we think or on a consensus of what others think is right or wrong. Something is right because God says it is right. Something is good because God says it is good. Needless to say, this flies against the cultural bias of today. Nowadays we hear more about children's rights than we do about their responsibilities. Children are not only expected to rebel, but they are even encouraged to do so. However, this is not God's order.

There is a two-fold promise associated with obeying your parents: First, that it may be well with you, which promises a quality of life. Second, that you may live long on earth, which promises a quantity of life.

VULNERABLE PLACES

"You shall not commit adultery." (Exodus 20:14)

The seventh command tells us we are not commit adultery. Many people might say, "Well, I've never done that." But then Jesus said again in the Sermon on the Mount, "You have heard that it was said to those of old, 'You shall not commit adultery.' But I say to you that whoever looks at a woman to lust for her has already committed adultery with her in his heart." (Matthew 5:27–28). Of course, this applies to women as well: adultery also can be looking at a man lustfully.

This word Jesus used for "look" does not just mean a casual glance, but in the original language, refers to the continuous act of looking. In this usage, the idea is not that of an incidental or involuntary glance, but one of intentional and repeated gazing.

Jesus is not speaking here of unexpected and unavoidable exposure to sexual temptation. He is speaking of one who intentionally puts himself or herself into a vulnerable place. You understand the difference. We all live in a very wicked world, and tragically today, we don't need to go very far to see things that would be sexually explicit. Television is one place to start. Then of course, there is the Internet. Even if have been careful to avoid these things in your home, when you walk into a mall or a store today, there will be monitors playing videos, plus billboards and advertisements all around you. So we are constantly being exposed to these things.

The person Jesus is describing who commits adultery in his or her heart is one who would intentionally put himself or herself into a place of obvious temptation. Those who love God and want to please Him won't want to do this.

Weekend

WHAT REALLY MATTERS

In those days Hezekiah was sick and near death. And Isaiah the prophet, the son of Amoz, went to him and said to him, "Thus says the Lord: 'Set your house in order, for you shall die, and not live.'" (2 Kings 20:1)

Over the years, I have done a lot of funerals and memorial services. I have visited people who were literally at death's door, and I can tell you that when life comes to an end, there are three things that will really matter to you: faith, family, and friends.

Of number-one importance will be your faith, your relationship with God. I have heard more people say with regret, "I wish had I spent more time walking closely with God. I wish I had made more time for spiritual things." They recognize the fact that they will stand before God Almighty. How sad it is when people realize they have squandered their lives.

Next will be your family. "I wish that I had been a better father," or, "I wish that I had been a better mother," some say. You will not be concerned about how much money you made, whether you spent enough time at the office, or if you have plenty of possessions. You will be leaving all that behind. Sadly, we spend so much time on that which doesn't really matter in the long run and, in the process, neglect that which really does matter.

It all will come down to faith, then family, and then friends. These are things that we want to think about. We want to make sure that our lives are right before God. When King Hezekiah was close to death, the prophet Isaiah told him, "Set your house in order" (2 Kings 20:1). Is your house in order today?

Monday

THE EIGHTH COMMANDMENT

"Do not steal." (Exodus 20:15 NLT)

Stealing has become such a widespread problem in our culture today that it is now commonplace. By that I mean, we are so accustomed to people stealing that we wouldn't even think of leaving our cars or homes unlocked. People break into cars. They break into houses. If you accidentally leave your wallet or purse somewhere, you don't ever expect to see it again. Stealing is so rampant in our culture that we are shocked when we see anyone being honest. It is such a rare quality today.

Yet the temptation to steal is constant. When you sell that house or car, it is tempting to inflate the price a little. When you receive too much change, the temptation is to keep it. But God says that we should live honest lives. Ephesians 4:28 says, "If you are a thief, stop stealing. Begin using your hands for honest work, and then give generously to others in need" (NLT). The idea in this verse is not to simply cease doing what is wrong (stealing), but to start doing what is right.

Also, in 2 Thessalonians 3 we read, "Even while we were with you, we gave you this rule: 'Whoever does not work should not eat.' Yet we hear that some of you are living idle lives, refusing to work and wasting time meddling in other people's business. In the name of the Lord Jesus Christ, we appeal to such people—no, we command them: Settle down and get to work. Earn your own living" (verses 10–12 NLT).

Know that God will honor the person who honors the principles of Scripture. The Bible says, "Do not steal," and it means what it says. If you steal, then you are unwise. And it will catch up with you.

Wednesday

TELLING THE TRUTH

"Do not testify falsely against your neighbor." (Exodus 20:16 NLT)

Some years ago, a book called *The Day America Told the Truth* was published. According to the authors' findings, 91 percent of Americans lie on a regular basis. "The majority of us find it hard to go through a week without lying," the book states. "And one in five cannot make it throughout a single day without lying." Apparently, we are a lying culture.

While some people consciously lie, many others try to couch the truth with a little diplomacy because they don't want to offend someone. But God's Word has a lot to say about lying, and Proverbs 6 includes it in a list of things God hates:

There are six things the Lord hates—no, seven things he detests: haughty eyes, a lying tongue, hands that kill the innocent, a heart that plots evil, feet that race to do wrong, a false witness who pours out lies, a person who sows discord among brothers (verses 16–19 NLT).

Notice that three of these seven things are closely associated with the ninth commandment: a lying tongue, a false witness who pours out lies, and a person who sows discord among the brothers. From this, along with the command not to testify falsely against our neighbor, we can safely conclude that God hates lying. God is the source of all truth. Jesus said, " 'I am the way, the truth, and the life . . .' " (John 14:6 nlt). He is the embodiment of truth. Scripture also tells us that it is impossible for God to lie (see Hebrews 6:18).

In dramatic contrast to this, Satan is described as "the father of lies" (John 8:44). So when we lie, we are behaving more like children of the devil than children of God.

Thursday

CONTENTMENT'S ENEMY

*"Do not covet your neighbor's house. Do not covet your neighbor's wife,
male or female servant, ox or donkey, or anything else your neighbor owns."*
(Exodus 20:17 NLT)

The tenth commandment, which deals with coveting, speaks to our deepest attitudes. Of course, the word, "covet," means to be dissatisfied with what we have and to desire more, regardless of what it may cost us or someone else.

One Christmas when I was a young boy, I received everything that I had wanted. I was so happy. I thought, "This is the greatest Christmas I've ever had!" Then I went over to my friend's house and saw his gifts. Suddenly, I was miserable, because he had been given something that I sort of wanted, but I had forgotten about it. All of a sudden, all that I had (as wonderful as it was) was no longer acceptable, because my friend had something that I wanted more. That is what coveting is.

As adults, we can do this as well. Everything is fine in our lives, but then we see what our neighbor has. We see what somebody else has. Then we begin to covet that. We want that—and sadly, some will even go out and take whatever it is they are coveting. We might even covet another person's spouse. It can ruin our lives. We are not to covet.

Jesus said that the first and greatest commandment is, " 'You must love the Lord your God with all your heart, all your soul, and all your mind' " (Matthew 22:37 nlt) and that a second and equally important command is to " 'Love your neighbor as yourself' " (verse 39 nlt). All the other commandments are based on these two. So, if you can get these down, then everything else will come naturally.

A FRIEND INDEED

Then He said to them, "My soul is exceedingly sorrowful, even to death. Stay here and watch with Me." (Matthew 26:38)

Do you know that sometimes the best thing you can do for a hurting person is to just be there? When I was a young pastor, I had a sermon for everyone. But since then, I have stood with many people who have experienced a tragedy or loss, and I have realized they don't always need a sermon. Often what they need is just a friend. They don't need someone to say, "I know what you are going through," or "Maybe this is the reason." They need someone to just love them, pray for them, and cry with them because of the great sense of loss they are experiencing.

Jesus experienced loneliness. He experienced anguish. In the Garden of Gethsemane, He asked Peter, James, and John just to be there with Him. But Matthew 26:56 tells us that a short while later, "all the disciples forsook Him and fled." Then, perhaps in the loneliest moment of His life, He cried out from the cross, " 'Eli, Eli, lama sabachthani?' that is, 'My God, My God, why have You forsaken Me?' " (Matthew 27:46). It is believed by many (myself included) that at that moment, God poured all the sin of humanity on His sinless Son. As the Heavenly Father, who is holy, turned His face, Jesus was separated momentarily from Him. In that moment, Jesus experienced loneliness like we never have known.

So the next time you are feeling down, the next time you are feeling misunderstood, the next time it seems like your friends have forsaken you, know this: Jesus has been there. He knows what it is like. And He will never leave you or forsake you.

Weekend

He Walked Among Us

For He shall grow up before Him as a tender plant, and as a root out of dry ground. He has no form or comeliness; and when we see Him, there is no beauty that we should desire Him. (Isaiah 53:2)

One thing that has fascinated people, especially artists, throughout the centuries is the question of what Jesus looked like. It is interesting that no actual physical description of Jesus is found in Scripture, except for a figurative one in the Book of Revelation. You would think that somewhere in one of the Gospels, someone would have taken the time to give us just an idea of what He looked like: "Oh, by the way, Jesus was five-feet eleven and had wavy, brownish hair, and green eyes." I mean, someone could have said something. We know nothing about Him physically except that He had a beard. We don't know much more. We don't really know what He looked like. Do you wonder why that is? I think perhaps it is because God knows our propensity for idol worship and left it out, knowing we would end up worshiping His image and forget all about Him.

Quite honestly, I would say that I seriously doubt He looked like the Jesus who has been depicted throughout history. I don't think Jesus had blond hair and piercing blue eyes. Being from the area in Israel that He was, His skin and hair very likely would have been dark. His eyes would have been dark as well. But that is not really important, is it?

God didn't give us a physical description of His Son. But God does want us to answer the question of who Jesus is. He is both the Son of God and God the Son, fully God and fully man.

Weekend

THE MOTHER WHO PRAYED

Then Jesus answered and said to her, "O woman, great is your faith!
Let it be to you as you desire." And her daughter was healed
from that very hour. (Matthew 15:28)

When we are praying for something that we believe is the will of God, we should not give up. Keep asking, keep seeking, and keep knocking—that is what Jesus told us to do. In fact, when Jesus saw the great faith of a mother from Canaan who was doing this very thing, He gave her carte blanche, so to speak: "Let it be to you as you desire."

This mother believed that what she was asking was the will of God, and she would not give up. Maybe you, like this mother, have a child who is under the devil's influence today. He or she has rejected your influence, at least for now. It is tough, because you have raised this child in the ways of the Lord. The very thing you have prepared your child for—to become independent—has happened. My advice is, hold on. You will come through it.

That thing you may believe is the worst-case scenario might be the step toward bringing your child to a true, heartfelt faith. The rebellion may be difficult to endure right now. But it also may be short-term, and it may be what it takes to bring your child to a place of realizing his or her own need for Jesus Christ. Our kids need to get these convictions in their hearts as *their* convictions, not just as Mom or Dad's convictions. It may mean a detour into the land of the prodigals. It may mean hitting bottom. But don't give up. Keep praying. Our children can escape our presence, but they cannot escape our prayers.

Monday

GOD'S FREE GIFT

For the wages of sin is death, but the gift of God is eternal life in Christ Jesus our Lord. (Romans 10:9)

Many years ago, I was given some free tickets to Disneyland. I was walking around the park having a good time, but I started to feel guilty because I had two extra tickets. I thought maybe there was someone outside who wanted to come in, but perhaps couldn't afford it. So, I decided to go outside and find someone to give the tickets to. I noticed some kids hanging out in front of the park. I walked up and said, "Hi. I have two free tickets to Disneyland. Would you like them?"

"What are you doing, man?"

"Just two free tickets," I said.

"How much is it going to cost us?"

"It won't cost you anything. I have some extra. I would just like you to have them."

"No."

I went to someone else. "Hi. I have these two free tickets to Disneyland. I would like to give them to you." Again and again, I received the same response. It took 40 minutes to give away those tickets.

People are suspicious, and the same goes when it comes to spiritual things. We say, "The way to be forgiven of your sin and to have eternal life is to turn from your sin, receive Jesus Christ into your heart as your Lord and Savior, and begin to follow Him." People respond, "That's too easy. What's the catch? What else do I have to do?" In our pride, we want to think we have something to do with our salvation. But if we will come to God on His terms and do what He says, then we will be forgiven of our sins and have the assurance of eternal life.

Tuesday

Speaking Up

And the Syrians had gone out on raids, and had brought back captive a young girl from the land of Israel. She waited on Naaman's wife. Then she said to her mistress, "If only my master were with the prophet who is in Samaria! For he would heal him of his leprosy." (2 Kings 5:2–3)

Scripture tells us about Naaman, a commander of the Syrian army, who was loved by the people and by the king. He had everything people could dream of, but he had one major problem. It was called leprosy.

So, who did God use to reach this man? Did He send the prophet, Elisha, to come knocking at his door? Did God send an angel to reach him? No. Instead, God sent a young Jewish girl who had been taken captive and had been carried away to Syria. How easily this girl could have been bitter against God for allowing this to happen. Yet she spoke to Naaman's wife about the prophet, Elisha, and Naaman's wife, in turn, spoke to Naaman. He made the trip to see Elisha, who gave him a rather peculiar prescription, and Naaman was healed that very day.

Thank God for this girl who spoke up to Naaman and told him about the prophet in Israel. Thank God for every believer who speaks up in his or her home. Thank God for the believers who speak up in their schools and in their workplaces and tell people there is a God who can forgive sins. People today are seeking. They are in search mode, especially as they see such an uncertain future in our country, as well as the rapid changes taking place around the globe. People are wondering what is going on. They are questioning. God's Word has the answers.

TRUE CHANGE

Therefore, if anyone is in Christ, he is a new creation; old things have passed away; behold, all things have become new. (2 Corinthians 5:17)

During a visit to the Pacific Northwest a few years ago, I met a man who told me he had been heavily into alcohol and drugs, and his marriage, in his own words, had been hanging by a thread. One day, he took a gun, loaded it, and was planning to kill himself. Then, he turned on the TV. There on the screen was a Harvest Crusade, where I was sharing a message called, "How to Get Right with God." He said, "God began to speak to me. When you led those people in prayer, I prayed and asked Jesus Christ to come into my life." After he found Christ, he realized he needed to reconcile with his father. So, he rode his motorcycle across the country to see his dad. That is a long ride on a motorcycle, but that sounds like a conversion to me. That sounds like a man who had met God, because there was a change in his life.

When God healed Naaman of his leprosy, he wanted to show his gratitude with a gift. Saul, at his conversion, said to the Lord, "What would You have me to do?" The Philippian jailer, after becoming a believer, washed the backs of those he had previously whipped. And Zacchaeus, after he became a believer, wanted to restore what he had stolen from others.

If you have truly found a relationship with God through Jesus Christ, you will change. That doesn't mean you need to change your life before you can come to Christ. But it does mean that when you come to Christ, you will change and your priorities will change.

Thursday

THE GOOD IN GUILT

For all have sinned; all fall short of God's glorious standard. Yet now God in his gracious kindness declares us not guilty. He has done this through Christ Jesus, who has freed us by taking away our sins. (Romans 3:23–24 NLT)

When Sir Arthur Conan Doyle, author of the Sherlock Holmes stories, wanted to play a practical joke on 12 of his friends, he sent a note to each of them that simply read, "Flee at once. All is discovered." Within 24 hours, all 12 friends had left the country. That is what you call a guilty conscience!

If you ask me, I think we could use a little more guilt in our society. Guilt does serve a purpose. What good can possibly come from guilt? The same good that comes from the warning system in our bodies called pain. If you step on a piece of glass, your body sends a warning signal: "Stop! Don't go any further!" In the same way, God has installed a warning system called guilt into our souls, and we experience it when we do something wrong. Just as pain tells us there is a physical problem that must be dealt with or the body will suffer, guilt tells us something is wrong spiritually and needs to be confronted and cleansed.

So you see, guilt is not necessarily a bad thing. The guilt feeling we experience is the symptom of the real problem, which is sin. All of the psychological counseling in the world cannot relieve a person of his or her guilt. We can pretend it is not there or try to find someone else to blame for our problems. But the only real and effective way to remove our guilt is to get to the root of the problem, which is sin.

THE SEARCH FOR GOD

No one has real understanding; no one is seeking God. (Romans 3:11 NLT)

Often we hear people say, "I'm on a spiritual journey. I am trying to find the truth. I am trying to find the light. I am trying to find God. I'm searching for God." Yet the Bible says that no one is really searching for God.

You would think that with all the religious belief systems in the world, this could simply not be. Yet God plainly declares in His Word, "If you look for me in earnest, you will find me when you seek me" (Jeremiah 29:13 NLT). Let me be blunt: If you are seeking God, then you will find your way to Jesus Christ. And if you don't find your way to Jesus Christ, then you are not seeking God. You might be playing religious games. You might be dabbling with various belief systems. But the true seeker will find the true God, and those who claim to be true seekers yet reject Jesus Christ are not being honest with God or with themselves. Religion is humanity's search for God. But Christianity is God's search for humanity.

I have heard people say, "I found the Lord 10 years ago," as though God had been lost. But God wasn't lost; we were. God is seeking to save us, and if we really want to know Him, then we will find Him. People do not come to Jesus Christ because they bristle at the thought of being sinful. They are unwilling to accept God's assessment of them. They are unwilling to acknowledge their guilt. That just bothers them. Instead, they want to believe they can get to heaven by their own merit, by their goodness, and by their own deeds. But the Bible says that simply isn't so.

Weekend

FEARING GOD

"They have no fear of God to restrain them." (Romans 3:18 NLT)

I think there was a time in history when God was misrepresented as a divine being who threw lightning bolts down from heaven on people who displeased Him. We've heard derogatory references to fire-and-brimstone preaching. But I don't think this is the problem today. We don't hear that much about preachers delivering fire-and-brimstone messages anymore.

What we do hear are messages about how we can be successful. We hear messages about how God will prosper us. But it is more rare to hear about a holy God who wants us to repent of our sins and walk with Him. That is not very popular anymore. In a way, I think many people have come to develop a new God, an all-loving, benign being who is hovering up there in the universe. If that is your God, then I'm sorry to tell you this is not the God of the Bible. That is a god of your own making. Without question, the real God is a God of love who loves you deeply. But the real God is holy. Not only should we love God, but we should also fear Him.

What I mean by "fearing God" is not necessarily to be afraid of Him. It is to have a respect for God, a reverence for Him. One of the best translations of the term I have heard is, "A wholesome dread of displeasing Him." I think this is lacking in lives of many people today, and sadly, even in the lives of people in the church. While it is true we will stand before a God of love one day, it is also true that we will stand before a holy God. So, we need the fear of God.

Monday

JUSTIFIED

In His forbearance God had passed over the sins that were previously committed, to demonstrate at the present time His righteousness, that He might be just and the justifier of the one who has faith in Jesus. (Romans 3:25–26)

"Justification" is an often-used word in the Christian vocabulary that carries great meaning. It is a word that declares the rightness of something—not symbolically or potentially, but actually. The Bible says that when I come to Christ and ask Him to forgive my sin, recognizing that He died in my place and took the penalty that I should have taken, then I have been justified.

One way to think of the word, "justification," is "just as if it never happened." When I come to Christ and ask His forgiveness, He says, "You are justified." That is, "just as if it never had happened." It is incredible to think about. Sometimes guilt from the past can plague you. The devil may whisper, "Do you remember what you did? Do you remember that sin you committed 23 years ago?"

But you can say, "I am justified—just as if it never happened." Only God makes that possible. As Psalm 103 says, "He has not dealt with us according to our sins, nor punished us according to our iniquities. For as the heavens are high above the earth, so great is His mercy toward those who fear Him; as far as the east is from the west, so far has He removed our transgressions from us (verses 10–12). That's a long way!

Corrie ten Boom used to say. "God has taken our sin and thrown it into the sea of forgetfulness and posted a sign that says, 'No fishing allowed.' " You are justified. Just as if it never had happened.

Tuesday

AN INVITATION TO REST

The Spirit and the bride say, "Come." Let each one who hears them say,
"Come." Let the thirsty ones come—anyone who wants to. Let them come
and drink the water of life without charge. (Revelation 22:17 NLT)

One December, I was on my way to New York and had a connection through Chicago. It was very cold outside, and as I was walking through the airport terminal, I noticed a large advertisement. It featured a sunny, tropical beach with beautiful, turquoise-blue water, white sand, and an empty beach chair. That picture was so alluring and so appealing because of where I was at that particular moment.

I think that photograph represented something all of us really want: rest, relaxation, and time off. Jesus has something to say to the person who is exhausted and worn out. He has something to say to people who have been chewed up and spit out by life—people who are frustrated, who are hurting. Here is His personal offer of rest to those who will respond: " 'Come to me, all of you who are weary and carry heavy burdens, and I will give you rest. Take my yoke upon you. Let me teach you, because I am humble and gentle, and you will find rest for your souls. For my yoke fits perfectly, and the burden I give you is light' " (Matthew 11:28–30 NLT).

Here we really have the Christian life in a nutshell. Here we see what it is to come to, to know, and to walk with Jesus Christ. This invitation stands today, but it will not stay that way forever. What is the invitation? Jesus says, "Come to Me." That's it. It is so simple, yet it is so profound. And we see this same invitation echoed throughout Scripture.

THE TWO-PART INVITATION

*" 'Take my yoke upon you. Let me teach you, because I am humble and gentle,
and you will find rest for your souls. For my yoke fits perfectly,
and the burden I give you is light.' " (Matthew 11:29–30 NLT).*

In Matthew 11, Jesus follows His invitation to rest with the invitation to take His yoke and learn from Him. He is telling us there is more; His invitation to rest is a package deal. If we are true followers of Jesus Christ, then we will take His yoke upon us. But what does that mean?

The concept of a yoke would have been readily understood by the people of Jesus' day. It was a steering device that was placed on animals to guide the plows or carts they were pulling. So Jesus, in essence, is saying, "Take my steering device upon you." He is saying, "Let me be in control of your life. Let me guide your life. Let me direct your life."

You might be thinking, "Here Jesus says that He will give me rest. Now He is saying to put on His yoke and learn. That sounds like work." I want you to know that it will be as much of a weight to you as wings are to a bird. It will be a joy, because now instead of wasting your life serving yourself or living for pleasure or success or whatever else one lives for, you will be channeling your energies into following and serving Jesus Christ.

You may give up some things to follow the Lord. But what you give up can't begin to compare to what He has given you. It is not just a great thing to do with your life. It is the most satisfying to do with your life.

Thursday

CLOTHED WITH CHRIST

But put on the Lord Jesus Christ, and make no provision for the flesh,
to fulfill its lusts. (Romans 13:14)

I like comfortable clothes. Most of the time you will find me wearing jeans, because they are comfortable. I don't like starched shirts, and when I send my shirts to the cleaners, I specify "no starch." For one of the cleaners we previously used, "no starch" meant "extra starch." I would put on these shirts and could barely move in them, they were so stiff. That is not the kind of clothing I want. I want clothes that move where I move.

This is also the meaning behind the phrase in Romans 13:14, "put on the Lord Jesus Christ. . . ." It means, "to enter into His views and His interests. Imitate Him in all things." "Put on the Lord Jesus" is the same concept as that of a person putting on clothing. It is the idea of letting Jesus Christ be a part of every aspect of your life. Let Him be with you when you get up in the morning. Make Him a part of your life today, going with you everywhere, and acting through you in every thing that you do.

J. B. Phillips puts the same verse this way: "Let us be Christ's man from head to foot" (PHILLIPS). I like that translation. Too often, we are on a collision course with God, fighting Him and resisting Him. Too often, instead of going where God wants us to go and doing what He wants us to do, we are pulling against Him at every turn. If this is the case, we will lose—and we will lose big. So why fight it? Recognize His plan for you is better than the plan you have for yourself.

WHEN STORMS COME

Now no chastening seems to be joyful for the present, but painful; nevertheless, afterward it yields the peaceable fruit of righteousness to those who have been trained by it. (Hebrews 12:11)

At the conclusion of Matthew 7, Jesus told the story of two men who built two types of houses. One house was built on a good foundation of rock, while the other house was built on a faulty foundation of sand. Then Jesus described a storm that came and beat against both houses. The house that was built on sand collapsed, while the house that was built on the rock stood firm. Jesus concluded that the man who built on the rock is the one who hears the Word of God and obeys it. He said the man who built his house on sand is the one who hears the Word of God and does not obey it

But one other thing I see in this teaching of Jesus is the fact that the storm struck both houses. Every life and every person will experience hardships. But the question is, how will you react when life's storms hit? Will they destroy you or strengthen you? Will they make you better or bitter?

Here is the good news for Christians: we know that whatever happens in our lives must first go through the protective screen of God's love. In other words, God will not let anything happen in the life of the believer that He is not completely aware of. As I have said many times, the word, "oops," is not in God's vocabulary. He is in full control of all the circumstances that surround the lives of His people.

So when hardship comes, we know that God has allowed it for a purpose. He has some plan in mind.

Weekend

THROUGH THE STORM

On the same day, when evening had come, He said to them, "Let us cross over to the other side." (Mark 4:35)

In the Gospel of Mark, we find an interesting story in which Jesus invited the disciples, some of whom were seasoned fishermen, to join Him on a little boat trip across the Sea of Galilee. But on the way over, they encountered a radical storm.

Now the question would arise, "Did Jesus know that a storm was coming?" The answer is yes. In fact, you might even say that it was a part of His curriculum that day. It was all part of teaching the disciples to believe what they claimed to believe.

We don't want to make light of what these disciples were experiencing, because I'm sure this was a very harsh storm. Several on board had seen many storms on the Sea of Galilee. So it had to be a very difficult storm for the disciples to be so gripped by fear. According to Mark's Gospel, the waves were breaking over the boat and filling it with water. The disciples were very afraid, but they didn't have to be. Jesus had made a significant statement they apparently had forgotten about: "Let us go to the other side." And when God says, "Let us go to the other side," it means you will get to the other side. He didn't say it would be smooth sailing. He didn't say it would be an easy trip. But He did say, "Let us go to the other side."

Often we are gripped by fear and cease to think logically when we forget God's Word to us. That is exactly what happened to the disciples. But Jesus was on board with them, and He was there to see them through.

Monday

GOD'S ANSWER TO WORRY

Don't worry about anything; instead, pray about everything. Tell God what you need, and thank him for all he has done. (Philippians 4:6 NLT)

In the Sermon on the Mount, Jesus had specific things to say about worry and anxiety. He said,

"So I tell you, don't worry about everyday life—whether you have enough food, drink, and clothes. Doesn't life consist of more than food and clothing? Look at the birds. They don't need to plant or harvest or put food in barns because your heavenly Father feeds them. And you are far more valuable to him than they are. Can all your worries add a single moment to your life? Of course not." (Matthew 6:25–27 NLT)

Why shouldn't we worry? First of all, Jesus tells us, it's because of the Father. Our Heavenly Father is watching out for us. Jesus points to the birds. You've never seen a bird sweat, have you? Birds are relatively calm. Certainly, the birds need to go out and gather their food. They do their part to get what they need. But they don't worry about it. The point Jesus is making is that if God cares for the birds, will He not take care of you? The answer obviously is yes, He will.

Second, worry does not bring about anything productive in your life. It is a destructive emotion. It doesn't lengthen your life and can even potentially shorten it. The next time you are tempted to worry about something, channel all of the energy you would have put into worry and put it into prayer instead. Say, "Lord, here is my problem. I am putting it in your hands. I am going to trust you." That is not an easy thing to do. But it is something we need to consciously do.

Tuesday

TIME WILL TELL

The Lord told Gideon, "With these three hundred men I will rescue you and give you victory over the Midianites. Send all the others home." (Judges 7:7 NLT)

Remember the story of Gideon in the Old Testament Book of Judges? Gideon had a fairly large army of 32,000 men. But he had a much larger adversary in the Midianites, who numbered in the thousands and thousands. God came to Gideon one day and told him that his army was too big. He told Gideon to call the men together and say, "Whoever is timid or afraid may leave and go home." Gideon obeyed the Lord, and 22,000 men said, "We're out of here." God thinned the ranks once more, and Gideon was left with 300 men. Why did God do that? He was looking for those who would stand up for Him, for those who would make a sacrifice.

In the same way, time will tell whether you are a true follower of Jesus Christ. It will be determined on the battlefield, not in a church service where everyone is praising the Lord together. Time will tell whether have truly gone forward spiritually. It will be determined by how you hold up when the first difficulties come, when the first temptations come, and when the first persecution comes.

I remember how things changed when I became a follower of Jesus Christ. I was harassed and mocked by friends whom I had known for many years. I recognized immediately that if I followed Christ, I would lose some so-called friends, and it would not always be easy.

If you are willing to endure, then you will have the greatest adventure imaginable in serving the Lord. God is looking for men and women to enlist in His army for His divine Delta Force.

In His Strength

"Finally, my brethren, be strong in the Lord and in the power of His might."
(Ephesians 6:10 NLT)

Just as police officers call for back-up when they sense that danger may be imminent, the first thing we must realize about spiritual battle is that in our own strength, we are no match for the devil. I think a healthy respect of our adversary is in order for believers today. We don't want to underestimate him, nor do we want to overestimate him. We want to accurately assess who he is and what his abilities are. We need to recognize that he is powerful; we don't want to try and take him in our own strength.

When I hear some preachers on television or the radio calling the devil silly little names, laughing at him, or making jokes about him, I remember what Jude 9 says: "Yet Michael the archangel, in contending with the devil, when he disputed about the body of Moses, dared not bring against him a reviling accusation, but said, 'The Lord rebuke you!' " Even the high-ranking Archangel Michael did not dare to condemn the devil with mockery. He simply said, "The Lord rebuke you!" There was a respect of the enemy.

The reason we need to "be strong in the Lord and in the power of His might" is because Satan wants to get us away from that. It is our power base. He wants to separate us from God, because the moment he gets us away from Him, we are open prey. Thus, the devil wants to put a wedge between God and us.

The only power that can effectively drive Satan out is the power of Jesus Christ. Be strong in the Lord. Stay close to Him. Don't let anything come between you and God.

Thursday

SAFE WITH THE SON

*We know that those who have become part of God's family do not make
a practice of sinning, for God's Son holds them securely, and the evil
one cannot get his hands on them. (1 John 5:18 NLT)*

I want to address a popular doctrine that has been floating
around in the church for several years. Some have actually made theology out of what I believe is a false assump-
tion. There are people today who will tell you the reason you
are having certain problems or struggling with certain vices
and sins is because of a generational curse that is on you and
your family. It may be that your father or grandfather or
great-grandfather were involved in the occult, and therefore,
a generational curse has been passed on from them to you,
which is why you are the way you are. Thus, you need to come
against this generational curse by first identifying and then
rebuking it and finding out the specific demons that are a part
of this curse.

It is all very interesting. But it is not biblical. The Bible
doesn't tell me to do these things. There is no generational
curse on me, because that curse was broken on the day I gave
my life to Jesus Christ. I am not under any curse.

Satan, however, is under the curse. So, I am to stand in
God's power and recognize, as 1 John 5:18 says, that God's Son
holds me securely, and the evil one cannot get his hands on me.
That phrase, "get his hands on," means that he cannot attach
himself to me. No generational curses here. No possession of
a Christian here. I am under the protection of God Almighty.
"So if the Son sets you free, you will indeed be free" (John
8:36 NLT).

Friday

ENEMY TACTICS

I do so with Christ's authority for your benefit, so that Satan will not outsmart us. For we are very familiar with his evil schemes. (2 Corinthians 2:10–11 NLT)

The devil tends to use the same tactics over and over again. I suppose he operates by the old adage, "If it ain't broke, don't fix it." He has used these techniques, plans, and strategies since the Garden of Eden, and they have worked with great effect to bring down countless people. Therefore, he just keeps bringing them back, generation after generation.

That is the bad news. The good news is that we know what they are, because they are clearly identified in the Bible. The devil is a dangerous wolf that sometimes disguises himself as a sheep. Sometimes he roars like a lion. But more often he comes like a snake. Sometimes he comes to us in all of his depravity and horror. Other times he comes to us as an angel of light. This is why we always need to be on guard.

He will tempt you and whisper, "Trust me on this. Go ahead and sin. You will get away with it. No one will ever know." So you take the bait and fall into sin. Then the devil shouts, "What a hypocrite! Do you think God would ever hear *your* prayers? And don't even bother going to church!" Sadly, some people will listen to this, believe it, and be driven away.

Just remember, no matter what you have done, no matter what sin you have committed, God will always be ready to forgive you if you will turn from that sin and return to Him. Don't let the devil isolate you from God's Word and God's people, because that is exactly what he is trying to do.

Weekend

SUIT UP!

Use every piece of God's armor to resist the enemy in the time of evil,
so that after the battle you will still be standing firm. *(Ephesians 6:13 NLT)*

When the apostle Paul wrote his letter to the Ephesians, he was chained to a Roman guard. So when we come to his description of the armor of God beginning in chapter 6, it's worth noting that Paul had a lot of time to observe Roman armor. There it was, 24 hours a day: breastplate ... helmet ... shield ... sword. This description was not given in a haphazard manner off the top of Paul's head to pass the time. Rather, these words are inspired by God. There is significance behind every word Paul attached to each piece of armor.

Paul identifies six pieces of armor altogether. The first three, the belt, breastplate, and shoes, were for long-range protection and were never removed on the battlefield. The second three, the shield, the helmet, and the sword, were kept in readiness for use when actual fighting began. So we see that each piece was important.

After all, you could wear your helmet, breastplate, and shield, but without a sword, you would find yourself in the unfortunate position of only defending or holding ground. Or, you might be wearing your sandals, your belt, and have your sword in hand, enabling you to attack enemy strongholds, but you would quickly lose what you gain due to inadequate defense.

So, we need all of the armor. It is not for us to pick and choose; it is a package deal. God has given us clear and defined spiritual weapons to fight with. Understanding what they are and how to use them can make all the difference in our spiritual battles.

Monday

ARMED WITH THE TRUTH

Stand your ground, putting on the sturdy belt of truth and the body armor of God's righteousness. (Ephesians 6:14)

In his description of the armor of God in Ephesians 6, Paul doesn't start with the high-profile objects like the sword or the shield. Instead, he begins his list by telling us to put on "the sturdy belt of truth." What was Paul speaking of? We need to think "Roman soldier" here for a moment. The Romans didn't wear pants like we do today. They wore robes or togas—generally short togas on the battlefield. So to move quickly on the battlefield, the Roman soldier would need to pull the toga up above his knees. Having the belt tightened simply meant that he would pull up his toga and tighten his belt a couple of notches, which gave him the freedom of movement he needed.

Now the belt is not a dramatic piece of armor, but it was essential to everything else. The breastplate was attached to the belt, as well as the sheath for the sword. So, if your belt fell off, your breastplate would fall off, and your robe would come loose. You may have the sharpest sword on the block, but you're destined to trip over your own toga and look quite foolish in the process. So, the belt was important. That is why Paul put it at the top of the list.

To have your belt tightened means you are ready for battle and ready to move. We need to be on duty at all times. We cannot afford to take a couple of days off spiritually. We must keep our armor on at all times, because the moment we take it off is the moment the devil will be there to hit us with full force.

Tuesday

OUR DEFENSE

Stand therefore, having girded your waist with truth, having put on the breastplate of righteousness. . . . (Ephesians 6:14)

Next on the Apostle Paul's list of the armor of God is the breastplate of righteousness. Key to the armor, the breastplate protects the vital organs. On the Roman battlefield, this is where the enemy would strike, so the breastplate would protects this important area.

In the same way, Satan will strike here because a well-placed blow to this area could prove fatal. Now, when we sin, we are very vulnerable, because the devil comes to us and says, "You have sinned. You are not worthy of God's forgiveness. You are not deserving of His blessings. God won't listen to your prayers. You're a hypocrite."

What will you say when that day comes? We all will sin. We all will fail. We all will fall short. The Bible says, "If we say that we have no sin, we deceive ourselves, and the truth is not in us" (1 John 1:8). What will you say on that day? Will you boast about the Bible verses you've memorized or the people you've led to the Lord or how often you go to church?

If you rely on what you've done, then you are guilty of self-righteousness, which simply means you believe that you somehow merit God's blessing because of all the things you've done. If this is your attitude, then you have a breastplate made of Styrofoam™. One strike of the enemy's sword will cut it apart and leave you open and exposed.

When you have sinned and the enemy condemns and accuses you, don't boast of all that you have done for God. Instead, boast of all that God has done for you. That is putting on the breastplate of righteousness.

THE RIGHT SHOES

Stand therefore, having girded your waist with truth, having put on the breastplate of righteousness, and having shod your feet with the preparation of the gospel of peace.... (Ephesians 6:14–15)

No matter how powerful the breastplate of a Roman soldier was or how much he had tightened his belt, these wouldn't do much good if he slipped and fell. So, in his list of the armor of God, Paul mentions "having shod your feet with the preparation of the gospel of peace...."

The Roman sandal or boot was essentially a sole with straps held firmly on the foot at the bottom. It would have been studded with nails, providing the soldier with better footing and thus preventing him from slipping and sliding on the terrain. It would be like wearing cleats today.

These shoes also provided protection, because one of the common battlefield tactics of ancient times was to place sharpened sticks in the ground at an angle. If a soldier came along and wasn't wearing sandals or boots, he would suffer a wound to his foot and probably die from infection. The irony is, he would be wearing his breastplate and have his sword and shield ready, but could end up dying because his foot got cut. So, footwear was of the greatest importance.

So when Paul said, "Have your feet shod," he is telling us to wear the right footwear. It will not only protect us from the enemy's tactics, but also will enable us to keep our footing. The devil would love for you to lose some of the ground you've gained since becoming a Christian. He will try to get you to start slipping and lose your footing, because he knows it will be the beginning of the end.

Thursday

READY TO MOVE

For shoes, put on the peace that comes from the Good News, so that you will be fully prepared. (Ephesians 6:15)

The sandals or shoes Paul describes in Ephesians 6 not only provide stability to help the believer hold ground. They also provide mobility. These are not dress shoes that are uncomfortable or that you want to keep perfectly clean. These shoes will allow you to move at a moment's notice.

As 1 Peter 3:15 tells us, "If you are asked about your Christian hope, always be ready to explain it." In the original language, these words communicate the idea of giving a defense, as in a court of law. So we should always be ready to give a defense of what we believe. We need to be ready at a moment's notice to seize opportunities to share the gospel.

Some people say, "The Lord never opens up opportunities for me to share my faith." I think He does, but I think often we are not paying attention. Opportunities are all around us. Sometimes we simply need to push on that door of opportunity a little bit. We need to talk to people. Jesus sat down with the woman at the well, asked her for a drink of water, began to converse with her, and transitioned into a spiritual conversation. People rarely will come knocking on your door to ask what they must do to be saved. Generally there will be other kinds of opportunities, but you need to have your spiritual antenna up, so to speak, and seize the moment when it comes.

The armor of God is not only for holding ground; it is also for gaining ground. We gain ground when our shoes are on and we walk through the doors of opportunity God opens for us.

THE SHIELD OF FAITH

In every battle you will need faith as your shield to stop
the fiery arrows aimed at you by Satan.
(Ephesians 6:16)

What is this shield of faith Paul refers to? Remember, as he was writing this letter to the Christians at Ephesus, he was chained to a Roman guard. He had plenty of time to observe Roman armor. The shield would have been made of wood—a rectangular object about four feet high and two feet wide. Prior to an actual face-to-face engagement with the enemy, a soldier often would encounter a barrage of flaming arrows coming from all directions. The sole purpose of this was to demoralize and confuse. Thus, the Roman soldiers would put their shields together to protect themselves from this onslaught of arrows that had been set on fire. They needed their shields above and beyond what their breastplates could provide for protection.

The same goes for us. The devil will direct his flaming arrows toward Christians. They could be arrows of immorality, hatred, pride, envy, covetousness, doubt, worry, or any other kind of sin. They will be delivered primarily in the realm of our thoughts. He will barrage us with his flaming arrows at strategic times, like when we decide to read the Bible or go to church. Flaming arrows will come our way during times of trial and hardship.

It is during these times that you hold up the shield of faith—not the shield of feelings, not the shield of emotions, but the shield of faith. You base your faith on what God has done for you, not on how you feel at a given moment. Emotions come and go. Sometimes you feel great; and sometimes you don't feel anything. It is then that you learn to use the shield of faith.

Weekend

WEAR YOUR HELMET

And take the helmet of salvation, and the sword of the Spirit,
which is the word of God. (Ephesians 6:17)

There are a lot of motorcyclists today who don't like helmet laws. I am among their ranks, I must say, because it is fun to get on a motorcycle and ride along with nothing on your head. But quite honestly, if you are in an accident on your bike and you become airborne, a helmet suddenly sounds like a really good idea. A helmet could literally keep you alive.

For the Roman soldier, the helmet was important because it obviously protected his head. It was made of leather, shrouded in metal, and designed to withstand a crushing blow to the head.

As believers, we need to put on the helmet of salvation the apostle Paul speaks of, because our minds, thoughts, and imaginations must be protected. It is here that most temptations start. Proverbs 23:7 says, "For as he thinks in his heart, so is he. . . ." Satan recognizes the value of first getting a foothold in the realm of the thoughts and imaginations, because this will prepare the way for that thought to translate into action. As it has been said, "Sow a thought; reap an act. Sow an act; reap a habit. Sow a habit; reap a character. Sow a character; reap a destiny." It starts with a thought.

While we cannot control all the things in this world that we are exposed to, we can control a few things. We can control what we watch at home on television. We can control what movies we decide to see. We can control what we choose to read and what we listen to. Be careful what you allow into your mind. Put on the helmet of salvation.

Monday

REMEMBER YOUR SWORD

Put on salvation as your helmet, and take the sword of the Spirit,
which is the word of God. (Ephesians 6:17 NLT)

Many believers have all their spiritual armor in place, but they never use their sword. They talk about it. They study it. They compare swords with others. But they never use their sword in spiritual battle. In fact, the devil would be pleased if believers would just keep their sword in its sheath. The devil knows too well the power and the authority of the sword of the Spirit, which is God's Word.

Hebrews 4:12 says, "For the word of God is full of living power. It is sharper than the sharpest knife, cutting deep into our innermost thoughts and desires. It exposes us for what we really are." God says of his own word in Isaiah, "I send it out, and it always produces fruit. It will accomplish all I want it to, and it will prosper everywhere I send it" (55.11). There is power and authority in the Word of God. That is why the devil doesn't want you to use this incredible weapon God has given you.

Remember how effectively Jesus used the sword of God's Word to defend Himself when He faced spiritual attack in the wilderness? Jesus was God. He didn't have to stand around and deal with the devil. He could have gotten out of the situation very easily. But instead, He stood and modeled for us the right way to fight temptation: with the Word of God.

So when the devil tries to attack you with temptation, fear, doubt, or brings up past sins you've already confessed and of which you've been forgiven, remember the sword of the Spirit. Pull it out of its sheath and use it aggressively to defend yourself.

Tuesday

ON THE OFFENSIVE

We are human, but we don't wage war with human plans and methods.
We use God's mighty weapons, not mere worldly weapons, to knock down
the Devil's strongholds. (2 Corinthians 10:3–4 NLT)

The sword of the Spirit that Ephesians 6 speaks of is not only for deflecting a blow from the enemy; it is also for inflicting one. This is something the devil doesn't want you to know. He doesn't want you to start attacking, because if you are always defending, then he is in the superior position. But if you are attacking, then you are in the superior position. So, we are not just using the sword of the Spirit to defend ourselves against the enemy's temptations and condemnations, but we are also using it to attack.

In Acts 8, we find this modeled for us in the life of Philip, who went to share the gospel with a man who had come from Ethiopia and was searching for God. Philip had been sharing the gospel in Samaria, and people were coming to faith. But then God said to him, "Go south." And Philip, like a good soldier prepared for battle, went. He pulled out the sword of the Spirit, the Word of God. From that point on, Philip preached Jesus to this man, because he knew God's Word and was able to use it when the right time came.

Make no mistake about it: there is authority and power in the Word of God. My words will fall to the ground, but God's Word sticks. God's Word breaks through. We could spend all day trying to defend and explain the Bible, but I have a better idea: use the sword of the Spirit. That is what Philip did, and that is what we need to do as well.

A Change of Direction

*"For we must all stand before Christ to be judged. We will each receive whatever
we deserve for the good or evil we have done in our bodies."*
(*2 Corinthians 5:10 NLT*)

One morning as Alfred Nobel was reading the newspaper, he was shocked to find his name listed in the
obituary column. It was a mistake, but nonethe-
less, there it was. He was stunned to see that he was primarily
remembered as the man who invented dynamite. At that time
in history, dynamite was used in great effect for warfare. It
distressed Nobel to think that all he would be known for was
inventing dynamite, something that was used to take the lives
of others. As a result of reading this mistaken obituary, Nobel
decided to change the course of his life. He committed himself
to world peace and established what we know today as the Nobel
Peace Prize. When the name Alfred Nobel is mentioned today,
dynamite is rarely the first thing that comes to mind. Rather,
we think of the prize that bears his name. It's all because Alfred
Nobel decided to change the course his life was taking.

Another man, living centuries before, also changed the
negative course his life was on. His name was Paul, formerly
known as Saul of Tarsus. Known as a relentless persecutor
of the early church, he was determined to stop the spread
of Christianity. But after a dramatic conversion on the
Damascus Road, Paul devoted the rest of his life to preaching
the gospel and building the church. Today we remember
him as a missionary, church planter, and author of 13 New
Testament epistles.

If you were to read your own obituary today, what do you
think people would remember you for? It isn't too late to
change your direction.

Thursday

SIMPLE OBEDIENCE

"Go and do what I say. For Saul is my chosen instrument to take my message to the Gentiles and to kings, as well as to the people of Israel." (Acts 9:15 NLT)

Prior to his conversion, Saul was a leading Pharisee and possibly even a member of the Jewish Sanhedrin. He presided over the death of the first martyr of the Christian church, Stephen. After his encounter with Jesus on the Damascus Road resulted in his conversion, the Christians of Saul's day were at first suspicious of his conversion, and understandably so.

So when God directed a believer in Damascus named Ananias to seek out Saul and pray for him, Ananias was reluctant, of course. But Ananias did what God told him to do. He found Saul in the place where God said he would be. He prayed that the Lord would restore Saul's sight (he had been blinded by the light as Jesus spoke to him on the Damascus Road), which the Lord did.

It is interesting that when God wanted to use someone to minister to Saul, He didn't call an apostle like Peter or John. He called an ordinary man. Ananias didn't write any book of the New Testament, raise a dead person back to life, or give a notable sermon that we know about. But he did, by faith, take a man under his wing who would do all of the above and far more. Ananias discipled the newly converted Saul who, in time, became the legendary apostle Paul and probably the greatest preacher in the history of the church.

Thank God for the Ananiases of the kingdom, those who faithfully work behind the scenes to make such a difference in our lives. They may be unknown to man, but they are beloved of God.

CHARACTERIZED BY PRAYER

"The Lord said, 'Go over to Straight Street, to the house of Judas. When you arrive, ask for Saul of Tarsus. He is praying to me right now.'" (Acts 9:11 NLT)

When God told Ananias to look for Saul, He said he would be praying. Sure enough, that is exactly what Ananias found him doing. I think Saul probably was asking God to forgive all the wrongs he had done. Can you imagine how hard it would be to accept God's forgiveness if you not only had been a murderer, but also had deliberately hunted down the followers of Jesus Christ and brought about their premature deaths? How hard it would be to have that on your conscience!

But Saul prayed, and in the process discovered that intimacy could be found with this God whom he had only known in a distant way before. You can't help but notice as you read through his epistles that prayer characterized Paul's life. So many of them begin or end with beautiful prayers. It was Paul who told us to pray without ceasing (1 Thessalonians 5:17 NLT).

Paul also practiced what he preached. When he and Silas were thrown in prison for preaching the gospel, they prayed and sang praises to God at midnight, and the other prisoners heard them. Now, who would want to pray at a time like that? But instead of cursing the men who put them there, they were blessing God. No wonder the other prisoners were listening to them. This was the transformation that took place in the life of Paul. He was a man of prayer.

Are you a man or a woman of prayer? Does prayer characterize your life? It should. If you want live this Christian life effectively, then you need to learn how to pray.

Weekend

A Word to Dads

And now a word to you fathers. Don't make your children angry by the way you treat them. Rather, bring them up with the discipline and instruction approved by the Lord. (Ephesians 6:4 NLT)

A few years ago, someone asked the former President George Bush, "What is your greatest accomplishment in life?" I thought that was an interesting question to ask someone like him, who has quite a long list of achievements. After all, he was the U. S. Ambassador to China, the director of the CIA, the Vice-President for two terms under President Reagan, and then, of course, the President of the United States himself. That is not to mention, of course, that one of his sons is the President of the United States, while another is the governor of Florida. I would have expected him to point to the accomplishments of his children or to his own success. Yet here was his answer: "My children still come home to see me." There is a man who has his priorities in order.

As a pastor, I have visited people who are coming to the end of their lives. I have seen what really matters to them. And as I have said before, it always comes back to faith and family. When your life is over, it is not going to matter how many business deals you made, how many investments you have, or how many things you've accumulated. When it is all said and done, it will come down to these basic values.

Tragically, so many men today are abandoning their families to chase after something they rationalize as a mid-life crisis. Men, we have to stand by the commitment we have made to our wives and children. We cannot even for a moment consider turning our backs on them.

Monday

SHAPED BY SUFFERING

Since I know it is all for Christ's good, I am quite content with my weaknesses and with insults, hardships, persecutions, and calamities. For when I am weak, then I am strong. (1 Corinthians 12:10 NLT)

On a recent visit to North Carolina, I drove through a town named Mocksville. I should have been born there. Prior to becoming a Christian, I always loved to mock other people. So when I became a follower of Jesus, I was shocked to discover that I was the one being mocked. People were laughing at me because of my faith in Christ.

This is what happened to Paul, but in a far more intense way. Right after his conversion, he started preaching the gospel in Damascus. But he was so powerful and persuasive that the religious leaders wanted him dead.

The Christians found out and devised a plan to help Paul escape. They put him into a basket and lowered it over the city wall at night. Think of the irony! Just a short time before, he was Saul of Tarsus, the notorious persecutor of Christians. The hunter had become the hunted. He was getting a taste of his own medicine.

His name change from Saul to Paul offers insight into the real transformation that took place. The first king of Israel was named Saul. In contrast, Paul means "little." It would be like deliberately changing your name from Spike to Squirt. Obviously, God had changed Paul into a man of humility.

Sometimes we want God to take certain things out of our lives that cause us pain. We pray over and over for those things to be removed. But do we ever stop to think that God is using those things in our lives to transform us and make us more like Him?

Tuesday

DESTINED FOR GREATNESS

He comforts us in all our troubles so that we can comfort others.
When others are troubled, we will be able to give them the same
comfort God has given us. (*2 Corinthians 1:4 NLT*)

It has been said that it takes a steady hand to hold a full cup.
God was planning to give a full cup to the apostle Paul. So
He took Paul away and put him into obscurity in the desert
of Arabia for a time. We are not told what happened there,
but we can only presume that he drew close to the Lord in
fellowship and communion. It was there that Paul refined his
theology, evidenced in the New Testament epistles that God
inspired him to write.

This was typical of how God dealt with many people He
was preparing for greater ministry assignments. When Elijah
obediently delivered God's message to King Ahab and Queen
Jezebel in their court, he was led away to the brook Cherith for
a few years to wait on God. Moses had forty years of training
that prepared him to lead the children of Israel out of Egypt.
Even after the young teenager David was anointed king of
Israel, it wasn't until he reached the age of thirty that he actually ascended the throne. Joseph was used greatly in the house
of Potiphar, but was then sent to prison for two long years. God
was preparing these men for what was ahead, and He was doing
the same for Paul.

When you have gone through the desert of hardship, God
uses you to more effectively minister to others. Do you find
yourself in a "desert experience"? Maybe God has some
training in mind for you. Remember, you can never be too
small for God to use; only too big.

FINISHING WHAT WE START

You ran well. Who hindered you from obeying the truth? (Galatians 5:7)

Imagine, for a moment, that we are competing in a race. When the starter pistol is fired, we take off, and I leave you in my dust. I'm running really well. Let's say we are going for ten laps, and we are coming to the last one. I say to myself, "I am creaming the competition. I am going to go get a Krispy Kreme doughnut now." So I wander off the track. Let's say that you cross the finish line ten minutes later. It is clear that I beat you, but if I didn't do the tenth lap and cross the finish line, then I have lost the race. It doesn't matter if I led for nine out of ten laps. I had to finish the race I began.

In the same way, there are people who started off with a great burst of energy as they followed the Lord. Maybe you were one of those people. Maybe you came to Christ during the days of the Jesus Movement. Or perhaps you came more recently. That is great. But listen: That was then, and this is now. How you were running a year ago, or even a month ago, is no longer significant. But how you are running right now is. Are you keeping up the pace? Are you going to make it across the finishing line? You can make it if you want to.

There will be times as you live the Christian life when it will be hard. You will have to hold on to God's Word and the promise that He will complete the work He has begun in your life (Philippians 1:6). But will you make the effort to cross the finish line?

Thursday

A Wing or a Weight?

"Therefore, since we are surrounded by such a huge crowd of witnesses to the life of faith, let us strip off every weight that slows us down, especially the sin that so easily hinders our progress ... " (Hebrews 12:1 NLT)

I heard about a great concert violinist who was asked about the secret to her great performances. She answered, "Planned neglect. Anything that would keep me from practicing and playing well must be neglected."

I think that some of us could use some planned neglect in our lives, because there is a lot more junk in them than we may realize. If you don't believe me, then try moving from one house to another. Isn't it amazing how much junk you have collected? The same is true in our lives. We take on things we don't need. Periodically, we needed to jettison this excess weight and let it go.

When the race of life gets difficult, we like to blame circumstances, other people, or sometimes even God. But we need to remember that if we stumble or fall, it is our own fault. The Bible says that Jesus' "divine power gives us everything we need for living a godly life" (2 Peter 1:3 NLT).

The Bible also tells us to lay aside the weight and the sin that hinders our progress (Hebrews 12:1 NLT). Notice the distinction: we are not just to lay aside the *sin*; we also are to lay aside the *weight*. In fact, I would suggest periodically asking yourself this question about the uncertain areas of your life: *Is it a wing or is it a weight?* In other words, does it speed you on your way in this race you are running? Or, is it a weight—something that slows you down?

In Focus

And let us run with endurance. … keeping our eyes on Jesus,
on whom our faith depends from start to finish. (Hebrews 12:2 NLT)

When I was in high school, I went out for track and field. I was a fairly decent short-distance runner, but I was horrible at long-distance runs. I hated to practice. But if ever I saw a pretty girl in the grandstands, I had new motivation for running.

As we run this race of life, we have a better motivation than I had in high school. We run for an audience of one: Jesus Christ. He is watching us. He is praying for us. In fact, the Bible tells us that He lives to intercede for us (Hebrews 7:25 NLT).

This is what gave young Stephen courage when he stood before his accusers who were ready to put him to death. Full of the Holy Spirit, he was given a glimpse of Jesus in heaven and said, "Look, I see the heavens opened and the Son of Man standing in the place of honor at God's right hand" (Acts 7:56 NLT). Seeing Jesus gave Stephen the ability to run the race and finish it.

Seeing Jesus also gave Simon Peter the ability to walk on the water. As he kept the Lord in sight, He did the impossible.

It is important to keep our eyes on Jesus. Why? Because circumstances will disappoint, and at times, devastate us. People will let us down and fall short of our expectations. Feelings will come and go. But Jesus will always be there to cheer us on.

He has run before you. He is the ultimate winner. He will show you how to run. But you have to keep looking to Him.

Weekend

Dealing with Distraction

So I run straight to the goal with purpose in every step. (*1 Corinthians 9:26 NLT*)

I n first-century track competitions, each runner would be assigned to a lane on the track. Each was expected to stay in his assigned lane. In the same way, as you and I run the race of life, our competition is not with other believers. Rather, our competition is with our enemies, who are the world, the flesh, and the devil. The goal is not to outrun someone else. The goal is to outrun those wicked influences that could bring us down.

You might justify your slow pace by pointing to other people still running behind you. True. But there are probably some people ahead of you too. You are not to concern yourself with who is behind you or who is ahead of you. You are to run the race before you. God has not called you to run someone else's race. We are each called to run our own race.

An incident from the life of Peter illustrates this truth. After Peter had been restored to the Lord following His denial, Jesus said to him, "Follow me." Then the Lord proceeded to tell Peter how his life would end. As they were talking, Peter noticed another disciple, John, was walking behind them. Peter asked, "What about him, Lord?" (John 21:21 NLT).

Jesus said, "If I want him to remain alive until I return, what is that to you? You follow me" (John 21 22 NLT). A loose paraphrase would be, "Peter, it is none of your business. You just do what I have told you to do."

I ask you today, are you just offering a half-hearted effort in the race of life? Or are you running as well as you can?

Monday

RUNNING TO WIN

*Remember that in a race everyone runs, but only one person gets the prize.
You also must run in such a way that you will win. (1 Corinthians 9:24 NLT)*

Not long ago, I celebrated my 50th birthday. Getting older is not a depressing thought, because from the day I gave my life to Jesus Christ, it has been an adventure. I don't regret a single day of my life that I have spent following and serving the Lord.

Sure, my life has had some surprises. One of them has been seeing people who I never thought would make it in the Christian life make it, and seeing people who I never thought would fall, fall. Some people have a powerful start and then crash and burn. Others have a rather weak start, but somehow pull it together in the end. Best of all, there are some who start and finish the race with flying colors. I want to be one of those people. Don't you?

Here is what we need to remember. We *do* have a say so as to how the race we run will turn out. Let me put it another way. If you want to be a winner in the race of life, then you can be. If you want to be a loser, then you can be. It really comes down to the choices you make on a daily basis. As I have said before, people fall away from the Lord because, for all practical purposes, they choose to. They neglect certain things, and at the same time, allow other things into their lives.

As we make our decisions, our decisions will make us. What practical steps can you take today to ensure that you will be running well in the Christian race 25 years from now?

Tuesday

GOING HIS WAY?

Can two people walk together without agreeing on the direction?
(Amos 3:3 NLT)

I have a German shepherd that was a former guide dog for the blind. Because he had slight hip dysplasia, he was put up for adoption. When we got him, he was perfectly trained. We could take him anywhere. He was happy to sit next to us. Another dog would walk by, and he could care less.

Then I got a hold of him. I would unleash him and let him run around in the park. Day by day, he started getting worse. The next thing you know, he was lunging at dogs. He was chasing rabbits all the time.

I called the people we got him from and asked what went wrong. They told me I couldn't let him do all that "dog stuff." I couldn't let him stop and sniff where he wanted to sniff. I couldn't let him chase rabbits. They gave me a little muzzle-like device to put on him. Gaining control of his muzzle meant he would obey, because it would hurt to pull away. When I took the device off of him, he was in sync with me again.

We can be like that with God sometimes. We are running around and being crazy, doing what we want to do. So the Lord has to pull us back into line, because He wants us to walk with Him.

To walk with God means that I must get into harmony with Him. I must go the direction that God wants me to go.

How about you? Are you walking with God today? Or, are you pulling against Him, trying to do things your own way? If so, then it's time to stop, ask God's forgiveness, and get in sync with Him once again.

Wednesday

AN APPOINTMENT WITH GOD

The Lord God called to Adam, "Where are you?" (Genesis 3:9 NLT)

In addition to walking in harmony with God, Amos 3:3 provides another nuance of meaning. It also gives the idea of keeping an appointment. Did you know that you have an appointment with God? You do. It is there, written in eternity. In fact, God wants to meet with you on a regular basis.

I wonder just how many times each day that God wants to speak to us and He can't get a word in edgewise? The Lord might say, "I have wanted to talk to you for a long time, but you are too busy. This morning I wanted to talk to you, but you didn't have any time for me. You read the newspapers and watched TV and talked on the phone. You never opened the Word. You never prayed. At lunch I tried to say something, but your prayer was so fast. Later I tried to talk with you. You have been so busy. You have an appointment with me. Why don't you keep it?"

Remember how Adam had an appointment with God every day in the Garden of Eden? He would hear the voice of the Lord in the garden in the cool of the evening. One day Adam missed that appointment because of sin. God said to Adam, "Where are you?"

I wonder if the Lord would say that to some of us each day: "Where are you? Where were you? I have been looking for you. I wanted to speak to you. I want you to walk with Me, and I want to walk with you."

Just imagine, the Creator of the Universe wants to spend time with you. Is there any appointment that is worth keeping more than this one?

Thursday

A LIGHT IN THE DARK

Enoch lived 365 years in all. He enjoyed a close relationship with God throughout his life. Then suddenly, he disappeared because God took him. (Genesis 5:23–24 NLT)

Enoch lived at a unique time in history, prior to God's judgment by the Flood. People of Enoch's day were really wicked. So wicked, in fact, that God was sorry He ever created them. Scripture tells us of that time that all their thoughts were "consistently and totally evil" (Genesis 6:5 NLT). Yet in the midst of this dark environment was an individual who walked with God. Enoch shows us that it is possible to live a godly life in an ungodly world.

We also read in Hebrews 11:5 that Enoch was pleasing to God. We, too, can live our lives in a way that pleases God. How? We can start by finding out what God specifically says is pleasing to Him. Here are a few from the pages of Scripture:

1. God is pleased when, in spite of the fact that we are in the right, we patiently endure when misunderstood (1 Peter 2:19).

2. God is pleased when children obey their parents (Colossians 3:20).

3. God is pleased when we worship Him and help others (Hebrews 13:15).

4. God is pleased when we give to the work of the kingdom (Philippians 4:17).

Of course, as you read and study God's Word, you'll discover other things that please Him. Some people have the mistaken notion that God is very difficult to please. He is not. He loves you. He knows all about you. Your failures do not come as a surprise to Him. He wants the very best for you. His resources are at your disposal. He is patient with you.

Enoch had this testimony: he pleased God. How is your testimony today?

FAITHFUL TO THE END

So Joshua blessed Caleb son of Jephunneh and gave Hebron to him as an inheritance. Hebron still belongs to the descendants of Caleb . . . because he wholeheartedly followed the Lord, the God of Israel. (Joshua 14:13–14 NLT)

Today I want to look at one of the unsung heroes of the Bible. His name was Caleb, and he never lost his edge spiritually. In his own words, he said, "I am as strong now as I was when Moses sent me on that journey, and I can still travel and fight as well as I could then" (Joshua 14:11 NLT). What makes that statement so significant is that Caleb was 85 years old when he made it!

What was the secret to Caleb's spiritual longevity? Caleb wholly followed the Lord. If we want spiritual longevity, we must do the same. But this means giving 100 percent to God.

Often when our lives are in trouble, we expect God to drop everything, run to us, and take care of our problems. Then when it comes to us doing our part for Him, it is amazing how busy we can be. *My schedule is so full. I don't have time for Bible study. I have tons of time for TV and reading magazines and talking on the cell phone, but I don't have time for the Word of God. I don't know if I have time to go to church this week, either.*

If your heart is right with God, it will be shown in the way you spend your time. It will be shown in the way you live your life. If you are wholly following the Lord as Caleb did, then you will want to give God your best, not your leftovers. That was the secret to Caleb's spiritual longevity.

Weekend

KEPT BY HIS LOVE

Nothing in all creation will ever be able to separate us from the love of God that is revealed in Christ Jesus our Lord. (Romans 8:39 NLT)

When you go to a place like Disneyland with your children, you know where they are. You don't leave the park and forget them, because you protect what you love.

In the same way, God never forgets what He loves. Writing to first-century believers, Jude addressed his epistle, "to all who are called to live in the love of God the Father and the care of Jesus Christ." In the original language, it is in the perfect tense of which the nearest equivalent would read, "You are continually kept by Jesus Christ." It is a continuing result of a past action.

Whatever your difficulties may be today, you need to know that you are preserved in Christ, and that He will maintain His investment, which He purchased at the Cross. He will protect you, preserve you, and keep you.

Yet the Bible also tells us to *keep ourselves* in the love of God (Jude 21). Is this a contradiction? No. It is merely two sides of the same coin. The Bible is teaching that God will keep us, but at the same time, we must keep ourselves in His love. We don't keep ourselves *saved*, but we keep ourselves *safe*.

There are things we must do on a daily basis to keep ourselves in a place where God can actively bless us, to keep ourselves away from all that is unlike Him, and from those things that would drag us down spiritually.

Attacks will come our way. Were it not for the preserving grace of God, none of us would make it. Clearly we are preserved, protected, and kept by the power of God.

Monday

NO EXCEPTIONS

But if you do not do so, then take note, you have sinned against the Lord;
and be sure your sin will find you out. (Numbers 32:23)

I read a newspaper article about a hungry thief who grabbed some sausages in a meat market. What he didn't realize was that the sausages were part of a 45-foot long string. As he was making his getaway, he tripped over them and couldn't escape. The police found him collapsed in a tangle of sausages. He was caught in the act. Literally.

In the same way, many people today play with sin, thinking they will get away with it. If hey don't get caught at first, they will go and do it over and over again. Sometimes people misinterpret God's loving patience and willingness to forgive as leniency. They think God is a soft touch, a pushover. Because they get away with their sin, they think God doesn't really mind. Then they deceive themselves into thinking God approves of what they're doing.

We must not misinterpret God's mercy as God's lenience. The Bible says, "The Lord is not slack concerning His promise, as some count slackness, but is long-suffering toward us, not willing that any should perish but that all should come to repentance" (2 Peter 3:9). Is God cutting you slack right now? By that I mean, if you are committing a sin that has not yet caught up with you, please don't misperceive that as leniency. Recognize it as mercy. Recognize that, sooner or later, it will catch up with you. The best thing you can do is turn from that sin, run to Jesus, fall down at His feet, and ask for His mercy. But if you continue, you will one day discover that your sin will find you out.

Tuesday

GOD'S MOTIVATING LOVE

Then Jesus stood up again and said to her, "Where are your accusers?
Didn't even one of them condemn you?"
"No, Lord," she said.
And Jesus said, "Neither do I. Go and sin no more." (John 8:10—11 NLT)

I wonder what was going through the mind of the woman whom the Pharisees brought before Jesus, claiming she had been caught in the act of adultery. The Bible doesn't mention that she was innocent. So we may assume that she was guilty. Trapped or not, she participated in this sin, and she bore responsibility for what she did.

As she watched these self-righteous, hypocritical, religious elitists try to have her put to death, she must have been amazed as Jesus wrote in the sand and dismissed them one by one. Maybe she thought, "What will He do to me now? If He dismissed these religious men, how will I fare today? He knows all my secrets."

But I am confident that, when she looked into His eyes, she did not see condemnation. I believe she saw real compassion when He said, "Neither do I."

How is it that Jesus didn't condemn her? Because in a short time, He would personally take upon himself that very condemnation.

When we realize how much God has done for us, how He has wiped our slates clean when we deserve judgment for what we have done, our reaction should be, "I want to serve a God like that." When God looks at us in our miserable, fallen, state and says, "I don't condemn you. Now go and sin no more," we should want to live a godly life. We should want to please Him, not because we are bound to or are afraid of righteous retribution, but because the love of God motivates us.

SIN NO MORE

"Therefore if the Son makes you free, you shall be free indeed." (John 8:36)

There are three things Jesus promised to the woman whom the Pharisees caught in the act of adultery and brought before Jesus. I believe they apply to us as well. *One, her sins could be forgiven and put behind her.* Jesus never mentioned her past. He didn't drag it out. The Bible says that when you become a Christian, you are justified by faith (see Romans 5:1). That word, "justified," is an interesting word that means, "just as if it had never happened." God looks at you as a forgiven person and He looks at your past as though it never took place. You are justified, just as if it had never happened.

Two, she did not have to fear the judgment day. "Neither do I condemn you," Jesus said (John 8:11), and neither does He condemn us. The Bible says, "There is therefore now no condemnation to those who are in Christ Jesus . . ." (Rom. 8:1).

Three, she had new power to face her problems. "Go and sin no more," Jesus told her. He wouldn't have asked her to do something that was impossible. He was not saying that she should be perfect. But He essentially was telling her to no longer live in a lifestyle of sin. In the same way, we no longer have to be under the control of sin. We can be free from it.

Does some sin have you in its grip right now? I want you to know that Jesus Christ can set you free. But you need to ask Him for His help. You need to take practical steps to distance yourself from it. "Go and sin no more." This is what we need to do.

Thursday

ASK FOR HELP

"For everyone who asks receives, and he who seeks finds, and to him who knocks it will be opened." (Luke 11:10)

The Bible tells the story of Simon Peter, who was out walking on the water with Jesus. He began to realize the impossibility of the situation and started sinking. He cried out, "Lord, save me!" How easily Jesus could have said, "Where is your faith, Peter? You made your bed; now lie on it. Try swimming." But the Bible says, "Immediately Jesus stretched out His hand and caught him" (Matthew 14:31). *Immediately.* I like that.

When you begin to sink and cry out, "Lord, save me!" He will immediately reach out. But you must cry out for His help. That is hard for some of us to do.

As a kid, I spent a lot of time at the beach. When I was out bodysurfing one day, a big set of waves started coming in. So, I did what I was supposed to do: I swam toward the waves and went under them. When I looked up, there was another set. I swam under those too. One set after another came. The people on the beach were looking like little ants. I was exhausted. I had no strength left. I had nothing to hold onto. And I was in trouble.

I realized I had two choices. I could cry, "Help!" and the lifeguard would come running with his life preserver. When we got to shore, my friends would laugh, and I would never live it down. Or, I could drown with dignity.

A lot of us don't want to admit our need. We don't want to cry out to God. We want to maintain our dignity. But I need the best God has to offer. And you do too.

THE QUESTION WE MUST ANSWER

He said to them, "But who do you say that I am?" (Matthew 16:15)

I magine boarding an airplane and hearing the pilot announce, "Ladies and Gentlemen, welcome to Flight 239 with service to Honolulu, Hawaii. Our cruising altitude today will be 22,000 feet. By the way, I'm not so sure about this whole fuel thing. As I look at the fuel gauge, it doesn't appear as though I have enough to get to Hawaii. But I want you to know that I feel good about this, so there is no need to panic. And by the way, folks, I'm not going to use any of my navigation devices, nor am I going to break out any maps, because I feel that maps are so narrow and bigoted, so absolute. I believe that we can just flow with it, because all roads lead to Hawaii. Don't worry, because I am very sincere in what I am saying. So have a good flight." Of course you would say, "Get me off this plane—right now!"

Yet regarding the things of God with eternal ramifications, people make statements like this. People want to believe that all roads lead to God and that whatever path they choose, if they are sincere enough, it will eventually get them there. But every belief system is different, and they largely contradict one another. Therefore, they can't all be true. You can't say all roads are the same and that all religions teach the same thing, because they don't. Only one can be true.

So you must make the decision as to whom you will believe, because that is what it comes down to. Hundreds of years ago, Jesus asked His disciples a question: "Who do you say that I am?" He is still asking that question today.

Weekend

THE CHOICE WE MUST MAKE

*"He who is not with Me is against Me, and he who does not
gather with Me scatters." (Luke 11:23)*

When we come to the message of the gospel, we must say yes or no to it. Either we are in or we are out. Either we are for or we are against Jesus Christ.
Moses told the people of Israel, "I call heaven and earth as witnesses today against you, that I have set before you life and death, blessing and cursing; therefore choose life . . ." (Deuteronomy 30:19).

After Joshua led Israel into the Promised Land, he confronted them with a choice: " 'Choose for yourselves this day whom you will serve. . . . But as for me and my house, we will serve the Lord' " (Joshua 24:15).

On Mt. Carmel, Elijah challenged the people with the same choice and said, " 'How long will you falter between two opinions? If the Lord is God, follow Him; but if Baal, follow him' " (1 Kings 18:21).

We, too, must make a choice.

Narrow is the way that leads to life. Christianity is not the most popular way to live. If you truly follow Jesus Christ, then you will be a part of a minority. And in case you haven't noticed, it is open season on followers of Jesus. We have seen Christians ridiculed. We have seen Christianity exaggerated. We have seen our message distorted. If you truly follow Jesus Christ, then you will have some difficulties in life.

Although it is true that it costs to follow Jesus, it is also true that it costs a whole lot more not to follow Him. Whatever it costs to follow Jesus Christ, it is worth it. And whatever you give up, He will make up to you.

Monday

READ THE MANUAL

Then I said, "Behold, I have come—in the volume of the book it is written of Me—to do Your will, O God." (Hebrews 10:7)

If you want to learn about Jesus, then learn to study this wonderful book God has given to us, the Bible. It is the user's manual of life. It tells us what is right and wrong and what is good and evil. It tells us how to live, how to do business, and how to have a successful marriage. But most importantly, the Bible tells us how to know and walk with God. In fact, everything you need to know about God is found in the pages of the Bible.

Abraham Lincoln said of the Bible, "All of the good from the Savior is communicated through this Book. All things that are desirable to man are contained in it."

Sadly, many people today own Bibles but seldom read them. As many as 93 percent of Americans own at least one Bible, but little more than half read it, only 25 percent read it every day.

Yet success or failure in the Christian life is determined by how much of the Bible you get into your heart and mind on a daily basis and how obedient you are to it. Think about that for a moment.

What amazes me are Christians who have known the Lord for many years, yet do not read the Bible. They attend church and Bible studies and listen a little here and there, but they don't actually open the Word of God and read it.

If you want to grow spiritually, then this must become a regular part of your life. It is essential. It is not something you will outgrow, any more than you will outgrow eating or breathing.

Tuesday

Full Minds, Full Hearts

Your word I have hidden in my heart, that I might not sin against You.
(Psalm 119:11)

My computer screen flashes a little warning sign on those occasions when I try to load too much information on my hard drive. It tells me my memory is full—there is no more room for any more information. In the same way, if we would fill our hearts and minds with God's Word, then when the devil comes with his perverse thoughts and ungodly schemes, he will see a sign that notifies him that our memory is full. It is so important for us to fill our minds and hearts with the Word of God.

Certainly it is good to carry a Bible in your briefcase, pocket, or purse. But the best place to carry the Bible is in your heart. It is good to go through the Word of God. But the Word of God must go through you. Is great to mark your Bible. But your Bible must mark you. It must affect the way that you live.

I have found that one of the best ways to remember Scripture is to write it down. I remember it more easily that way. In fact, the Bible tells us to store up these words in our hearts, teach them to our children, and write them down (see Deuteronomy 11:18–20).

Maybe when you are memorizing a verse, it doesn't feel like the most supernatural experience of your life. But it is a discipline. And the next time you are faced with a difficult situation, suddenly that verse will come to you with freshness from the throne of God. It will speak to your situation and strengthen your heart.

So get God's Word into your heart and mind. And put it into practice.

Swim Upstream

"Enter by the narrow gate; for wide is the gate and broad is the way that leads to destruction, and there are many who go in by it." (Matthew 7:13)

Any dead fish can float downstream, but it takes a live fish to swim upstream. You can just go with the flow, do what everyone else is doing, end up wasting your life, and face a certain judgment. Or, you can go against the flow and choose the narrow way that leads to Jesus Christ.

True rebellion in our day is following Jesus Christ. If you want to be a real rebel, then say that you believe there is a God, that He sent His Son to die on the cross for you, and that you believe trusting in Christ as your Savior and Lord is the way to find forgiveness of sins. Say that you believe God has given us His standards in the Bible not to make our lives miserable, but to make our lives full. Statements like these will make you a rebel in our culture and society today. Yet this is the narrow way—and it is the good way. As Jeremiah 6:16 says, "Stand in the ways and see, and ask for the old paths, where the good way is, and walk in it; then you will find rest for your souls."

The other option is the broad way. It is not a hard road to walk. No rules. No regulations. Just go with the flow. The problem is that it leads to destruction. The Bible says, "There is a way that seems right to a man, but its end is the way of death" (Proverbs 14:12).

God has given us the right way to live. It is the narrow way that leads to life.

Thursday

THE GREAT THING ABOUT PRAYER

Keep on praying. (1 Thessalonians 5:17 NLT)

I clearly remember when I was a new Christian and first began to pray. I had never prayed in my life. I wasn't aware that I could know God in such a way as to call on Him and listen to Him. I also remember the first time I prayed with a group of other Christians. I was so nervous. With every word, I was convinced I was bombing in prayer. My heart was pounding.

Sometimes we think we don't know how to pray properly. We don't know how to phrase certain things. We wonder if we should be using King James English. We wonder if we should pray in a certain posture. But these are not the main issues. The most important thing is our hearts. The great thing about prayer is that God looks primarily at our hearts. Even if our prayers aren't perfectly structured, even if they aren't eloquent, if they come from a heart that is directed toward God, they are pleasing to Him. God keeps up with all the latest terminology, so don't worry about that. He knows what you are saying. He knows what you are thinking. The main thing is to start praying. Just start where you are, and be honest with God.

Luke 18:1 tells us that Jesus told his disciples a story "to illustrate their need for constant prayer and to show them that they must never give up" (NLT). So spend time in prayer. You can pray at home. You can pray while you're stuck in traffic. We read in the Bible that people of all ages from different walks of life prayed every day, always, in any posture, and under all circumstances. God can hear prayer at any time in any place.

Friday

A PATTERN FOR PRAYER

Now it came to pass, as He was praying in a certain place, when He ceased, that one of His disciples said to Him, "Lord, teach us to pray. . . ." (Luke 11:1)

When Jesus gave us the model prayer known as The Lord's Prayer, He said, "In this manner, therefore, pray . . ." (Matthew 6:9). Notice He didn't say, "When you are really in trouble, this is the prayer to use. It's the big one." I'm not making fun of The Lord's Prayer or the person who prays it. But Jesus didn't tell us to pray these words verbatim. He said, "In this manner, therefore, pray. . . ." He was providing a structure for prayer.

If we were to design our own pattern for prayer, it probably would follow along the lines of, "Our Father in heaven, give us this day our daily bread." We would cut to the chase and tell God what we want.

But when Jesus taught on prayer, He taught that should first say, "Our Father in heaven, hallowed be Your name. Your kingdom come. Your will be done. On earth as it is in heaven" (verses 9–10). Before we utter a word of personal need, we need to acknowledge that we are speaking to the Creator of the universe—and we need to let that sink in. We need to think about His glory, His power, and His splendor before we bring our prayers before Him.

Then, before a word of petition comes out of our mouths, we should pray, "Your kingdom come. Your will be done. On earth as it is in heaven." Essentially, we are acknowledging that we have limited understanding, that we want God's will more than our own. This is how Jesus taught us to pray.

Weekend

WHY PRAY?

For we do not wrestle against flesh and blood, but against principalities, against powers, against the rulers of the darkness of this age, against spiritual hosts of wickedness in the heavenly places. (Ephesians 6:11)

Why should we pray? Among many reasons, there is a devil. The Bible says, "Be sober, be vigilant; because your adversary the devil walks about like a roaring lion, seeking whom he may devour" (1 Peter 5:8). The Bible teaches that we are engaged in a spiritual battle—not against flesh and blood, but against principalities, powers, and spiritual might in the supernatural realm. We are able to see things accomplished in the supernatural realm through prayer. God has given us prayer as a way of dealing with the adversary.

We should also pray because it is God's appointed way for us to obtain things. The Bible says, "You do not have because you do not ask" (James 4:2). Of course, some have taken this idea to extremes and have taught that if you name something and claim it in the name of Jesus, then God will give it to you. They have misunderstood a wonderful promise of God regarding prayer. We also can go too far in the other direction and fail to receive what God has for us, simply because we don't ask. You might be sick. Pray and ask God to touch you. Maybe you are in need of financial help. Pray. Maybe you wonder why certain things are not happening in your life. Have you prayed about it? Have you taken it before the throne of God and said, "Lord, here is a need in my life. I need your help"? God is interested in you, and He wants to answer your prayers. But He wants you to participate in the process.

Monday

JUST PRAY

"I desire therefore that the men pray everywhere, lifting up holy hands, without wrath and doubting." (1 Timothy 2:8)

Three ministers were debating the best posture for prayer. One claimed the best way to pray is to always have your hands pressed together and pointing upward. The second insisted the best way to pray is on your knees, while the third was convinced the best way to pray is stretched out on the floor, flat on your face. As they were debating, a repairman from the telephone company overheard their conversation while he was working in the next room. He walked in and said, "Excuse me, gentlemen. I don't mean to interrupt, and I am certainly no theologian. But I have found that the most powerful prayer I have ever prayed was when I was dangling upside down from a power pole, suspended 40 feet above the ground."

When we look at instances of prayer in the Bible, we discover that any posture will do. People prayed while standing, lifting their hands, sitting, lying down, kneeling, lifting their eyes, bowing, and pounding their chest.

We also see that any place will do. People prayed during battle, in a cave, in a closet, in a garden, on a mountainside, by a river, in the sea, in the street, in a home, in bed, in a prison, in the wilderness, and in the belly of a whale. So any place will do.

Last, we find that anytime will do. People prayed early in the morning, in the mid morning, in the evening, three times a day, before meals, after meals, at bedtime, and at midnight. Both day and night are good times for prayer. Isn't that great to know? You can pray any time, anyplace, and in any posture. So just pray.

Tuesday

NO WORRIES

"Therefore do not worry about tomorrow, for tomorrow will worry about itself. Each day has enough trouble of its own." (Matthew 6:34)

Have you ever been gripped by worry? I have. I think I worry now more than at any other time in my life. Maybe it is because I have two sons. But worry is not a good thing to do. It is not productive. It doesn't help. In fact, it really hurts. Medical research has proven that worry is physically harmful to you. It can actually affect your central nervous system and make you less resistant to disease. Worry also can affect your digestive organs and your heart. Experts have said that excessive worry can even shorten the human life. So the irony is that you can be worrying all the time about whether something bad might happen to you—if you might get sick, for example, or whether you will die one day soon. But the irony of it is that you can actually shorten your life by worrying about it too much.

Are you someone who is gripped by worry right now? It has been said that worry is the advanced interest that you pay on troubles that seldom come. God says when we are tempted to worry, "Do not be anxious about anything, but in everything, by prayer and petition, with thanksgiving, present your requests to God. And the peace of God, which transcends all understanding, will guard your hearts and your minds in Christ Jesus" (Philippians 4:6–7). Isn't that a wonderful promise? Instead of worrying, the Bible tells us to bring our requests to God, and His peace will keep our hearts and minds. So the next time you want to worry, the next time you are gripped by anxiety, pray about it.

Wednesday

Waiting for Answers

Then he said to me, "Do not fear, Daniel, for from the first day that you set your heart to understand, and to humble yourself before your God, your words were heard; and I have come because of your words." (Daniel 10:12)

An interesting story in the Old Testament book of Daniel offers us a rare, behind-the-scenes look at what happens when we pray. The Bible tells us that Daniel was praying, and his prayer reached heaven. God heard Daniel's prayer and dispatched an angel with a special message for Daniel. But the angel who was sent from heaven with the answer to Daniel's prayer was stopped for 21 days, because he was engaged in spiritual warfare with a powerful demon spirit. So God dispatched Michael the archangel. You might say that Michael is a head honcho among angels. Michael was sent, who overruled the demon power, and the answer was eventually brought to Daniel. But it took 21 days for the answer to get there.

Sometimes when God doesn't answer our prayers as quickly as we would like Him to, we think that He is letting us down. We need to understand that delays are not necessarily denials.

When we pray and don't see an answer as quickly as we would like, I wonder if there is not a spiritual battle going on behind the scenes. Maybe you have been praying for someone to come to know the Lord. Maybe you have been praying for God to heal you. Maybe you have been praying for God to open up doors of opportunity for you to serve Him. Don't give up. Don't be discouraged. Keep praying. Jesus said to keep asking, keep seeking, keep knocking, and the door would be opened. So be persistent. And watch what God will do.

Thursday

STRENGTH IN NUMBERS

"Again I say to you that if two of you agree on earth concerning anything that they ask, it will be done for them by My Father in heaven. For where two or three are gathered together in My name, I am there in the midst of them." (Matthew 18:19–20)

No question about it, when Christians get together and pray, things will happen. It is good to join forces with other believers. But let's not misunderstand. It doesn't mean that if two Christians agree to pray together that God will give them a Learjet, God will answer their prayers. What Jesus was saying is that if two people get their wills in alignment with the will of God, agree together in that area, and keep praying about it, then they will see results.

That is why we need to pray with our Christian friends. That is why we need to call up people and say, "Let's pray about this together." That is why Christians need to be involved in church. If you want to grow spiritually, then you must be a part of a congregation of believers. It isn't optional. You need to become part of a group of believers, build friendships with them, and become a productive part of that body. If you are not involved in a church on a regular basis, then I would venture to say you that you are probably floundering spiritually.

Just as you must eat and drink and breathe to live, you must read the Bible, you must pray, and you must be involved in a church to spiritually live. You will never outgrow these things. You will need them until your final day on this earth. And if you neglect these things, I guarantee that you will have a spiritual breakdown.

IMPEDED PRAYERS

"But when you are praying, first forgive anyone you are holding a grudge against, so that your Father in heaven will forgive your sins, too." (Mark 11:25 NLT)

One hindrance to having our prayers answered is, without question, unforgiveness in our hearts. When you go before the Lord in prayer, if you harbor bitterness and hatred toward someone else, then it can hinder your prayers.

Maybe you're thinking, "Wait a second! What do you mean, 'forgive'?" That person ripped me off. He took advantage of me. I'll pray for him—I'll pray for bad things to happen." But that kind of an attitude can hinder our prayers. If you hate certain people, then it will hurt your prayer life. Resolve those things. Work it out. Forgive.

An idol in your heart is another thing that can hinder your prayers. Ezekiel 14:3 says, " 'Son of man, these leaders have set up idols in their hearts. They have embraced things that lead them into sin. Why should I let them ask me anything?' " (NLT). An idol is anything or anyone that takes the place of God in your life. It can be an image that you bow down before, but an idol also can be your career. It can be possessions. It can be your body. It can be anything that is more important to you than God himself. And it will hinder your prayers.

Also, unconfessed sin will bring your prayer life to a screeching halt. Psalm 66:18 says, "If I had not confessed the sin in my heart, my Lord would not have listened" (NLT). An old adage says, "If you feel far from God, guess who moved?" Have you allowed something to get in the way of your relationship with Him? You can change that today.

Weekend

TIME WITH THE FATHER

But Jesus went to the Mount of Olives. (John 8:1)

During a visit to Israel, I had the opportunity to see a replica of a home from the time of Christ. I was surprised by how sophisticated this home was. It had what appeared to be different rooms, one of which even had a bathtub. It was rather nice. Not all homes in Jesus' day were that way, of course, but some were.

We do know, however, that Jesus probably didn't live in a home like this, because in Matthew 20:8, Jesus said, " 'Foxes have holes and birds of the air have nests, but the Son of Man has nowhere to lay His head.' " The Gospel of John offers additional insight: "And everyone went to his own house. But Jesus went to the Mount of Olives" (7:53–8:1).

In this particular passage of John's Gospel, we don't read that Jesus' disciples were with Him. While everyone else went to their comfortable homes, Jesus literally went to sleep outside in the open air. He also went to commune with His Father. While the Pharisees were busy thinking up the newest way to set a trap for Jesus, He was spending time in the presence of His Father. While His enemies were communing with hell, Jesus was communing with heaven. In doing this, He left us an example to follow.

There are times when we need to get away from the crowd and spend time in communion with our Heavenly Father. While we don't need to abandon our homes necessarily, we may need to abandon some activities or pursuits. There are times when we need to get away from the busyness and pressures of life to spend time with the Lord. I can guarantee that it will be time well-spent.

Monday

WHAT IS HAPPINESS?

"Happy indeed are those whose God is the Lord." (Psalm 144:15 NLT)

A distraught, miserable man was looking for help and sought the counsel of a liberal minister. Looking at the unhappy condition of the man, the minister said, "Forget about those things. Go and see this famous comedian that is appearing at a local comedy club. I hear that he is keeping everyone in stitches. Go listen to him, and you will forget how miserable you feel." After a moment of silence, the man said, "I am that comedian."

What is happiness? I think the world's version of it is quite different than the Bible's version. The happiness of this world depends on circumstances. If you are in good health, the bills are paid, and things are going well, then according to the world's philosophy, you are happy. But if someone cuts you off on the freeway or if something else goes wrong, then suddenly you are unhappy. Your happiness hinges on what is happening at a given moment.

The Bible gives us a completely different view of this thing called happiness. According to Scripture, true happiness is never something that should be sought directly; it always results from seeking something else. When we are trying to be happy, when we are trying to be fulfilled, we rarely are. But when we forget about those things and get back to the very purpose for which God put us on the earth, suddenly we find the wonderful byproduct of happiness popping up in our lives. When we seek holiness, we will find happiness. When we seek righteousness, we will become happy people, because our will is aligned with the will of God as we walk in harmony with Him. The rest of our lives will then find their proper balance.

Tuesday

POOR IN SPIRIT

Then He opened His mouth and taught them, saying: "Blessed are the poor in spirit, for theirs is the kingdom of heaven." (Matthew 5:2–3)

When Jesus said, "Blessed are the poor in spirit," the word, "poor," that He used is a verb that means, "to shrink, cower, or cringe." It describes a destitute person or someone who is completely dependent on others for help.

But Jesus didn't just say, "Blessed are the poor." He said, "Blessed are the poor in spirit." Jesus was not addressing a person's economic situation. Rather, He was dealing with a person's spiritual condition. Let's not miss what this is saying: Blessed, or happy, is the person who recognizes his or her spiritual poverty apart from God. Happy is the man or woman who sees themselves as they really are in God's sight: lost, hopeless, and helpless.

Apart from Jesus Christ, everyone is spiritually poor. Regardless of our education, accomplishments, or religious knowledge, we are all spiritually destitute. How often we will look at someone in prison or the down-and-outer or the drug addict and think, "Now there's someone who is spiritually destitute." Then we look at ourselves. Maybe we have lived a relatively refined life. Maybe we have a good education or have accomplished certain things. We say, "I am not as destitute as that person." In one sense, that may be true. But in another sense, it isn't true at all. Before God, all people are spiritually destitute and unable to help themselves.

Some people have a hard time admitting this. It is hard for us to acknowledge that we need to reach out to God, that we need His forgiveness. But if we want to be forgiven, if we want to be happy, then we must humble ourselves and admit our need.

HAPPY ARE THE UNHAPPY

"Blessed are those who mourn, for they shall be comforted." (Matthew 5:4)

The apostle Paul, after assessing his own spiritual condition on one occasion, said, "O wretched man that I am! Who will deliver me from this body of death?" (Romans 7:24). Paul saw himself for who he really was: someone in need of help, in need of change. Paul saw himself for what he really was. He saw his true condition in the light of God's truth and realized he was spiritually destitute and in desperate need. It caused him to be sorry. It caused him to mourn over it.

"Blessed are those who mourn," could be rephrased, "Happy are the unhappy." It almost sounds like a contradiction. How can I be happy if I am unhappy? But according to the Bible, before you can be truly happy, you have to first be unhappy. Why? Because "godly sorrow produces repentance" (2 Corinthians 7:10). If you are really sorry for your sin, then you won't just mourn about it. You won't just blubber about it. You will do something about it. Specifically, you will repent of it and turn from it.

The Bible says, "Blessed are those whose lawless deeds are forgiven, and whose sins are covered. Blessed is the man to whom the Lord shall not impute sin" (Romans 4:7–8). When we see our spiritual condition and our need for God, we realize this is the way to become happy. We reach out to God. We ask for His forgiveness. Then we will be comforted, because we have come to Jesus Christ. Although this happiness comes through pain initially, it ultimately brings the greatest happiness of all. Thus, our sorrow leads to joy. But without that sorrow, there is no joy. So you see? Happy are the unhappy.

Thursday

POWER UNDER CONSTRAINT

"Blessed are the meek, for they shall inherit the earth." (Matthew 5:5)

What does it mean to be meek? Jesus didn't say, "Happy are the weak." He said, "Happy are the meek." A good definition of meekness is "power under constraint" or "strength under control." Its origins are found in a word used to describe the breaking of a powerful stallion. A stallion hasn't lost its will or strength when it has been broken. But the horse has, in essence, surrendered its will to its rider.

What a contradiction of this world's kind of thinking, which says that if you want to get ahead, you must assert yourself. You must stand up for your rights and look out for number one.

Meekness means taking your will, your desires, and your ambitions and surrendering them to God. It doesn't mean that you have no will, desires, or ambitions. But it does mean that you have surrendered your will to God's and have said, "Lord, I want to channel the energy You have given me for Your glory now. I want to do something for Your glory. I want to make a difference in this world for You, not for me. I'm not looking out for me anymore; I'm looking out for You." Then, as you begin thinking more about God and less about yourself, you discover that you are happy. But it wasn't a result of seeking happiness. It was a result of forgetting about yourself.

In the only autobiographical description of His personality, Jesus said, "For I am gentle and lowly in heart" (Matthew 11:29). Philippians 2:5 says, "Let this mind be in you which was also in Christ Jesus. . . ." When we follow His example, our priorities change. A new spiritual quality is produced in us: meekness.

HUNGRY FOR GOD

"Blessed are those who hunger and thirst for righteousness,
for they shall be filled." (Matthew 5:6)

Have you ever been really hungry? My wife has told me, "Everything with you is always extreme. When you are hungry, you always say, 'I'm starving to death.' Can't you just be *sort of* hungry?" But that is how it happens. I'm not hungry, and then all of a sudden, it hits me: I'm ready to eat. My wife's hunger, on the other hand, is the kind that builds up over time.

If you ever have been really hungry or thirsty, then you have an idea of what Jesus was speaking of in Matthew 5:6. It is a picture of someone who is hungry and thirsty for God himself, someone who hungers and thirsts for righteousness. This is a person who is fed up with sin and self-pursuit and is hungry for God—a person who wants God more than anything else. The psalmist said, "As the deer pants for the water brooks, so pants my soul for You, O God" (Psalm 42:1). This should be our attitude as well.

Are you hungry for God? Do you really want to know Him? Do you crave a holy life? Do you hunger for God's best for you? That's the attitude we need if we want to be truly happy people. We need to hunger for the things of God. If you want to be happy, then live a holy life. Happiness will come from pursuing holiness, from pursuing godliness. What a great pursuit that is for life. No man or woman will ever look back on a life that was dedicated to God and say, "I really wasted my life." So put yourself in the way of righteousness. Put yourself in the way of God.

Weekend

BEING MERCIFUL

"Blessed are the merciful, for they shall obtain mercy." (Matthew 5:7)

There is a sequence, an intentional order, if you will, to these statements in Matthew 5 known as The Beatitudes. They are not given haphazardly. First we see ourselves as we are (verse 3). Then we mourn and take action (verse 4). Then we assess our condition and become truly meek. (verse 5). Then, as we are emptied of ourselves, we find a great hunger for God himself (verse 6). This leads to the next step: becoming people of mercy who understand and sympathize with those who do not yet know God, those who are outside of His forgiveness and who are without His help.

A good litmus test to determine whether you have gone through these steps is your attitude toward others who have sinned. When another Christian has fallen into sin, what is your attitude? Do you think, "What an idiot! I would never do that"? When you see someone who is without Christ, do you say to yourself, "What a fool. I don't know how anyone could live that way"? If this is your attitude, then you are not merciful.

How much do you know of God's forgiveness? Do you remember that you were once in the same place? God has graciously reached out to us and forgiven us, and we, of all people, should be merciful toward others.

Those who look down at others show they know little about God's mercy and grace. The more righteous a person is, the more merciful he or she will be. The more sinful a person is, the more harsh and critical he or she will be. "Blessed are the merciful. . . . " May God help us to be merciful—to see people as He sees them.

Monday

AN UNDIVIDED HEART

"Blessed are the pure in heart, for they shall see God." (Matthew 5:8)

The apostle Paul said, "Brethren, I do not count myself to have apprehended; but one thing I do, forgetting those things which are behind and reaching forward to those things which are ahead . . ." (Philippians 3:13). Now there is a person who had an undivided heart. Many of us today could say, "These *eight* things I do …" or "These *four* things I do …" instead of saying, "This *one* thing I do. …" It's the problem of a divided heart.

The word, "pure," in Matthew 5:8 means "undivided." In other words, blessed, or happy, is the person who has an undivided heart. Happy is the man or woman with a pure heart. Happy is the person who knows where he or she is going in life, who has priorities and lives by them. Happy is the person who isn't trying to live in two worlds.

We live in such a wicked time in which we are exposed to so many things that could be spiritually harmful. It seems that we are lacking purity today. But according to Romans 16:19, we as believers are "to be wise in what is good, and simple concerning evil." Another translation reads, "I would have you well versed and wise as to what is good and innocent and guileless as to what is evil" (AMPLIFIED).

God is offering you true happiness, which is not contingent on how much you have, but *who* you know. If you don't get your life properly aligned with God, you will always be chasing an elusive dream. But if you get your life aligned with God and start seeking Him, you will find purpose in life. You will find the happiness you are seeking.

Tuesday

EMPTY PURSUITS

I have seen all the works that are done under the sun; and indeed,
all is vanity and grasping for the wind. (Ecclesiastes 1:14)

During a visit to the home of Billy and Ruth Graham, I noticed a dog that chased his tail. I watched as he got closer and closer to the edge of a little hill, but because he was so preoccupied with his tail, he didn't notice and rolled down to the bottom. He climbed back up and started chasing his tail again. On a return visit a few months later, I didn't see this dog anywhere. So I said, "Where is the dog that chased his tail?"

"He got it," they said. "He bit it off and he died."

Like that dog, we chase after empty pursuits, but once we get them, we are more miserable afterward. We have been created to know God, and nothing is going to satisfy us except Him.

God wants you to be a happy person, but more than that, He wants you to be a forgiven person. When you find His forgiveness, you will find happiness. Do you want to find true happiness? Then you need to be poor in spirit; you need to see yourself as you really are. The Bible says, "All have sinned and fall short of the glory of God" (Romans 3:23). Every one of us falls miserably short of God's standards.

Therefore, God has reached down to us. Jesus walked this earth as God in human form, went to the cross, and died for our sins and paid the price for us. If we will turn from our sin, acknowledge our condition, and ask Him to be our Savior and Lord, we can be forgiven and ultimately find the happiness we are seeking in life.

COME AND DINE

What makes us think that we can escape if we are indifferent to this great salvation that was announced by the Lord Jesus himself? It was passed on to us by those who heard him speak. ..." (Hebrews 2:3 NLT)

It amazes me how flippant people can be when they consider God's offer of forgiveness to them, as though they had all the time and resources in the world. They believe they can invent the rules as they go, casually picking and choosing what appeals to them on a celestial salad bar of life. They will take a small amount of Christianity (but hold the guilt, because they are on a guilt-free diet), add a little Hinduism, and then maybe a side of Buddhism. Finally, they season it all with a few New Age spices.

But here is the real picture: We are in the middle of a hot desert, dehydrated, and starving. We have no resources to purchase food or water. Suddenly, God appears. He sets out a beautiful table in the shade with the finest, freshest gourmet offerings available and invites us to come and dine. The price for this sumptuous feast has already been paid. All we have to do is take a seat and feast away. There are no other options. It's simple: Eat and live or don't eat and die.

God offered only one way for us to be forgiven of our sins when He came to this earth, walked among us, went to the cross, and died in our place. We aren't doing God a favor by considering His offer to us. God is, in fact, doing us a favor by offering it in the first place. We should be running to Him to receive His offer of forgiveness before it is too late.

Thursday

BEWARE OF BACKSLIDING

"Your own wickedness will correct you, and your backslidings will rebuke you. ..."
(Jeremiah 2:19)

I have been a Christian now for more than three decades and I can tell you, with absolute assurance, there is no spiritual plateau. By that I mean, you will never arrive at a place in which you suddenly are above problems, above temptation, and incapable of falling. There isn't a super-spiritual state in which you will no longer grapple with temptation. There isn't a level of Christian living you will reach that will somehow guarantee you are above it all. The Christian life is one of constant growth and constant change, and that transformation will continue until our lives come to an end on this earth and we meet the Lord in heaven.

But consider this: The moment you cease to progress as a Christian is the moment the process of backsliding will potentially begin. When you cease to go forward, it will be only a matter of time until you start going backward, and yes, even backsliding.

The word, "backsliding," may seem kind of extreme, but did you know that you can attend church every Sunday and still be a backslider? It's a matter of what is happening in our hearts.

Falling away and backsliding is something that we as Christians need to be constantly aware of, because the Bible warns that in the last days, an apostasy, or a falling away from the faith, will take place: "Now the Spirit expressly says that in latter times some will depart from the faith, giving heed to deceiving spirits and doctrines of demons ... " (1 Timothy 4:1). So keep your guard up, because if you're not moving forward as Christian, then you will be going backward. It is either one or the other.

NOT THE TIME TO STOP

But you, dear friends, must continue to build your lives on the foundation of your holy faith. ... (Jude 1:20 NLT)

A sign posted at the end of the road on an airport runway reads: "Keep moving. If you stop, you are in danger and a danger to those who are flying." We could apply the same principle to the Christian life: Keep moving. If you stop, you are in danger. . . .

Why should we keep moving? Because we have a natural tendency to slip back into our old, sinful ways. Just as a car parked on a hill will naturally roll backward when shifted into neutral, we will naturally go the wrong way if we shift our Christian lives into neutral and stop seeking to learn and grow as believers.

Take a flower and a weed, for example. Our old nature, that part of us that doesn't want to obey God, is like a weed. Our new nature is like a flower. Now, my wife Cathe loves to grow flowers. She will tend them, care for them, fertilize them, and pull any weeds that get remotely close to them. And in the time it has taken for those flowers to grow a few inches, a weed will have found a crack in the sidewalk and has grown 18 feet tall. How much nurturing did the weed need? None. It simply took off. Like Cathe's flowers, our new nature needs nurturing. We need to do the things that will build us up spiritually. But if we cease to do those things, that old nature will come back to haunt us. The Christian life is not just about obeying commandments. It is also about wanting to please the Lord, wanting to grow, and wanting to become more like Him.

Weekend

NOTHING WE CAN'T HANDLE

And God is faithful. He will keep the temptation from becoming so strong that you can't stand up against it. When you are tempted, he will show you a way out so that you will not give in to it. (1 Corinthians 10:13 NLT)

S ome people like to blame the devil every time they fall into sin. They will say, "The devil got me the other day. I was just minding my own business, walking with the Lord, and the devil just grabbed me." Please. If you are a Christian, the devil can't "just grab you." You are under God's protection.

This doesn't mean you won't be tempted by Satan. It doesn't mean he won't try to hassle you. But he cannot pick you off at will. He must ask God's permission. However, some people will put themselves unnecessarily in the way of temptation, and then blame God when they fall. But don't blame God when you put yourself into a vulnerable place and then get tempted. When that happens, you really have no one to blame but yourself.

God knows what you can take. He won't give you more than you can handle. When my son Jonathan was younger and we would carry in the groceries, I would give him things like a roll of paper towels and a half-gallon of milk to take into the house. "This is too heavy," he would say.

"Buddy, you can do it," I would tell him. I knew he had more strength than he realized. It is often that way with us. We may think, "This is too much. I can't handle it." But God knows what we can endure. He knows what we can take. He knows our weaknesses. And He won't ever let us face more than we can handle.

Monday

HOPING FOR JUDGMENT

The Lord gave this message to Jonah son of Amittai: "Get up and go to the great city of Nineveh! Announce my judgment against it because I have seen how wicked its people are." (Jonah 1:1–2 NLT)

When God told Jonah, "Get up and go," we might wonder why Jonah didn't just obey. But we need to understand that Jonah was a patriotic Israelite. He loved his people. Ninevah was the capital of Assyria, the enemy of Israel. So when God told Jonah to go and preach to the Ninevites, he probably thought, "I know God. He has this tendency to forgive. My fear is that He will let them off the hook. I'm kind of happy to know He is planning to judge them. It's one less enemy we will have to contend with." Jonah didn't care about the Ninevites. His procrastination and personal prejudice was stronger than any passion for the lost. The truth of the matter was, judgment for Nineveh suited Jonah just fine. In his mind, they certainly deserved it. In fact, he probably hoped God would carry out His judgment quickly.

Some of us can be that way. There might be some of us who take perverse pleasure in knowing that certain people who really irritate us or harass us will someday be going to hell. But certainly that is not the attitude we should have as believers. In fact, we all deserve to go to hell. We all deserve the judgment of God. Jesus did not say, "Hate your enemies and hope judgment comes to them soon." Rather, He said, "But I say, love your enemies! Pray for those who persecute you!" (Matthew 5:44 NLT). Remember, you once were on your way to hell. I was too. I try never to forget that.

Tuesday

RUNNING THE WRONG WAY

But Jonah got up and went in the opposite direction in order
to get away from the Lord. ... (Jonah 1:3 NLT)

I t is interesting that, with the passing of thousands of years,
it always has been the same old antics with humanity.
When we human beings don't want to do something that
is the will of God, we try to run from Him, just like Jonah did.
When God told Jonah to go and preach to the city of Nineveh,
Jonah went, all right—in the opposite direction. He was trying
to escape from God and from his own conscience.

It may seem easy to criticize Jonah, but in reality, haven't we
as Christians been given our own marching orders from the
Lord himself? He said, "'Therefore, go and make disciples of
all the nations, baptizing them in the name of the Father and
the Son and the Holy Spirit ... ' " (Matthew 28:19). Have we
done that? In many ways, some of us may be just like Jonah.

The real message in the book of Jonah is that of God's long-
suffering, patience, and willingness to forgive those who are
willing to stop running from Him and instead run to Him.

Maybe, like Jonah, you have been trying to run away from
God. Maybe you know the will of God for your life, but you
have said, "I know what God wants me to do. I know I shouldn't
be doing what I'm doing, but I want to do it anyway. It's what
I choose to do." Even if you have turned your back on God,
I want you to know that God has not turned His back on you.
No matter what you have done, God stands ready to forgive.
But you must return to Him.

LOOKING FOR HIS LEADING

But Jonah arose to flee to Tarshish from the presence of the Lord. He went down
to Joppa, and found a ship going to Tarshish. ... (Jonah 1:3)

When Jonah was running in the opposite direction of
God's will, the Bible tells us that "he went down to
Joppa, and found a ship. ..." We must realize something: Satan opened all the doors for Jonah's disobedience. It's
amazing how skilled Satan is at manipulating circumstances.
But circumstances manipulated by the devil will always lead us
in the wrong direction, because God isn't the only one who can
open doors.

I have had people walk up to me and say, "The Lord brought
this person into my life. It's wonderful." So I will ask whether
this person is a Christian. "No, but the Lord brought this
person. It just happened. I was praying, and it happened.
Surely it must be of the Lord." It hasn't occurred to them that
the devil might have brought someone along to lead them the
wrong way.

God speaks to us primarily through His Word, the Bible.
So, there are certain areas in which we don't need to pray for
God's direction. You don't need to walk up to me and say,
"Would you pray with me about murdering someone?" No,
I won't pray with you about it, because I don't need to. God
says in His Word, " 'You shall not murder' " (Exodus 20:13).
You don't need to say, "Would you pray with me? I am think-
ing about having an affair and leaving my wife." No, I won't,
because the Bible says, " 'You shall not commit adultery' "
(Exodus 20:14). There are some things we don't need to pray
about, because God has already shown us His will for us in
His Word.

Thursday

THE LAST WORD

But the Lord sent out a great wind on the sea, and there was a mighty tempest on the sea, so that the ship was about to be broken up. (Jonah 1:4)

Jonah was God's child—a wayward one who ran from the Lord, but he was His child nonetheless. The Bible says that when it comes to dealing with His children, God chastens those whom He loves (see Hebrews 12:6). Because God loves us, He will seek to get our attention when we are going the wrong way.

I think we all know what this is like. When we are about to do something we know we shouldn't do, there will be that internal red flag, that sense of conviction from the Holy Spirit, which says, "Don't do this. You are going the wrong direction." Sometimes God will even put blockades in our path in the form of other believers. Maybe you are about to do something you know you shouldn't do, when all of the sudden, you run into that Christian friend from church. You think, "Lord, you are making this hard." But God loves you. He doesn't want you to make a mistake and go in the wrong direction.

David said, "Before I was afflicted I went astray, but now I keep Your word" (Psalm 119:67). In other words, before he tasted the sting of discipline, David was doing what he wanted to do. But the Lord got his attention.

Jonah 1:4 tells us, "But the Lord sent out a great wind on the sea. ..." I love those three words: "But the Lord. ..." Know this: God will always have the last word. No matter what you do, there will always be, "But the Lord. ... " He will always do what He wants to do.

A TIME SUCH AS THIS

"Yet who knows whether you have come to the kingdom for such a time as this?"
(Esther 4:14)

The Book of Esther contains a wonderful and dramatic story of a beautiful, young Jewish girl named Esther who actually won a beauty contest, and as a result, was made the queen of the kingdom. She was taken into the palace of the king, where she could enjoy the finest food, wear the most beautiful clothing, and have numerous servants at her bidding. She was living in the lap of luxury.

But there was a wicked man named Haman working for the king. He hated the Jewish people and devised a wicked plot to exterminate all the Jews living in the kingdom. Haman was going about his business, seeing to it that his plan would come to pass.

Esther had an uncle named Mordecai, who was concerned that his niece was in a place where she could influence the king to turn away from Haman's horrible plan, yet was afraid to act. So Mordecai sent this message to Esther: " 'Do not think in your heart that you will escape in the king's palace any more than all the other Jews. For if you remain completely silent at this time, relief and deliverance will arise for the Jews from another place, but you and your father's house will perish. Yet who knows whether you have come to the kingdom for such a time as this?' " (Esther 4:13–14). So Esther went to the king and appealed to him, and Haman's wicked plot was averted.

Who knows that God has not put you where you are right now for such a time as this? In whatever situation you find yourself, seize the moment. Do what you can. That's what Esther boldly did.

Weekend

THE GOODNESS OF GOD

"Oh, give thanks to the Lord, for He is good! For His mercy endures forever."
(Psalm 118:1)

One thing that is clear in the Bible is that God is good. We see this truth repeated over and over again. David said, "Oh, taste and see that the Lord is good ... " (Psalm 34:8). In Jeremiah, God said, "I know the thoughts that I think toward you, says the Lord, thoughts of peace, not of evil, to give you a future and a hope" (29:11).

Of course, God has an obvious advantage over all of us. He has complete foreknowledge. He knows everything that will happen in our lives; therefore, He is trying to mold us into men and women of God. He is seeking to unfold His plan for our lives as individuals.

Maybe we don't think that God is good. Maybe we think that God is out to ruin our lives. I don't know why we come to that conclusion. Perhaps someone has misrepresented God somewhere along the line, whether it was a bad experience in church or it was a pastor or Sunday School teacher who did or said something that disillusioned you.

Then again, maybe you had a father who mistreated you and abused you. Sadly, this happens a lot in our culture. Many children today come from broken homes in which their fathers have neglected them or even abandoned them. Perhaps you have taken those traits of your earthly father and have transferred them to your heavenly Father to the extent that you think of God in the same way you have thought of your earthly father.

But you need to know something: God is good. You need to realize that about His nature. You need to realize that about His purposes for your life.

Monday

GOD'S UNFAILING LOVE

He who does not love does not know God, for God is love. (1 John 4:8)

The Bible not only tells us that God is good; it tells us that God is love. He loves us. It is not merely that God has love or that He is loving. The Bible actually says that God is love.

Today we have a Hollywood version of love that is very shallow. It is probably closer to lust than anything else. Basically, the Hollywood version of love is one that says, I love you as long as you are lovable." Or, "I love you as long as you are beautiful or handsome. But the moment you cease to interest me, I will trade you in on the new model. I will move on to another relationship."

In contrast, God's love is unchanging. It is consistent. It is inexhaustible. He always loves us. He loves us when we are sitting in church with smiles on our faces and a Bible in our laps, but He also loves us when we are failing and when we are sinning. Though God is displeased by our sin, He still loves us, no matter what we do. So we need to remember that about God.

But I want you to know something about sin: sin will cost you. Sin is very expensive. Many advertisements today will urge us to "Buy now, pay later." We love that, because it almost seems as though we're getting something free. But payday will come—with interest.

In the same way, the devil says, "Play now. You won't have to pay." But sin will always cost. Adam's sin cost him paradise. David's sin cost him his family and his reputation. Samson's sin ultimately cost him his life. What is your sin costing you?

Tuesday

LISTEN CLOSELY, SPEAK CAREFULLY

So then, my beloved brethren, let every man be swift to hear, slow to speak, slow to wrath. (James 1:19)

How different our lives would be if we heeded the admonition of James 1:19. Most of us are swift to speak, slow to listen, and quick to anger. Yet James tells us to do just the opposite.

In this day of instant information when we don't need to wait for much of anything, it's hard to slow down and listen—especially to God. Many of us are like Martha in Luke's Gospel: we run around in our little, self-made circles of activity instead of calmly sitting at the Lord's feet like Mary. We need to be quick to listen.

We also need to be slow to speak. How many times have you blurted out something, only to regret it the moment it left your lips? Right after you said it, did you wonder why? Or sometimes you want to say the right thing, but you say the worst possible thing. It is easier to save face if you keep the lower half shut. It is difficult to put your foot in your mouth if you keep it closed. As the saying goes, "A closed mouth gathers no foot."

We should be quick to listen and slow to speak, because Jesus said, " 'For every idle word men may speak, they will give account of it in the day of judgment' " (Matthew 12:36).

It has been estimated that most people speak enough words in one week to fill a five hundred-page book. In an average lifetime, this amounts to three thousand volumes, or 1.5 million pages. Can you imagine a record like that? There is one—in heaven. So we should be quick to listen, slow to speak, and slow to anger.

HEARING WITH OUR HEARTS

Therefore lay aside all filthiness and overflow of wickedness, and receive with meekness the implanted word, which is able to save your souls. (James 1:21)

The Word of God cannot work in our lives unless we receive it in the right way. It is possible to hear God's Word with our ears, but not with our hearts.

The picture that is used in James 1:21 is one of soil. The human heart is like receptive soil to the seed of the Word of God. We determine what kind of soil our hearts will have by our response to God's Word. That is why James says, "Lay aside all filthiness and overflow of wickedness." For the seed of God's Word to take root properly, we must first clear the ground of all that would hinder its growth. We need to uproot weeds of bitterness, wickedness, or anything that would hinder the seed from taking root. Jeremiah 4:3 says, " 'Break up your fallow ground, and do not sow among thorns.' "

Once the ground is broken up and cleared out, what are we to do? "Receive with meekness the implanted word." This would be the opposite of pride. It means coming humbly, with an open ear to apply God's precious Word, and not with some hypercritical, already-heard-that attitude. It is an openness to the Word of God.

It was after years of walking with the Lord that the apostle Paul said, "Not that I have already attained, or am already perfected; but I press on, that I may lay hold of that for which Christ Jesus has also laid hold of me" (Philippians 3:12). There is so much to learn, so much to know. We need to come to God's Word with a willingness to accept and apply what it says.

Thursday

LISTEN, LEARN, LIVE

For if anyone is a hearer of the word and not a doer, he is like a man observing his natural face in a mirror; for he observes himself, goes away, and immediately forgets what kind of man he was. (James 1:23–34)

If you have ever looked at yourself carefully in a magnifying mirror, then you know what it is like to see every pore and every imperfection. But imagine walking away and immediately forgetting what you just saw. That would be difficult to do. But according to James 1:23–24, this is what it is like to hear God's Word, yet fail to apply it to our lives.

As you are reading your Bible or listening to a message, maybe a certain truth really speaks to you. It's as though the Holy Spirit has said, "You have been wondering about this, so this is for you." It seems as though it is being directed to you and you alone.

Here is what it comes down to: What are you going to do about it? You might have thought, "That really spoke to me. I need to do something." But then you close your Bible or leave the church service and forget about it. God has spoken to you through His Word and you know that you should do something, but you basically ignore it.

This is what James is speaking of. We look at ourselves in the mirror of God's Word and realize we need to do something, but then we don't take action. But unless God's Word has made a change in our lives, then it has not really entered our lives. We need to act on what we see in God's Word. It is not enough to just hear it. We also need to apply it.

THE LAW THAT LIBERATES

But he who looks into the perfect law of liberty and continues in it, and is not a forgetful hearer but a doer of the work, this one will be blessed in what he does. (James 1:25)

One afternoon, a brightly colored little bird landed in my backyard. My German Shepherd was a few feet away, and I knew the moment he saw that bird, it would become an appetizer for him. So I went over to the bird and bent down. It was shaking, its feathers fluffed. When I held out my finger, the little bird hopped on. I walked into the house and said to my wife, "Cathe, look at this little bird." She turned around to see it perched on my finger.

"Where did you get that?"

"Our backyard."

"It must be someone's pet."

"Yeah, but I don't know who it belongs to."

Just then, my son Jonathan walked in. He told us about a girl down the street who had a bird that died. He offered to run and get the cage. When he brought it back, we put it on the kitchen counter, opened the door, and placed the bird inside. The bird, which had stayed frozen on my finger all this time, suddenly came alive. He started chirping and hopping from perch to perch. His feathers smoothed down. It was obvious that he liked his new surroundings. Then it dawned on me: what we saw as a means to contain this little bird was, from his standpoint, a means of security and protection.

In the same way, God gives us His law. He gives us His standards. While we might see them as restrictive, they are, in reality, our source of protection. This is "the perfect law of liberty" that James is speaking of.

Weekend

Three Qualities
of a Godly Person

*If you claim to be religious but don't control your tongue, you are just
fooling yourself, and your religion is worthless. Pure and lasting religion
in the sight of God our Father means that we must care for orphans and widows
in their troubles, and refuse to let the world corrupt us. (James 1:26–27 NLT)*

I n James 1, we find three tests that determine whether
we are truly spiritual. If you are truly a godly person,
then these three things should characterize your life.

One, you will control your tongue. A true test of a person's spirituality is not the ability to speak one's mind but to hold one's
tongue. We may pride ourselves in the fact that we are not
immoral or violent. But we may inflict a pain on others that
is much worse by wounding someone with our words and stealing his or her good name or reputation. So we need to control
our tongues.

Two, you will care about others. Jesus spoke of the fact that, when
we give a drink to a stranger, invite people into our homes, or
clothe them or visit them when they are sick or in prison, we
are doing it for Him and to Him (see Matthew 25:40). Do
you know someone right now who could really use your help
in a tangible way? Show them the love of God by helping them.
That is true spirituality.

Three, you will keep yourself uncorrupted by the world. God will
keep us, but we need to keep ourselves by making sure we don't
conform to the world and its standards. It is faith alone that
justifies, but faith that justifies can never be alone. If your faith
is real, there will be changes in your life as a result of it.

Monday

A FAITH THAT WORKS

Do you still think it's enough just to believe that there is one God? Well, even the demons believe this, and they tremble in terror! (James 2:19 NLT)

It may come as a surprise to you that the devil and his demons are neither atheists nor agnostics. They believe in the existence of God. They believe in the deity of Jesus Christ. They believe that the Bible is the very Word of God. They believe that Jesus is coming back again. You could say, in a very limited sense, that the devil and his demons are quite orthodox in their beliefs. But are they followers of Christ? No. They are enemies of God.

We already know about the devil's fall, his agenda, and his final, impending judgment. We know that he is the enemy of God. Yet he believes—in the sense that he would recognize that certain truths are correct.

So you see, just because you believe something to be true doesn't mean you have real faith. You can even have a belief that is relatively orthodox, but that is not enough, in and of itself. Although it is important, it is not enough. That faith must impact your life. It comes back to not just acknowledging something to be true, but following the Lord and being obedient to His Word.

Faith and works go together like two wings of an airplane. A person could get on a plane and say, "I really like the right wing better." Another person could say, "Well, I like the left wing." I personally prefer both wings, because if one is missing, we aren't going anywhere. The two are intertwined.

You can't have real faith without works, because if you have a faith that is real, it will impact the way you live.

Tuesday

WHERE TEMPTATION COMES FROM

Let no one say when he is tempted, "I am tempted by God"; for God cannot be tempted by evil, nor does He Himself tempt anyone. (James 1:13)

We all know what it is like to be tempted. Unfortunately, we all know what it is like to give in to temptation. We all would like to know how to better resist the temptation that comes our way.

Where does temptation come from? I can assure you, it does not come from God. We play a key role in our own temptation. For the devil to succeed in tempting us, we must listen, yield to, and most importantly, desire what he has to offer. Where there is no desire, there is no temptation. So the devil will vary the types of bait he uses with various people.

When I went on a fishing trip to Alaska, we used bright orange salmon eggs to bait the King Salmon. For some reason those stinky, little eggs attract these great fish. Then we went to another place and used another type of lure. In the same way, the devil will use different kinds of bait and different kinds of lures to pull us in.

The devil also works with two close allies in our temptation: the world and the flesh. So the three enemies we face are the world, the flesh, and the devil. In using the term, "the world," I'm speaking of a world system that is hostile to God. I am not speaking of the plant Earth, *per se*, but a way of thinking or a mentality. That is why the Bible tells in Romans 12:2, "Do not be conformed to this world," or as one translation puts it, "Don't let the world around you squeeze you into its own mould" (PHILLIPS).

Wednesday

THREE ENEMY STRATEGIES

For all that is in the world—the lust of the flesh, the lust of the eyes, and the pride of life—is not of the Father but is of the world. (1 John 2:16)

You can take any temptation you have ever faced in your life, and it would fall under one of these three categories: the lust of the flesh, the lust of the eyes, and the pride of life.

The lust of the flesh primarily speaks of the gratification of our physical desires. It is not wrong to desire food or sleep or even to have a sexual drive. All these can be satisfied within God's natural order (the sexual drive being satisfied exclusively within the bonds of marriage), but we can let these things control our lives. Instead of simply wanting to eat, you can become a glutton. Instead of just wanting to rest, you can become lazy, and so forth. So the lust of the flesh is physical temptation.

The lust of the eyes is a little different. This speaks primarily of mental temptations, such as the thought life or fantasy life, which usually turn into eventual action.

Last, there is the pride of life, which is more subtle than the lust of the flesh and the lust of the eyes. The clever strategy of the pride of life is that you can pursue knowledge and seek to better yourself, even be a relatively religious person, and yet love the world. That is the irony of the pride of life.

These are the strategies the enemy uses in each of our lives. It is good to know these things. The Bible says we should not be ignorant of the devil's schemes, strategies, and deceits. It helps if we know what our enemy is up to.

Thursday

THE TRAP OF COMPROMISE

For we are not ignorant of his devices. (*2 Corinthians 2:11*)

When I was a kid, I collected snakes. I don't know why, but I thought snakes were very cool. It was my goal in life to become a herpetologist. I read up on snakes and owned a number of them. My mom, who was very tolerant of my hobby, took me to the pet store one day to pick up a new snake. We put it in the trunk of the car in a little box, but by the time we got home, the box was empty. The snake was gone. My mom said, "I am never driving my car again." But a situation arose in which she had to drive. As she was waiting at a traffic light, she felt a cold coil drop onto her ankle. She thought the missing snake was making a reappearance, so she opened the car door and jumped out, screaming at the top of her lungs. A police officer happened to be there and asked what was wrong. She told him that a snake was in her car. He went over to investigate, and as it turned out, the "snake" she felt actually was a hose that had come loose and fell down onto her leg. We never found the snake. There had been just a little opening in that box, and it escaped.

The devil is like that snake. When you give him a small opening in your life, watch out. You may think, "I'll just compromise a little bit here. I'll just lower my guard a little bit there. I can handle it. This is no problem." But the next thing you know, the devil has sunk his fangs into you, and you are going down fast. So be careful.

Temptation's Timing

Immediately the Spirit drove Him into the wilderness. And He was there
in the wilderness forty days, tempted by Satan. ... (Mark 1:12–13)

When does temptation come? In a broad sense, it can come at any time. Of course it often comes after great times of blessing, after the Lord has done a wonderful work in your life.

Remember, Jesus was tested, or tempted, in the wilderness for forty days and nights. When did this happen? It happened immediately after His baptism in the Jordan River, when the Spirit of God came upon Him in the form of a dove, and a voice came from heaven saying, "You are My beloved Son, in whom I am well pleased" (Mark 1:11). After the dove came the devil. After the blessing came the attack. Often after times of great blessing, the enemy will be there, wanting to rob you of what God has done in your life.

Maybe you have experienced a time of great blessing in your life, when all of a sudden, you were plunged into some kind of valley, so to speak. Maybe things have been going really well for you lately. Things are going well for your family, with your career, with your ministry, or with your walk with the Lord. That is good. Enjoy it, because the enemy will show up and try to rattle your cage. He will attack you. He will tempt you. It is not a matter of "if." It is a matter of "when." So keep your guard up. The devil will wait for the opportune time to attack. The devil will be sizing you up. He will be waiting for that moment when you are the most vulnerable. And we are often the most vulnerable when we think we are the strongest.

Weekend

Temptation's Targets

And these are the ones by the wayside where the word is sown. When they hear, Satan comes immediately and takes away the word that was sown in their hearts. (Mark 4:15)

Although temptation comes to everyone, the enemy often focuses his attacks on those who are young in the faith or those who are making a difference in the kingdom.

You probably remember that after you became a Christian, the devil was there to tempt you. One thing you most likely faced was a tendency to doubt your own salvation. Satan whispered in your ear, "So you think you are saved? You think Christ really came into your life? You psyched yourself into this. It is a bunch of nonsense. What are you getting yourself into? Are you crazy?"

But this goes back to the Garden of Eden. Remember what the devil said to Eve? "Has God indeed said, 'You shall not eat of every tree of the garden'?" (Genesis 3:1). It's the same thing. The enemy will say things like, "Is God's Word really true? Do you think God has really forgiven you?" It is simply a tactic he keeps using over and over again. So the enemy will be there to attack right after someone believes.

But temptation also comes to those who are making a difference in the kingdom of God. As C. H. Spurgeon said, "You don't kick a dead horse." In all honesty, the devil doesn't really need to spend a lot of time on some people, because they are essentially where he wants them: immobilized. When you say, "Lord, use me. Let my life make a difference," then know this: the enemy won't give you a standing ovation. Instead, he will attack you. You had better expect it and brace yourself for it.

Monday

THE LAST TO BELIEVE

For even His brothers did not believe in Him. (John 7:5)

I t is noteworthy that neither James nor any of the other brothers of the Lord believed in Him prior to His resurrection. In fact, the Bible tells us they even came to take Him home at one point, thinking that He had taken leave of His senses. This just goes to show that even if we as believers were to live perfect and flawless lives, it would not necessarily convince someone of the truth of the gospel.

We will hear people say, "The reason I am not a Christian is because there are so many hypocrites in the church." What are we going to say? That it isn't true? Of course there are hypocrites in the church. We all have been hypocritical at one time or another. When it comes to living out the Christian witness we ought to live, all of us will fall short at times.

But Jesus lived a flawless, perfect life. He never sinned in any capacity. He never lied or stole or lost His temper. He never even sinned inwardly. Yet some of those who were closest to Him did not believe in Him—at least not right away. As John's Gospel tells us, "For Jesus Himself testified that a prophet has no honor in his own country" (John 4:44).

This should serve as a reminder that the hardest people to reach are often those who are the closest to us, especially in our own families. Those who were raised in non-Christian homes know how difficult and hostile an environment like that can be. Here was the Lord himself who lived a perfect life. Yet it took His resurrection from the dead to finally bring them around. That is when they all finally believed.

Tuesday

COUNT IT ... JOY?

My brethren, count it all joy when you fall into various trials, knowing that the testing of your faith produces patience. (James 1:2–3)

Have you ever gone through a tough time and someone has tried to comfort you with a greeting-card type slogan such as, "When life gives you lemons, make lemonade," or "Don't worry. Be happy." How about that old favorite, "When the going gets tough, the tough get going"? I don't know about you, but this approach doesn't comfort me. In fact, it makes me even more miserable when I hear things like that.

Yet James, who was writing to people who were suffering, said, "My brethren, count it all joy when you fall into various trials. ..." Now, what kind of thing was that to say to someone who was suffering? Was James advocating a sort of mind-over-matter method of coping? Was he encouraging these people to engage in possibility thinking or positive thinking? Not at all.

Let's understand, James was not saying that we should be experiencing an all-encompassing emotion of joy or happiness during times of hardship. Nor was he demanding that we enjoy the trials in our lives. He was not saying that trials are joyful, because they are not. They can be tough. They can be hard. In fact, Hebrews 12:11 says, "Now no chastening seems to be joyful for the present, but painful. ..." James was saying that you need to make a deliberate choice to experience joy. Why? Because those trials are accomplishing something in our lives. So we can rejoice that God is in control of all circumstances that surround the life of the Christian. We can rejoice in the fact that the word, "oops," is not in God's vocabulary. Isn't that great to know? God is in control.

Pop Quizzes

But at midnight Paul and Silas were praying and singing hymns to God,
and the prisoners were listening to them. (Acts 16:25)

When Paul and Silas were imprisoned for preaching the gospel, the Bible says they sung praises to God at midnight. Their backs had been ripped open by a whip. They had been put in stocks in a dungeon. Do you think they felt like singing praises at the moment? I doubt it. But they were able to realize that God was in control. It was not mind over matter. It was faith over circumstances. It was not rejoicing in what they were going through. It was rejoicing in the fact that God had not abandoned them. He had not forgotten about them. He would accomplish His work.

One of the first things that comes to mind when we go through difficulties is why it's happening to us. We wonder what we've done to deserve such a thing. But it is important for us to know that God does have lessons He wants to teach us during these trials. Of course, I would like to learn what God is trying to teach so I can move on. I don't want to repeat any courses, if possible.

Remember in school when the teacher would announce a pop quiz? If you were like me, you would get a sinking sensation when such an announcement was made. Well, I have some news for you: God gives pop quizzes too. Often He doesn't announce them. We may think we are really learning and growing in the Christian life. So God will give us a little pop quiz to see if we are really learning as much as we think we are. It is then we will see how much faith we really have.

Thursday

SPREADING OUR WINGS

For when your faith is tested, your endurance has a chance to grow. So let it grow, for when your endurance is fully developed, you will be strong in character and ready for anything. (James 1:3–4 NLT)

When a mother eagle teaches an eaglet to fly, she will very unceremoniously kick it out of the nest, which is usually 90 feet or more above the ground. As the little bird is falling, she will wait until it almost hits the ground. Then she will swoop down, pick it up, put it back into the nest, and then kick it out again. She will do this again and again. After awhile, that little eaglet starts using its wings. Now, this may seem like a cruel way to teach something, but that is how eagles learn to fly.

Sometimes God will kick you out of your nest. You might be in a comfort zone in which everything is going the way you want it to. Then the Lord will say, "It's time for you to grow up. It's time for you to stretch your faith. It's time for you to spread your wings."

God will test you because He wants you to mature. He wants you to develop a walk with Him that is not based on your fluctuating emotions, but on your commitment to Him as you learn to walk by faith.

Notice that James 1:2 does not say, "Count it all joy if you fall into various trials. …" Rather, it says, "Count it all joy when you fall into various trials. …" It is only a matter of time until the next trial will come along. It is not an option. We all will be tested. The question is, when these tests come, will you pass or fail?

Transforming Trials

For whom He foreknew, He also predestined to be conformed to the image of His Son, that He might be the firstborn among many brethren. (Romans 8:29)

We must remember that God never tests us without a purpose or a reason. God will allow us to go through trials, but He has a long-term goal in mind. It is to conform us into the image of Jesus Christ.

There are times in our lives in which we will go through a trial, and then things will work out great. At times like these, we are reminded of Romans 8:28: "And we know that all things work together for good to those who love God, to those who are the called according to His purpose." A lot of things that make no sense at the time will work out in the end.

A classic example of this is Joseph. One day, he was on top of the world, and the next day, he was literally at the bottom of a pit. In the end, Joseph, with the advantage of twenty-twenty hindsight, was able to look back and say to his brothers who betrayed him, "You meant evil against me; but God meant it for good" (Genesis 50:20). I have seen a lot of things happen in my own life that I did not understand at the time. But after a few years passed, I was able to look back and see why the Lord allowed them.

Not everything works out that way, however. There will be things you go through in life that will not have a convenient explanation. There will be some unanswered questions. But we know on that final day, when we stand before God, all of our questions will be answered. All of our problems will be resolved.

Weekend

THROUGH THE FIRE

*So we don't look at the troubles we can see right now; rather, we look forward
to what we have not yet seen. For the troubles we see will soon be over,
but the joys to come will last forever. (2 Corinthians 4:18 NLT)*

When I have gone through any kind of suffering in my life, it has always changed me in a way that I cannot describe. Hopefully trials will make us a little more compassionate, a little more sensitive, and a little more caring when someone else goes through a hardship. It might be difficult to understand, but God is working toward a goal in our lives: to make us more like Christ.

There will be things you go through that you will not understand and that you will not be able to easily explain. In reality, those things are inwardly forming you into the image of Jesus. You might not fully appreciate those things, at least in this life. But through the suffering and through the valleys, you will be made more and more into the likeness of Jesus Christ.

The good news is that trials are temporary. According to 2 Corinthians 4:17, "Our present troubles are quite small and won't last very long. Yet they produce for us an immeasurably great glory that will last forever!" (NLT).

When God permits His children to go into the furnace, He always keeps an eye on the clock and a hand on the thermostat. If we rebel, He may have to reset the clock. But if we submit, He will not permit us to suffer one minute too long. He won't give us more than we can handle.

Maybe you are going through a fiery trial right now. Maybe you are experiencing a difficulty right now. God is aware.

Monday

THE BATTLE WITHIN

Temptation comes from the lure of our own evil desires. These evil desires lead to evil actions, and evil actions lead to death. (James 1:14–15 NLT)

If we are not careful, testing on the outside can become temptation on the inside. When circumstances are difficult, we might find ourselves complaining against God, questioning His love, or resisting His will. At this point, Satan will provide an opportunity to escape the difficulty, and that opportunity becomes a temptation.

You will go through hardships. You will go through trials. When you do, you have a choice. You can turn to God in complete faith and humility and say, "Lord, I don't know what to do. I don't know what the answer is. I'm giving this situation to You." Or, you can get angry with God or even rebel against Him. This essentially will turn your testing into a temptation.

This is what happened to Abraham. When he arrived in Canaan. A great famine came, and he wasn't able to care for his flocks and herds. It was an opportunity to trust in God. But instead of learning from this trial, Abraham turned it into a temptation. The Bible says he went down to Egypt. To preserve his life, he asked his wife Sarah to say she was his sister, because she was very beautiful. God had to deal strongly with Abraham to bring him back to a place of obedience. Abraham turned a time of testing into a time of temptation.

When we fall into temptation, let's not blame it on God. It is our own fault. To pray for strength to resist temptation and then rush into a place of vulnerability is like putting your hands into a fire and praying you won't be burned. We bring it on ourselves.

Tuesday

KEEP YOUR DISTANCE

So humble yourselves before God. Resist the Devil, and he will flee from you.
(James 4:7 NLT)

People will sometimes walk into a place of temptation and think, "This is no problem. I can handle it. I am strong." Famous last words.

That is what Samson thought. The Philistines had repeatedly tried to kill him, yet he came out ahead every time. On one occasion, he killed one thousand Philistines with a bone he picked up off the ground. No one could stop him.

So the devil changed his tactics. He couldn't bring Samson down on the battlefield, so he decided to bring him down in the bedroom. He sent a beautiful young girl named Delilah into Samson's life. She was very up front about her intentions. She said, "Please tell me what makes you so strong and what it would take to tie you up securely" (Judges 16:6 NLT). That should have been a major sign this was not a good relationship. But Samson didn't take her seriously. He got closer and closer to revealing the truth, until one day, he told Delilah everything. He said that he had taken the vow of a Nazirite from birth, so his hair had never been cut. That was the key to his strength. So the next time Samson fell asleep, Delilah gave him a buzz cut. Then he found out what happens when you play around with sin: sin plays around with you. Samson's life ultimately ended as a result.

We need to have a healthy respect of our adversary. That doesn't mean love him or honor him, but respect him as a powerful foe. The devil is not more powerful than God. But he is a powerful spirit being whom we want to keep as much distance from as possible.

UNDER HIS CARE

Do you not know that to whom you present yourselves slaves to obey, you are
that one's slaves whom you obey, whether of sin leading to death,
or of obedience leading to righteousness? (Romans 6:16)

L uke's gospel tells us that at one point during the Last
Supper, Jesus turned to Peter and said, "Simon,
Simon! Indeed, Satan has asked for you, that he may
sift you as wheat. But I have prayed for you, that your faith
should not fail; and when you have returned to Me, strengthen
your brethren" (Luke 22:31–32). I don't know about you, but
I would be really concerned if Jesus said that to me. Here was
Peter, spending time with the Lord and the other disciples.
Everything was great. Then Jesus says, "The devil has been
asking for you. ..."

"By name?"

"Yes—that you would be taken out of the care and protection
of God." This wasn't sounding good at all. I wonder if the Lord
paused there for effect and looked at Peter. He went on to say,
"But I have prayed for you, that your faith should not fail; and
when you have returned to Me, strengthen your brethren."
That was good news. Jesus had been praying for Peter.

We need to stand in God's strength and realize our vulnerability. We play a part in our own temptation. Satan needs
our cooperation to draw us in. For him to succeed, we must
first listen to what he has to offer. Then we have to yield to it.
Finally, we have to desire what he is presenting to us. When
there is no desire on our part, there is no temptation of any
effect on his part. So we want to keep our distance. Flee temptation, and don't leave a forwarding address.

Thursday

THE HEART OF THE MATTER

What is causing the quarrels and fights among you? Isn't it the whole army of evil desires at war within you? (James 4:1 NLT)

Several years ago when El Niño weather patterns were noticeably affecting Southern California, I witnessed an interesting phenomenon. It became the one thing on which people could blame practically everything. No matter what was happening, El Niño was the culprit. "This has been a wet year." El Niño. "It's a little hot today." El Niño. "It's a little cooler than normal today." El Niño. "There's a crime wave going on." El Niño. "Why did that marriage fall apart?" El Niño. "Why did you show up late for work today?" El Niño.

It is great to have a scapegoat, especially in a time when no one wants to take responsibility for his or her actions. We are living in a day in which we love to blame someone or something for the things we do. Of course, the problem is never us. We find a million and one excuses to explain away our wrong behavior. It is so easy to blame someone else for our problems.

But what is really the source of our problems today? Is it low self-esteem? Is it our family? Is it our culture? Is it the government? Is it El Niño?

The Bible tells us the source of our problems: "What is causing the quarrels and fights among you? Isn't it the whole army of evil desires at war within you?" (James 4:1 NLT). The answer to that question is yes. That is exactly where these problems come from. This is the answer to questions we may have about conflicts in the church and in our own lives. It comes down to one, simple thing: the problem is us. The problem is inside.

NEVER SATISFIED

You lust and do not have. You murder and covet and cannot obtain.
You fight and war. Yet you do not have because you do not ask. (James 4:2)

"Whoever drinks of this water will thirst again," Jesus said to the woman at the well who was trying to fill the void in her life with men. He wasn't just referring to the water in the well there in Samaria where their conversation was taking place. Rather, He was speaking of the pursuits of life.

You can take that statement Jesus made and apply it to whatever it is you hope will give you fulfillment in life. You can apply it to a career: "Whoever drinks of this water will thirst again." You can apply it to a relationship: "Whoever drinks of this water will thirst again." You can apply it to possessions. "Whoever drinks of this water will thirst again." You can apply it to anything that might take the place of God in your life. You will thirst again.

No matter what we obtain, no matter what we achieve, we always want more. Scripture says, "Hell and Destruction are never full; so the eyes of man are never satisfied" (Proverbs 27:20). Never satisfied—that is how life goes when one's body, mind, and spirit are not yielded to God. Life becomes a vicious circle, because the natural heart of a person is never content.

This can even affect our prayer lives. James says, "You ask and do not receive, because you ask amiss, that you may spend it on your pleasures." (4:3). It comes down to our motives in prayer. It is very important what motivates us, because when God listens to our prayers, He looks into our hearts. And He knows what we are really asking for.

Weekend

THE PURSUIT OF PLEASURE

You ask and do not receive, because you ask amiss,
that you may spend it on your pleasures. (James 4:3)

The Bible tells us one of the signs of the last days is that people will be lovers of pleasure rather lovers of God (see 2 Timothy 3:1–4). That to me is an accurate assessment of our culture today. We are a pleasure-mad society. We want to be constantly entertained, titillated, and thrilled. We want constant activity taking place in our lives. We are entertaining ourselves to death.

The Bible does not say that pleasure in and of itself is necessarily wrong. There are certain pleasures that have been given to us by God himself. Psalm 16:11 says, "You will show me the path of life; in Your presence is fullness of joy; at Your right hand are pleasures forevermore." Also, the Bible speaks of a joy and happiness that can be experienced by the man or woman who is walking with God. Psalm 84:11 says, "For the Lord God is a sun and shield; the Lord will give grace and glory; no good thing will He withhold from those who walk uprightly." This reminds us there is nothing God tells us to avoid that is good. If He withholds it from us, it is only because it will harm us.

We must accept this by faith, because there will be times when certain things in the world will look really good. They will be appealing. They will be exciting. They will be tantalizing. But if God says no to something, then it is for our own good. He won't hold back anything from us that is good. Yet when pleasure becomes the focus of our lives, we will be miserable, because it rarely brings what we're searching for.

Monday

FAITHFUL IN THE LITTLE THINGS

Unless you are faithful in small matters, you won't be faithful in large ones. ...
(Luke 16:10 NLT)

When I was a young Christian attending Calvary Chapel of Costa Mesa, I would listen to Pastor Chuck Smith and some of the other pastors and think, "That is what I want to do. I want to serve the Lord like that. I want to speak." I had been a believer for three or four months when I went to see Pastor Chuck one afternoon. I sat down in his office and said, "I have been listening to you speak. I want you to know that I want to be used by God. Whatever you want me to do around here, I would be happy to do it." I was kind of hoping he might say, "Greg, why don't you teach for me Sunday morning?" or something like that Instead, he suggested that I talk to Romaine, another pastor at Calvary Chapel. Romaine was a former drill sergeant in the Marine Corps.

So I went to Romaine's office and told him, "I want to be used by God."

"You do?"

I said, "Yes I do. I want to serve the Lord."

"That's great," he said. "See that broom? See that tree? Start sweeping." There was a pepper tree on the church property, which I believed had only one function: to drop leaves. I would sweep under this tree, and one minute later, there would be two hundred more leaves. I would sweep it up. Two hundred more leaves. That was all I did for weeks, even months. I just swept that tree and did little things around the church. But that was good. They were testing my faithfulness. Do you want to be used by God? Then be faithful in the little things.

Tuesday

FRIENDS WITH THE WORLD

Adulterers and adulteresses! Do you not know that friendship with the world is enmity with God? Whoever therefore wants to be a friend of the world makes himself an enemy of God. (James 4:4)

When you see the term, "the world," in the Bible, it isn't speaking of planet Earth, per se. Sometimes it is, but generally it isn't. This term speaks of a system, a mentality, or a way of thinking that is controlled by the god of this world, Satan. Interestingly, the phrase, "friendship with the world," used here in James 4:4 appears only in the New Testament. In its original language, this word, "friendship," describes love in the sense of strong emotional attachment: to love, to have an affection for, or even to kiss.

The world has a value system, and it is all around us. It is on TV, in the movies, in the magazines and newspapers, on the radio, and on the Internet. It is taught as dogma in our classrooms. We are expected to march in step to what we are told is the right thing to believe. In this day of moral relativism in which everyone is afraid of declaring certain things as right or wrong, tolerance has become the watchword of the day. Don't judge other people, we are told.

This, of course, poses a problem for the Bible-believing Christian, because we do not subscribe to the theory of moral relativism. We believe there is absolute truth, right and wrong, and good and evil. So what are we to do when we are surrounded by this mentality, this system that is so contrary to what the Word of God teaches? The only way to counteract this world's message is to fill your heart and mind with the things of God.

How to Draw Near

"Draw near to God and He will draw near to you." (James 4:8)

There is only one way to draw near to God, and that is to first recognize we are sinners. We need to recognize it is the shed blood of Christ that gives us access to His throne. It is not our own worthiness.

You see, the devil will lie to you and say, "You are not worthy to pray. Why do you think God would hear you after what you did today?" The devil is clever. He will tempt you to do something, and then when you do it, he condemns you. He will say, "You can't go to God," and you will believe it. You will start to think you aren't worthy. But does that mean when you are doing well spiritually, you are suddenly worthy? Does it mean that you are worthy if you've read your Bile today, listened to Christian radio all day long, and prayed over your meals? I have news for you: you are not worthy. You aren't worthy when you are doing well, and you are not worthy when you are doing bad. Your access to God is not based on worthiness. It is based on the shed blood of Christ.

It is good to get into God's Word, pray, fellowship with other believers, and share your faith. But these things don't give you access to God. These are what should be happening in the life of a committed believer. My access to God is always on the basis of the blood of Christ. So when I have sinned, when I have failed, that is the time I should really make the effort to draw near to God. And when you draw near to God, He will draw near to you.

Thursday

A Vanishing Vapor

Whereas you do not know what will happen tomorrow. For what is your life? It is even a vapor that appears for a little time and then vanishes away. (James 4:14)

James asks an interesting question: What is your life? This is not a philosophical question. Rather, James is reminding us of the shortness of human life. This theme is echoed throughout Scripture. Job 9:25 says, " 'Now my days are swifter than a runner; they flee away, they see no good,' " and Job 14:1 says, " 'Man who is born of woman is of few days and full of trouble. He comes forth like a flower and fades away.' " Then in James 4, life is compared to a vapor that appears today and vanishes tomorrow. That really puts our lives into perspective.

James was addressing his words to Christian businessmen who seemed to be taking credit where credit wasn't due. They were boasting of their ability to make money and be successful. In the process, they were forgetting all about God. That is a dangerous thing to do, because God will not share His glory with another. As James said, "Instead you ought to say, 'If the Lord wills, we shall live and do this or that' " (James 4:15). James was not condemning the person who makes plans for the future. Rather, he was criticizing the person who makes those plans with no thought whatsoever of God's will.

There is nothing wrong with making plans, and we don't need to say, "If the Lord wills," every time we plan something. We have our plans. We have our purposes. We have our agenda. But we also need to recognize that God may have other plans in store for us, and we must be willing to accept that.

Giving Him the Glory

But now you boast in your arrogance. All such boasting is evil. (James 4:17)

When we become proud of our abilities and say that we can accomplish whatever we put our minds to, we are making a big mistake. The Bible tells us that it is the Lord who gives us the ability to do what we do. It is the Lord who gives us the very breath we draw in our lungs. It is the Lord who has given us our hearts that are beating away. It is the Lord who gives us the ability to earn a living. Everything we have is a gift from God. We must never forget that. Scripture says, "For you were bought at a price; therefore glorify God in your body and in your spirit, which are God's" (1 Corinthians 6:20).

Remember Nebuchadnezzar, the king of Babylon? One day, he went out to his royal balcony and surveyed this ancient wonder known as Babylon. He stood out there, took in all of its splendor, and said, " 'Is not this great Babylon, that I have built for a royal dwelling by my mighty power and for the honor of my majesty?' " (Daniel 4:28).

The Bible says these words were still on his lips when a voice came from heaven saying, " 'King Nebuchadnezzar, to you it is spoken: the kingdom has departed from you!' " (verse 29). Judgment came swiftly upon him.

We never want to look at any success we have had, be it in a career, in ministry, in relationships, or in another thing and say, "Look at what I have done. Look at what I have accomplished." It is the Lord who has given us this ability, and we should give Him the glory for all we have accomplished.

Weekend

FORGETFULNESS

For this reason I will not be negligent to remind you always of these things, though you know and are established in the present truth. (2 Peter 1:12)

Anumber of years ago, I received one of those dreaded notices in the mail. It was time for me to take my driving test again. I thought, "I have been driving for many years. I don't think I need to read the manual again." When I showed up at the DMV for my appointment, I was handed a written test. Some of the questions stumped me a bit, but I thought I did reasonably well. I realized that I could only miss three. I took my test back to the DMV employee and watched her as she pulled out a red pen and, with great relish, began to look over my test. She marked one. Two. Then three, four, five, six. … "You have to take the test again," she told me.

I passed the test … barely. It was a humiliating experience. I drive every day. I thought I knew all of the basics, but obviously I did not. It reminded me that I don't necessarily know as much as I think I do. There are things in life that we forget. That is one of the reasons Peter wrote his second epistle. He said, " 'Yes, I think it is right, as long as I am in this tent, to stir you up by reminding you, knowing that shortly I must put off my tent, just as our Lord Jesus Christ showed me' " (2 Peter 1:13–14). If you focus on these things you should never forget, God says you will never stumble or fall (verse 10), and He will give you an abundant entrance into His kingdom.

Monday

IF MY PEOPLE ...

If My people who are called by My name will humble themselves, and pray and seek My face, and turn from their wicked ways, then I will hear from heaven, and will forgive their sin and heal their land. (2 Chronicles 7:14)

When God revealed to the prophet Daniel that He would bring judgment on Israel, Scripture tells us that Daniel was personally moved when he considered this prophecy. Daniel said, "Then I set my face toward the Lord God to make request by prayer and supplications, with fasting, sackcloth, and ashes. And I prayed to the Lord my God, and made confession ... ' " (Daniel 9:3–4). Daniel was essentially saying, "I am personally moved. Lord, I am sorry for my sin."

As we think about the Lord's return, we might say, "God will judge this world. He will finally mete out the justice that is so desperately needed in our culture today." But it is interesting that when God points out what is wrong with the nation spiritually, He doesn't point His finger at the government. He doesn't point His finger at the media. He points His finger at the church.

Today when we look at what is spiritually and morally wrong in our nation, we are quick to place the blame with the White House. We are quick to place the blame with Congress, or with Hollywood, or with someone else.

But God says that when a nation is sick, it is because there is a problem with His church. God says it is His people. Here is what it comes down to. How should the teaching that Christ is coming back affect you? Don't worry about the rest of the world. Don't even worry about the other Christians you know. How should it affect *you*?

Tuesday

AN ATTITUDE OF READINESS

Therefore be patient, brethren, until the coming of the Lord. See how the farmer waits for the precious fruit of the earth, waiting patiently for it until it receives the early and latter rain. (James 5:7)

Remember how you felt as a child on Christmas Eve? If you were like me, you could hardly wait. You had a hard time getting to sleep. When morning came, you sprang out of bed. You were anxious to see what was under the tree.

This is the same attitude that James 5:7 speaks of. The word used for "patience" does not refer to a passive resignation. It is not an attitude that says, "He will come one of these days. Whatever." Rather, it is a patient, expectant, excited attitude as we look for the Lord's return. It is an attitude of readiness.

Yet some believers are not living this way. Instead, they are just biding their time. But God tells us we should be active as we await the return of Christ. "And do this, knowing the time, that now it is high time to awake out of sleep; for now our salvation is nearer than when we first believed." (Romans 13:11). God wants us to wake up to the urgency of the hour. He is telling us to be ready.

James compares this to the farmer who looks for the early and the latter rain. In Israel, the early rains will usually come in late October or early November. These will soften the hard-baked soil for plowing. The latter rains usually come in late April or May and are essential to the maturing of the crops. If a farmer were to rush out and harvest his crops before their time, he would destroy them. He has to wait. And so do we.

AT THE RIGHT TIME

But when the right time came, God sent his Son,
born of a woman, subject to the law. (Galatians 4:4)

By nature, I am an impatient person. I am one of those guys who, when the pizza comes, doesn't wait for it to cool off. I start eating it immediately. Of course, I have burned the entire roof of my mouth that way. But I just can't wait.

In this day and age when everything moves so fast, we don't need to wait for much of anything anymore. How did we ever make it without microwave ovens? Yet even these seem slow to me now. At the grocery store, even if it's necessary for me to leave a few things behind, I will try to get in the ten-items-or-less line. When I am on the freeway, if one lane starts to move, even if it's just slightly faster than my lane, I will move to the faster lane. I don't like to wait.

Yet the Lord tells us to be patient for His return. As we look at this world in which we live and the way our culture is changing, we may think, "Lord, come on. Return. Look at the way things are going." But God has His own schedule. He won't be late. He won't be early. He will be right on time.

When He came the first time, it was according to His perfect plan. Galatians tells us, "But when the right time came, God sent his Son ..." (4:4). I love that phrase: "when the right time came." At the appointed hour, Jesus Christ, the Son of God, fulfilled the Old Testament prophecies and was born in a manger in Bethlehem. And when the time is just right, Jesus Christ, the Son of God, will return.

Thursday

THE ROD AND THE STAFF

Your rod and Your staff, they comfort me. (Psalm 23:4)

The rod and staff David spoke of in Psalm 23 are two essential tools of a shepherd. The staff is that long, crooked instrument a shepherd uses to pull in wayward sheep—and sheep are definitely wayward. They have a natural tendency to go astray and get themselves into trouble. They also have a natural tendency to follow each other. If one sheep goes astray, the others will follow, even to their own death. Sheep are so compliant that they will do what the other sheep do. So, a shepherd will use his staff to pull the wayward sheep in.

At other times, the shepherd will use the rod to fight off intruders, such as wolves or lions. But the shepherd sometimes uses the rod on his sheep too—his sweet, little sheep that he loves so much. Why? Because he would rather use the rod than see them dead. For some stubborn sheep, the staff simply doesn't work. So the shepherd pulls out the rod and applies it.

The Bible says, "All we like sheep have gone astray; we have turned, every one, to his own way ..." (Isaiah 53:6). Because we have that same tendency, the Lord will use the staff in our lives. When we go astray and do something we shouldn't do, the Holy Spirit convicts us. If we keep doing it, the Spirit convicts us again. If we keep on going, then God will pull out the rod. Wham. Something dramatic happens. All of a sudden, the bottom drops out. It is the rod. The rod is not meant to destroy us, but to warn us of the danger of what we are doing. God uses the rod in our lives because He loves us.

WHEN WE'RE SUFFERING

Is anyone among you suffering? Let him pray. Is anyone cheerful?
Let him sing psalms. (James 5:13)

If you are suffering, the Bible says the first course of action is to pray. There is nothing wrong with asking God to remove your suffering. When hardship comes, I will pray and ask the Lord to remove that hardship. But then I will add, "Lord, if I have brought this on myself through some act of disobedience, then show me what it is so I might change the course my life has taken."

There are also times when our suffering is not of our own doing, but something the Lord has allowed, as in the case of Job. It is during those times we must wait on the Lord and trust He has a plan and purpose in mind.

The apostle Paul faced a great affliction. We don't know what it was exactly, but he described it as a thorn in the flesh. He said, " 'And lest I should be exalted above measure by the abundance of the revelations, a thorn in the flesh was given to me, a messenger of Satan to buffet me, lest I be exalted above measure. Concerning this thing I pleaded with the Lord three times that it might depart from me' " (2 Corinthians 12:7–8).

There are theories about the nature of his affliction, but all we know is that something was physically troubling the great apostle. He asked the Lord for deliverance, but God said, " 'My grace is sufficient for you, for My strength is made perfect in weakness' " (verse 9). God allowed this suffering in Paul's life.

In spite of what you are going through, remember that God is still in control. The word, "oops," is not in His vocabulary.

Weekend

PRAYING FOR HEALING

Is anyone among you sick? Let him call for the elders of the church, and let them pray over him, anointing him with oil in the name of the Lord. (James 5:14)

H ere in James 5, we are given the scriptural pattern for healing. I do believe that as Christians, God has given us the promise of divine healing. Among the verses on this subject, Isaiah 53:4 says, "And by His stripes we are healed." God can and will heal people today.

James tells us that if we are sick, we are to ask for the elders of the church to pray for us. It is interesting that nowhere in the Bible do we read of anyone having a miracle or faith-healing ministry. Although the Bible teaches there are and were miracles and healings, we don't read of anyone who was called a faith healer. Nor do we read of anyone who had a miracle ministry. We do read, however, that everyone had a gospel-preaching ministry. Their calling was to proclaim the Word of God, and the Lord would confirm with signs that followed. It was never the objective to place the focus on miracles or signs and wonders. The objective was always to place the focus on Jesus Christ and tell people how to believe.

At the church where I pastor, Harvest Christian Fellowship, we pray for people who are sick, and people are often healed. I am so thankful the Lord still heals us today. We should ask for God's touch and healing. We are certainly given that option in Scripture, and we ought to exercise it. Sometimes God will heal. But other times, He will not. So we need to remember that God always has a plan and purpose in mind, and we need to trust Him.

Monday

BE RECONCILED

Confess your trespasses to one another, and pray for one another,
that you may be healed. The effective, fervent prayer
of a righteous man avails much. (James 5:16)

When the Bible tells us to confess our sins or trespasses to one another, it is to be done among fellow believers. It does not mean that we must confess our sins to a pastor or a priest to be absolved. Rather, we should first confess our sins to God and then to each other. It also doesn't mean that every time you have sinned, you need to come to church, stand up at some point, and say, "Excuse me. I have an announcement to make. I went over the speed limit today. That was a sin." You don't need to go through a litany of every sin you have committed.

The idea here is that if you have specifically sinned against someone, then you ought to specifically repent of it. If there has been a specific wrong done, then you should try to rectify it. Jesus said, " 'If you are standing before the altar in the Temple, offering a sacrifice to God, and you suddenly remember that someone has something against you, leave your sacrifice there beside the altar. Go and be reconciled to that person. Then come and offer your sacrifice to God' " (Matthew 5:23–24). It is suggesting that if there is unresolved conflict between you and another believer, it can hinder your prayer life.

You might want to pray, "Lord, is there anyone I have sinned against? Is there anyone I have hurt? Is there anyone I have wronged? If I have, then show me who that person is." Until that area is dealt with, it can hinder your ability to approach the throne of God.

Tuesday

POWERFUL PRAYER

The earnest prayer of a righteous person has great power and wonderful results. Elijah was as human as we are, and yet when he prayed earnestly that no rain would fall, none fell for the next three and a half years! (James 5:16–17 NLT).

When you come to the words of James 5:16 that speak of "the earnest prayer of a righteous person," do you think, "That counts me out. I am certainly not a righteous person"? If you have put your faith in Jesus Christ, then I would beg to differ. According to 1 Corinthians 1:30, "God alone made it possible for you to be in Christ Jesus. For our benefit God made Christ to be wisdom itself. He is the one who made us acceptable to God. He made us pure and holy, and he gave himself to purchase our freedom" (NLT). Because of what Christ accomplished for you and me on the cross, you are positionally righteous—and so am I.

Part of the work of justification that takes place when you put your faith in Christ is that you are not only forgiven of every wrong you have ever done, but the righteousness of Christ is imputed into your account. It would be as though you were penniless and were $20 million in debt. Then one day, someone came along, paid your debt, and deposited $100 million into your account. That is the idea. So positionally before God, you are a righteous person.

James cites Elijah as an example. Most people think of him as a super prophet, yet Elijah was a very human guy. He had his lapses. But he prayed and God answered his prayer. So in spite of our flaws, we can know that our prayers still can be powerful and effective.

Wednesday

WHEN BELIEVERS STRAY

> *My dear brothers and sisters, if anyone among you wanders away from the*
> *truth and is brought back again, you can be sure that the one who brings*
> *that person back will save that sinner from death and bring about*
> *the forgiveness of many sins. (James 5:19–20 NLT)*

We all know people who once walked with the Lord, but have thrown in the towel. They have abandoned the faith. They have gone back to their old life. What should we do in these situations? Should we confront these people? Should we just leave them alone? Should we just forget about them? James tells us that we should do something about it. In the original language, the word, "wander," carries the idea of a planet leaving its orbit. It is speaking of someone who is leaving something they once knew in an intimate way.

Paul gives us additional insight in Galatians 6:1. He says, "Dear brothers and sisters, if another Christian is overcome by some sin, you who are godly should gently and humbly help that person back onto the right path. And be careful not to fall into the same temptation yourself" (NLT).

I have news for you: you have the potential to fall. So do I. You might think, "Not me! I have been walking with the Lord for twenty-seven years now. But there is always tomorrow. One thing we need to recognize about ourselves is our vulnerability, as the classic hymn, *Come Thou Fount,* reminds us, "Prone to wander—Lord, I feel it—prone to leave the God I love."

The first step down is self-confidence. Therefore, if we see someone else who has strayed from the faith, we should restore such a person in the spirit of meekness. After all, one day it could be you.

Thursday

HE KNOWS

"I know your works, your labor, your patience, and that you cannot bear those who are evil. ..." (Revelation 2:2)

The church of Ephesus that Jesus was addressing in Revelation 2 was a literal church. The apostle Paul, and possibly the apostle John as well, pastored it. When Revelation was written, not only had the Ephesian believers been under excellent leadership, but they also were in their second generation of believers.

There were many commendable things about this congregation at Ephesus. They were serving the Lord with great fervor and effort, as we can see from the words of Jesus in verse 2: "I know your works, your labor, your patience, and that you cannot bear those who are evil. ..." Jesus in no way criticized their works, labor, or patience.

Could that be said of us? Does God know of the work and labor we undertake for Him? Do you think He is aware of what we are doing?

I want you to know that God is aware of every little thing that we do for Him. Sometimes when we are serving the Lord, we may feel that we are unappreciated. Perhaps no one thanks us or encourages us. They may not notice us. When others get the attention or the acclaim or the awards or the affirmation, know this: Jesus is saying, "I have noticed. I am aware of it. I know your works, your labor, and your patience. I am pleased with what you are doing." That is why He tells us in Matthew 6:3, "But when you do a charitable deed, do not let your left hand know what your right hand is doing, that your charitable deed may be in secret; and your Father who sees in secret will Himself reward you openly." God sees.

WORK AND WORSHIP

I know you don't tolerate evil people. You have examined the claims of those who say they are apostles but are not. You have discovered they are liars. You have patiently suffered for me without quitting. (Revelation 2:2–3 NLT)

J esus commended the church of Ephesus for their discernment. How we need more discernment in our churches today. Far too many Christians are completely gullible, simply accepting anything that anyone says in the name of the Lord. But the believers in the church of Ephesus were careful. They tested all things according to Scripture.

This church also helped stop the spread of evil in their community. Have you ever wondered what kind of a place your community would be if God had not raised up your church and others in the area? How many lives would still be messed up? How many marriages would be falling apart? How many would have died and gone to hell? We will never know this side of heaven the impact we have had.

Today, the church as a whole (I'm speaking of the evangelical church in this context) has never been organized politically. We get the word out quickly when legislation comes up that isn't good for the nation morally and spiritually. We speak up. We make a difference. But have we left our first love? Has our passion for that which is temporarily good displaced our passion for that which is eternally good? When was it that our work for Jesus began overtaking our worship of Him? Are we more inclined to protest than to pray? Are we more interested in who is in the White House than who is in God's house? Are we more interested in boycotts than in the salvation of family and friends? Have we left our first love?

Weekend

No Substitute for Love

And you have persevered and have patience, and have labored for My name's sake and have not become weary. Nevertheless I have this against you, that you have left your first love. (Revelation 2:3–4)

Jesus acknowledged that the church of Ephesus had worked hard, even to the point of sacrifice. He said, "You have persevered and have patience, and have labored for My name's sake and have not become weary" (verse 3). These believers were working themselves to the bone. They were giving everything for the Lord.

Again, this is a commendable virtue. Jesus acknowledged this was good. But then He said, "You have left your first love" (verse 4). But what does that mean? It means these Ephesian believers were so busy maintaining their separation that they were forgetting their adoration. They were forgetting that labor is no substitute for love.

But is it really that big of a deal to leave your first love? Let's look at it this way. Imagine that your husband or wife walked up to you today and said, "Honey, I want to tell you something. I no longer love you. But rest assured, everything is fine. I will continue living with you. I will continue being a parent to our children. I will continue doing all the things that a spouse and a parent should do, but I just don't love you anymore." How would this hit you? Do you think this lack of love would impact your relationship? Of course it would, because all that you do for each other flows out of love.

This is what was happening with the church in Ephesus. And Jesus knows that when there is a breakdown of our love for Him, it is only a matter of time before it will affect our actions.

Monday

IS THE HONEYMOON OVER?

"Nevertheless I have this against you, that you have left your first love."
(Revelation 2:4)

What is the "first love" that Jesus was speaking of in Revelation 2? It's similar to the kind of love that two newlyweds experience. This is mentioned in Jeremiah 2, where God says, " 'I remember you, the kindness of your youth, the love of your betrothal, when you went after Me in the wilderness, in a land not sown' " (verse 2). God was saying to Israel, "I remember when we had that honeymoon type of relationship." It was a close, intimate love.

This is not to say that two married people can and should have that feeling of butterflies in their stomachs forever. I remember that when I first met my wife, I would experience a loss of appetite and would get sort of jittery around her. Today, I am more in love with her than I have ever been, but I am not necessarily feeling those emotions that I felt when we first met.

In the same way, God is not saying that He expects us to walk around with a constant emotional buzz in our lives as a result of being His followers. But He is speaking of a love that doesn't lose sight of the very things that brought it into being. When a husband and wife begin to take each other for granted, when their life begins to become a mere routine and the romance is dying, then you can know that marriage is in danger. This can happen to us as believers. We can start taking God for granted. We can start taking church for granted. We can start taking our faith for granted. Sure, we're still going through the motions, but have we left our first love?

Tuesday

SIMPLICITY AND PURITY

For I promised you as a pure bride to one husband, Christ. But I fear that somehow you will be led away from your pure and simple devotion to Christ. ... (2 Corinthians 11:2 NLT)

There are two earmarks of a believer who is continuing to live in a first-love relationship with God: simplicity and purity. I want to ask, are you living a simple and a pure life as a believer today? To be simple doesn't mean you are a simpleton or that you are naive. Remember, Jesus commended the believers at Ephesus for their discernment. But we should never outgrow our sense of wonder and awe of who God is. We should never lose our childlike faith. Yes, we should grow up and become mature men and women of God in our knowledge of Scripture and in our understanding of who God is. But we should always have a simple, childlike, faith and dependence on God. In other words, we should live simple and pure lives.

Yet this is an area that is breaking down in the lives of many believers today. They begin to compromise morally. They begin to compromise ethically. They begin to compromise spiritually. There is a breakdown, and the purity is gone. Don't let this happen.

There is a difference between someone who is in a first-love relationship with God and someone who is not. In a first-love relationship, our work for the Lord is a work of faith. But when our first love is lost, it is just work. There is a big difference between being tired *in* the work of the Lord and being tired *of* the work of the Lord. When our love for Him is full, our service to Him comes easily. It is the overflow of a Christ-filled life.

BACK TO THE BASICS

"Look how far you have fallen from your first love! Turn back to me again and work as you did at first. ... " (Revelation 2:5 NLT)

I once knew a guy who was always in the best shape. I would run into him a couple of times a year, and he always made a point of reminding me that he was in much better shape than I was. He would tell me, "Feel my arm!"

"That's hard."

"That's right!" he would say. But he was a stressed-out kind of guy. He was very intense. One day, I received the sad news that he had died of a heart attack. He had it all together on the outside. He was in great shape. But inside, his heart was in trouble.

You may have the greatest physique—bulging biceps and rippling abs. You may have incredible stamina and energy. But what good is all of that if you have heart disease? You might be able to flex your spiritual muscles in front of other people. You might say, "Look at my schedule! Look at all that I am doing for God. Look at what I have done. Listen to my accomplishments." That's good. Sort of.

When Jesus told the believers at Ephesus they had left their first love, He was getting to the heart of the matter, the root of success or failure in the Christian life. He was saying, "You are leaving this first love. You are neglecting these basic things." That is when the Christian life becomes drudgery. That is when you start saying, "There are so many rules. There are so many restrictions. I want to live as I please. I want to be free." When you begin to think like this, you are leaving your first love.

Thursday

DESTINED FOR A FALL

"Remember therefore from where you have fallen. ... " (Revelation 2:5)

Show me a believer who has fallen into any sin, whatever sin it may be, and I will show you a believer who, somewhere in time—maybe months ago, maybe years ago—left his or her first love.

Jesus told the believers at Ephesus to remember from where they had fallen. We might dismiss this as a trivial issue. You might think, "OK, so I am not as close to the Lord as I used to be. Don't be too hard on me."

Listen. It is of the greatest importance that we maintain our first-love relationship with Christ. David stands as an example of this. We rightly remember him as the man after God's own heart and the sweet psalmist of Israel. He was. But we also remember him as a murderer and an adulterer.

Of course, we ask ourselves how someone who had risen so high spiritually could fall so low morally? It's simple. He left his first love. That was at the root of it. We read in Scripture of David as a young boy who was out in the wilderness, worshiping the Lord, playing on his stringed instrument, and singing his songs of praise to God. But after he became king, and he was a great king for a time, we don't read that he worshiped the Lord as he once had. Instead of that wonderful spiritual activity, he became idle. It was only a matter of time until something led to his fall.

That is what many of us are like. We are setting ourselves up for a fall, because we are neglecting our passion and our devotion to Christ. Yet this is foundational. Let's make sure that we are not leaving our first love.

RETURNING TO OUR FIRST LOVE

"Remember therefore from where you have fallen;
repent and do the first works. ..." (Revelation 2:5)

When Jesus found a fatal flaw in the church at Ephesus—that they were leaving their first love—He also gave His prescription for renewal and revival. They are the three Rs of returning to our first love: remember, repent, and repeat.

First, you need to remember. This word could be translated, "Keep on remembering." What should you remember? You should remember where you were when Jesus Christ first found you. You were separated from Him by sin and on your way to a certain judgment. But He graciously and lovingly reached out to you and forgave you. All of us were separated from God and facing judgment. The essential thing Christ did for you is the same that He did for every person.

The psalmist described it this way: "He also brought me up out of a horrible pit, out of the miry clay, and set my feet upon a rock, and established my steps. He has put a new song in my mouth—praise to our God ... (Psalm 40:2–3). Every Christian can say this. That is what Christ did for us.

Second, you need to remember where you were at the highest point of your love for Jesus. When was that high point in your spiritual life? Was it a month ago? Was it a year ago? Was it ten years? Or is it today? Could you say, "At this moment in my life, I believe I am as close to the Lord as I have ever been." If you can say that, praise God. If not, remember when you were closest to the Lord, mark it in your mind, and make it your aim to return there once again.

Weekend

REMEMBER, REPENT, REPEAT

"Repent, and turn from all your transgressions,
so that iniquity will not be your ruin. ..." (Ezekiel 18:30)

The word, "repent," means to change your direction.
This means that if I realize I am not living in a first-love relationship with the Lord as I ought to, then I
need to repent. Make no mistake about it: leaving your first
love is a sin. Jesus said, "Remember therefore from where you
have fallen ..." (Revelation 2:5). This is not just stumbling;
this is being in a fallen state. Christ is telling us to repent
and to get out of the state we are in. The key is to "do the first
works" (verse 5).

For example, maybe you know you need to get into better
shape than you are in. You didn't necessarily aspire to be a
pear, but that is the shape you are today. So, you decide to do
something about it. What do you do? First, you remember.
You remember there was a time when you were in better shape.
So you decide to try the latest diet. You try the diet drinks.
You try the herbal remedies. You try it all and nothing works.
Suddenly, it dawns on you. You remember that you exercised.
You remember that you disciplined yourself in regard to your
eating habits. So you decide to return to that old regimen.
You remember. You repent. And you repeat.

Now let's apply that to the spiritual life. You remember there
was a time when you were doing well spiritually. Your fire was
burning brightly. What did you once do? Was there anything
different you once did that you are not doing now? If so, go
back and do what you did before. That is what Jesus tells us to
do. Remember. Repent. Repeat.

Monday

LOSING OUR LIGHT

Repent and do the first works, or else I will come to you quickly and remove your lampstand from its place—unless you repent. (Revelation 2:5)

When we come across the word, "lampstand," in Scripture, it is a symbol of the church and speaks of something that displays light. So when Jesus told the church of Ephesus that He would remove their lampstand from its place, He was telling them that in spite of the privilege they once had enjoyed in Ephesus, they were in danger of losing their light.

The church that has lost its love will soon lose its light. In the original language, the phrase, "you have left your first love," in Revelation 2:5 could speak of both a love for God and a love for people. When you are truly loving God as you ought to, you will have the love that you need for people. A church that has lost its love for the Lord and its love for people is a church that is losing its light, losing its effectiveness, and losing its testimony.

One of the most powerful testimonies a church can have is when someone comes into their midst and senses a genuine love for other people and for God. If a church loses that, it then will lose its testimony. Today our nation is filled with cavernous church sanctuaries that once had a powerful impact on their communities as the Word of God was faithfully proclaimed. But the original leadership grew old. Their legacy was not successfully passed on. Liberal tendencies crept in, and now those churches have lost their light in the community. It can happen anyplace. It can happen in an individual life as well. God help us to always have a testimony and lives that make a difference.

Tuesday

God's Promise to the Persecuted

"Write this letter to the angel of the church in Smyrna. ... 'I know about your suffering and your poverty—but you are rich! I know the slander of those opposing you. ...'" (Revelation 2:9–10 NLT)

The church of Smyrna was a group of believers who braved persecution in their day. Jesus' words to them are for all suffering believers. Of course, we think that suffering and persecution are the worst things possible. We don't want to face them. We don't want hardship. We don't want harassment. We don't want persecution of any kind in our lives. In fact, we try to avoid it at all costs.

But there is a special blessing promised to the persecuted believer. Jesus said, " 'God blesses you when you are mocked and persecuted and lied about because you are my followers. Be happy about it! Be very glad! For a great reward awaits you in heaven. And remember, the ancient prophets were persecuted, too" (Matthew 5:11–12 NLT).

Jesus also said that as His followers, we should expect persecution: " 'When the world hates you, remember it hated me before it hated you. The world would love you if you belonged to it, but you don't. I chose you to come out of the world, and so it hates you. Do you remember what I told you?' "A servant is not greater than the master." 'Since they persecuted me, naturally they will persecute you. And if they had listened to me, they would listen to you!' " (John 15:18–20).

God may allow persecution. He may allow hardship. He may allow difficulty. He may allow a thorn in the flesh to keep you dependent upon God. And whether you like it or not, it is for your own good spiritually.

THE PERSECUTED CHURCH

"Do not fear any of those things which you are about to suffer. Indeed, the devil is about to throw some of you into prison, that you may be tested, and you will have tribulation ten days. Be faithful until death, and I will give you the crown of life." (Revelation 2:10)

The message of Jesus to the church of Smyrna, which represents the persecuted church, is the briefest message given to any of the seven churches of Revelation. The word, "Smyrna," comes from the root word, "myrrh." In the Bible, myrrh is essentially an embalming element. The wise men who came to visit Jesus as a child brought gifts of gold, frankincense, and myrrh. When Jesus hung on the cross, He was offered vinegar with myrrh to help deaden the pain, but He refused it. As myrrh is crushed, it gives off a beautiful scent. The actual church of Smyrna developed, processed, and exported myrrh. But it had a broader application as persecution began to enter in. Like the myrrh from which its name was derived, the church of Smyrna was a church that was crushed.

Jesus told this particular church they would face persecution for ten days. In fact, secular historians agree there were ten great persecutions against the church, ten major attempts to wipe out Christianity from the face of the earth, beginning with the wicked Caesar Nero and ending with Diocletian. During this time, an estimated six to eight million Christians died an untimely death. But instead of destroying the church, persecution actually strengthened it.

Persecution has a way of separating the real believers from the false ones. If you knew you would lose your life for professing Christ as your Savior and Lord, would you speak up for Him? Or would you hide your faith?

Thursday

SILENCE FROM HEAVEN

"I know your works, tribulation, and poverty (but you are rich). ... "
(Revelation 2:9)

Interestingly, Jesus had nothing to say to the church of Smyrna in the way of correction or commendation. He corrected the other churches, but He did not correct this one. Why? Because there was nothing to correct. These believers were living godly lives. They were laying them down for the Lord.

It is also worth noting that He did not offer a single word of commendation. Obviously, these believers were extremely pleasing to the Lord, because a special crown awaited those who suffered like this. But instead of a pat on the back, there was a warning that it would get worse: "'Do not fear any of those things which you are about to suffer ... '" (verse 10).

It would have been nice if Jesus had said, "It is tough now, but everything will get better. Just hang in there." But He said, "It is going to get worse. But if you are faithful, there will be a crown waiting for you."

When we are going through an extreme trial, a time of testing, or persecution, we may long for a special word from the Lord. But here is something to think about: it may be that the Lord's silence is His highest commendation. It may be that silence is not a sign of disapproval, but of approval. A case in point: the church of Smyrna. There was not a word of commendation from the Lord, but He obviously was so pleased with them.

If you are going through a time of suffering or hardship, it could be that Jesus is saying to you, "I know what you are going through." And maybe that silence from heaven is not condemnation, but commendation.

Friday

IS THERE A CATFISH
IN YOUR TANK?

"Do not marvel, my brethren, if the world hates you." (1 John 3:13)

I heard a story about some fish suppliers who were having problems shipping codfish from the East Coast. By the time it reached the West, it was spoiled. They froze it, but by the time it arrived, it was mushy. So, they decided to send it alive. But it arrived dead. They tried sending it alive again, but with one difference. They included a catfish in each tank. You see, the catfish is the natural enemy of the codfish. By the time the codfish arrived, they were alive and well, because they had spent their trip fleeing the catfish.

This is my point. Maybe God has put a catfish in your tank to keep you alive and well spiritually. It's called persecution. Maybe there's a person at work who always has eight, hard questions for you every Monday morning regarding spiritual things. Maybe it is that neighbor who is giving you a hard time for your faith in Jesus. Maybe it is a spouse or family member who doesn't believe. You are wondering why this is happening. It is like that catfish. That person is keeping you on your toes.

Shortly before His crucifixion, Jesus told the disciples, "If you were of the world, the world would love its own. Yet because you are not of the world, but I chose you out of the world, therefore the world hates you" (John 16:19).

God will allow persecution in the life of the believer. If you're experiencing persecution, here are two things to remember:

1. Persecution confirms that you are a child of God.
2. Persecution causes you to cling closer to Jesus.

When you are suffering persecution for your faith, remember, this world is not your home.

Weekend

OUTWARDLY ALIVE,
INWARDLY DEAD

"Write this letter to the angel of the church in Sardis. ... 'I know all the things you do, and that you have a reputation for being alive—but you are dead.'"
(Revelation 3:1 NLT)

Have you ever seen something that looked quite charming at a distance, but as you got closer, you realized it was not what you thought? This is how the church of Sardis could be described. Outwardly they did the right things, but inwardly, something was missing.

Historically, Sardis was one of the greatest cities of the world, built on a mountain peak that rose 1,500 feet above a valley floor. Sardis was so confident their walls would be impossible to scale, they did not place enough guards outside to keep watch. Sardis was characterized by complacency, which seemed to find its way into the church as well.

The church of Sardis was essentially living in the past and resting on its laurels. To this church, Jesus said, "I know all the things you do ... " (Revelation 3:2 NLT). The Lord began with words of commendation for what good He found there. This was not a lazy or inactive church. They were well-known. Outwardly, they had every indication of a church on the move, but inwardly, something was wrong that only Jesus could see: they were dead. So He told them, "Strengthen what little remains, for even what is left is at the point of death. ... Go back to what you heard and believed at first; hold to it firmly and turn to me again" (verses 2–3 NLT).

Have you been in a state of spiritual deadness? Maybe you are doing all the right things outwardly, but inwardly, you know something is not right. Remember Jesus' words to a spiritually deadened church.

Monday

READY TO GO?

Denying ungodliness and worldly lusts, we should live soberly, righteously, and godly in the present age, looking for the blessed hope and glorious appearing of our great God and Savior Jesus Christ. (Titus 2:12–13)

If the rapture happened today, would you be ready to go? The Bible says that Christ is coming for those who are watching and waiting. Does the thought that Jesus could come back today make your heart leap? Or does it make your heart sink?

Any person who is right with God should be excited about the imminent return of Jesus. It is a good litmus test of where you are spiritually. If the thought of His return brings joy to your heart, then that would indicate to me that you are walking with God. But if it causes fear, then that would be an indication that something is not right spiritually.

As Jesus spoke to His disciples about end times events, He closed His teaching with a personal exhortation: "But take heed to yourselves, lest your hearts be weighed down with carousing, drunkenness, and cares of this life, and that Day come on you unexpectedly. For it will come as a snare on all those who dwell on the face of the whole earth" (Luke 21:34–35).

As followers of Christ, we need to be living in such a way that we are ready for His return. We need to be living in such a way that every moment counts. One day, each of us will be held accountable for how we spent our time, our resources, and our lives. Let's not waste them. Let's allow the anticipation of the Lord's imminent return to keep us on our toes spiritually. Let's allow it to motivate us to live godly lives.

Tuesday

WANTED: DISCIPLES

Then Jesus said to His disciples, "If anyone desires to come after Me, let him deny himself, and take up his cross, and follow Me." (Matthew 16:24)

The great English preacher, John Wesley, once said, "Give me a hundred men who fear nothing but sin and desire nothing but God, and I do not care if they be clergymen or laymen. Such men alone will shake the gates of hell and set up the kingdom of heaven on earth." I don't know if Wesley ever found such men. But I know that Jesus did.

Jesus called these men to be His disciples. In the Book of Acts, they were described as "these who have turned the world upside down" (Acts 17:6). When that statement was initially given, it was not meant as a compliment. In fact, it was more of a criticism. But in a sense, that statement was a supreme compliment, because it acknowledged the impact these men were making.

If there was ever a time in history when a world needed to be turned upside-down, or should I say, right side up, the time is now. But if it is going to happen, then it will need to be through committed believers like the ones John Wesley was looking for: people who fear nothing but sin and desire nothing but God. No fair-weather followers need apply. God is looking for disciples.

So what does it mean to be a disciple? It simply means that you take your plans, your goals, and your aspirations and place them at the feet of Jesus. It simply means saying, "Not my will, but Yours be done."

Let's commit ourselves to being true disciples of Jesus Christ. Not mere fair-weather followers, but disciples.

Not Ashamed

For I am not ashamed of this Good News about Christ. It is the power of God at work, saving everyone who believes—Jews first and also Gentiles.
(Romans 1:16 NLT)

In his book, *The Devaluing of America,* former Secretary of Education William Bennett made this statement. "During my tenure as U. S. Secretary of Education, nothing I said seemed more unforgivable than my good words about religion. I was attacked as an Ayatollah when I supported voluntary school prayer and the posting of the Ten Commandments in school."

His experience is so typical of our culture today. You can say anything. You can believe anything. But if you stand up and say there are absolutes, if you say there is right and wrong and the Bible says so, then you are accused of hurting our society. You are the worst possible thing that could happen to our culture. Ironically, the very problems that are the result of society's rejection of God are then placed at the feet of the Christian, as though the Christian has brought these troubles on our culture.

But this is not the first time in history that Christians have become scapegoats for the ills of a culture. Christians were blamed for the burning of Rome when it was Caesar Nero who was largely responsible for its destruction.

We live in a time in which people are standing up for all sorts of causes. We have people standing up for the rights of animals. We have people standing up for the environment. We have people standing up for perverse sexual lifestyles. We have people standing up for everything imaginable, even willing to die for their cause.

Isn't it time that we, as Christians, stand up for what we believe? It's time to stand up and be counted.

Thursday

SAVED SOUL, WASTED LIFE

For no other foundation can anyone lay than that which is laid,
which is Jesus Christ. (1 Corinthians 3:11)

A poll was taken not long ago that asked Americans what they thought was their main purpose in life. The responses were interesting. You would think some would maybe say, "To make a contribution to society," or "To have a meaningful life." But what most people said was, "The main purpose of life is enjoyment and personal fulfillment." It's interesting to note that 50 percent of those polled identified themselves as born-again Christians.

According to the Bible, the purpose of life is not enjoyment and personal fulfillment. The Bible teaches that we are put on this earth to bring glory to God. We need to mark that well in our minds and hearts. Speaking in Isaiah 43:7, God said, "All who claim me as their God will come, for I have made them for my glory. It was I who created them." Therefore, we are to glorify God in all that we do with our lives.

Are you using your resources and talents for His glory? Sometimes we think that it God has given us this life to do with what we will. We will say, "Lord, this is mine. This is my week. Here is your time on Sunday morning. The rest of it belongs to me." Or, "Here is the plan for my life, Lord. Here is what I want to accomplish." Or, "This is my money. Here is your 10 percent, Lord. I give a waitress more, but 10 percent is all you get." We develop a false concept of God.

It's possible to have a saved soul, but a wasted life. If you were asked today, "What is the main purpose of life?" what would you say?

THE TIME IS NOW

"Now when these things begin to happen, look up and lift up your heads, because your redemption draws near." (Luke 21:28)

"It was the best of times, it was the worst of times. ..." These are the opening lines to Charles Dickens' classic book, *A Tale of Two Cities.* He was describing France during the revolution. In many ways, you could use the same words to describe our world today.

In 1948, General Omar Bradley made this statement: "We have grasped the mystery of the atom and we have rejected the Sermon on the Mount. The world has achieved brilliance without conscience. Ours is a world of nuclear giants and ethical infants." If that was true in 1948, it's definitely true now.

In many ways, things have never been darker spiritually in our world and in our country. Despite all of the incredible technological advances we have made in recent years, it seems like we actually have regressed morally. At the same time, we see rays of hope where God is intervening, where people are coming to faith.

As we see our world going the direction it is going, these are signs of the times, reminders that the Lord is coming back. Jesus told us there would be certain things we should look for that would alert us to the fact that His coming is near. Then He said, "Now when these things begin to happen, look up and lift up your heads, because your redemption draws near" (Luke 21:28).

If ever there was a time to be sure that our lives are right with God, if ever there was a time to be certain that we are walking with Him so we can gladly look up as our redemption draws near, the time is now.

Weekend

IMMORTALITY

These perishable bodies of ours are not able to live forever. But let me tell you a wonderful secret God has revealed to us. Not all of us will die, but we will all be transformed. (1 Corinthians 15:50—51 NLT)

Historian Will Durant, when he reached the age of 70, said, "To live forever would be the greatest curse imaginable."

Will we live forever? The answer is "yes" and "no." Will our bodies live forever? No. Will our bodies cease to exist at one point? Absolutely. But the soul is immortal. Every one of us has a soul. It is the soul that gives each of us uniqueness and personality. That part of us will live forever.

Today, many people are searching after immortality, that elusive fountain of youth. Sometimes it is hard for us to accept the fact that life is passing and that death is approaching. One day, you will wake up and realize you have more life behind you than you have in front of you. But the question we should be asking is not, "Can I find immorality?" Rather, it should be, "Where will I spend my immortality?"

If you have put your faith in Jesus Christ and have asked Him to forgive you of your sin, the Bible teaches that when you die, you will go immediately into the presence of God in heaven. That is God's promise to you.

But God not only promises life beyond the grave. He also promises life during life, not just an existence, but a life that is worth living. Jesus said, "My purpose is to give life in all its fullness" (John 10:10 NLT).

That is the hope and promise for all Christians. That is why the believer does not have to be afraid to die. Or afraid to live.

Monday

THE TRUTH ABOUT THE DEVIL

"The time of judgment for the world has come, when the prince of this world will be cast out." (John 12:31 NLT)

Martin Luther had it right when he wrote the words of the hymn, *A Mighty Fortress Is Our God*: "For still our ancient foe doth seek to work us woe—his craft and power are great, and armed with cruel hate, on earth is not his equal."

If you are a Christian, then you need to know that you have an adversary out there. He wants to trip you up. He wants to drag you down.

We should never underestimate the devil. He is a sly and skillful adversary. He has had many years of experience dealing with humanity. That's why there are some important things we need to remember about the devil—things that the devil doesn't want us to know.

We need to understand that Satan is nowhere near to being the equal of God. God is omnipotent, which means that He is all-powerful. God is omniscient, which means that He is all-knowing. God is omnipresent, which means that He is present everywhere.

In sharp and direct contrast, we need to know that the devil does not reflect any of these divine attributes. Although he is very powerful, Satan is not omnipotent. Nor is Satan omniscient. He can't see everything you are thinking. His knowledge is limited. Finally, he is not omnipresent. While God can be everywhere at the same time, Satan only can be in one place at one time.

Most important of all, we need to know that the devil was soundly defeated at the Cross. There he lost his stranglehold on the life of the human race. As a Christian, you have been set free by the power of Jesus Christ.

Tuesday

A TIME LIKE THIS

"Who knows whether you have come to the kingdom for such a time as this?"
(Esther 3:14)

The Old Testament Book of Esther is a wonderful love story—a story of what God did in the life of a woman to literally save a nation. Esther was a Jew who was plucked out of obscurity through an unusual chain of events and was made queen over the kingdom. Meanwhile, a wicked man named Haman had been devising a plot to put to death the 15 million Jews in that kingdom. So Mordecai, Esther's uncle, came to the palace, wanting Esther to use her influence to help her people.

He sent word to Esther, "Do not think in your heart that you will escape in the king's palace any more than all the other Jews. For if you remain completely silent at this time, relief and deliverance will arise for the Jews from another place, but you and your father's house will perish. Yet who knows whether you have come to the kingdom for such a time as this?" (Esther 4:13–14).

Wherever you may find yourself today, know that God has put you where you are for such a time as this. He has put you in that job or at that school. He has put you in that neighborhood. There are opportunities to seize. You need to take hold of them.

Yet the dilemma of Esther is similar to that of many believers today. They have been delivered from sin. They have found safety in the church. And they have grown lazy. They have no vision. Of course, the devil is happy with this, because that is exactly how he wants Christians to live. Be a complacent, apathetic Christian, and the devil will be generally pleased.

AT EVERY TURN

Put on salvation as your helmet, and take the sword of the Spirit,
which is the word of God. (Ephesians 6:17 NLT)

During the Korean War, a unit known as Baker Company was separated from the regiment, and enemy forces were advancing on them. For several hours, no word came from Baker Company. Finally, radio contact was made, and when asked for a report of their situation, Baker Company replied: "The enemy is to the east of us. The enemy is to the west of us. The enemy is to the south of us. The enemy is to the north of us." Then, after a brief pause, a voice continued, "And this time, we're not going to let them escape."

It seems that way in the life of the believer. The Enemy is at every turn. Yet some Christians don't realize that the Christian life is not a playground, but a battleground. They are oblivious to the fact that a war is raging. And in this war, they are either winning or losing.

In a battle, it's always better to be an aggressor instead of a defender, because the defender is simply waiting for the enemy's next attack, hoping he will survive. If we, as believers, are always defending, then the devil is in the superior position. But if we are attacking, then we are in the superior position. When the Apostle Paul wrote about the armor of God in Ephesians 6, he mentioned one offensive weapon: "the sword of the Spirit, which is the word of God" (verse 17 NLT).

Make no mistake about it: there is authority and power in the Word of God. God's Word sticks. God's Word breaks through. God's Word impacts. When the Enemy has you surrounded, keep him on the defensive with the Word of God.

Thursday

PRONE TO WANDER

Finally, my brethren, be strong in the Lord and in the power of His might.
(Ephesians 6:10)

When he was little, my son had a habit of wandering. One day, we were in a hotel and came to an elevator. He ran ahead to push the button. I told him, "If the elevator comes, wait until Dad gets there." Just as I arrived at the elevator, the doors were closing, and he was inside. He was gone. I frantically pushed the button for the other elevator, and waited for what seemed like an eternity. Finally, the doors opened, and I jumped in. I went down to lobby. He wasn't there. I ran back to the elevator, pushed every button for every floor, and as the doors opened, I would scream out his name. I didn't care about decorum. I wanted to find my son. And I found him, about three floors up, wandering around. But you know what? After that experience, he didn't wander anymore. He got separated from his dad, and it was scary for him. He learned how important it was to stay close to me.

As Christians, we should want to stay as close to our Heavenly Father as possible. The devil is a powerful adversary, and we are no match for him in our own strength. We don't want to venture out in this life on our own abilities and suffer spiritual defeat. I have a healthy respect for the devil's ability. Thus, I want to stay as close to the Lord as possible. I want to be strong in Him.

If ever there was a time to be walking closely with the Lord, it is now. This is not the time to be playing games with God. This is not the time to wander away.

WHAT DO YOU THINK?

For as he thinks in his heart, so is he. (Proverbs 23:7)

When Jesus walked this earth, He blew the cover of the religious elite of the day: the Pharisees who smugly thought that if they did not commit certain sins, they were okay. But they somehow had rationalized that they could do these things in their minds and it was not sinful. Jesus said, "You have heard that it was said to those of old, 'You shall not commit adultery.' I say to you that whoever looks at a woman to lust for her has already committed adultery with her in his heart" (Matthew 5:27–28). They didn't like that a whole lot.

What was Jesus pointing out to these men and to us as well? He was emphasizing again and again the importance of our minds. Our hearts. Our attitudes. That's because sin is not merely a matter of actions and deeds. It is something within the heart and the mind that leads to the action.

Sin deceives you into thinking that because you have not committed the act, you're okay. In reality, if you keep thinking about it, it may be only a matter time until that thought becomes an action. Even if it doesn't, that thought still is spiritually destructive. So, you need to go out of your way as a Christian to protect your mind and your thoughts. Satan recognizes the value of first getting a foothold in the realm of your thoughts and imaginations, because he knows this will prepare the way for that thought to eventually become an action.

As it has been said, "Sow a thought, reap an act. Sow an act, reap a habit. Sow a habit, reap a character. Sow a character, reap a destiny." It all starts with a thought.

Weekend

A Work in Progress

He has made everything beautiful in its time. Also He has put eternity in their hearts, except that no one can find out the work that God does from beginning to end. (Ecclesiastes 3:11)

I am an artist. I like to draw and design. Sometimes when I am sketching, someone will come along, look over my shoulder, and see only a certain shape or form. I realize that all that is visible for the time being. But I am still working.

"What is it going to be?" the person asks.

"Just wait."

"I think you should do it this way. . . ."

"Just let me do it," I say. "Why don't you let me alone until I'm finished, and then I will gladly show it to you." Every artist loves to display his work. But when I am working on my art, I know it is a work in progress. When I am done, then I am happy to show it to others.

You, too, are a work in progress. God is doing a work in your life. When it is done, He will show you. If it is not done yet, be patient. God sees the end from the beginning. We can't see what it is, but God can. That is important to remember. As God told the exiled nation of Israel, "For I know the thoughts that I think toward you, says the Lord, thoughts of peace and not of evil, to give you a future and a hope" (Jeremiah 29:11)

For Israel, it meant they would be in Babylon for awhile, but ultimately, God would get them out. For us, what it means specifically to us on a day-to-day basis, time will tell. Whatever it is, it is good, because God is in control of it.

A PLACE FOR JESUS

And I pray that Christ will be more and more at home in your hearts as you trust in him. May your roots go down deep into the soil of God's marvelous love.
(Ephesians 3:17 NLT)

Can you imagine going home tonight and getting ready to go to bed, when all of a sudden, you see someone walking up to your front door and knocking? Lo and behold, it is Jesus. How would you react?

Of course, we know this isn't going to happen. The Lord isn't going to bodily come to our homes and knock on the front door. But let's just let our imaginations run wild for a moment and pretend that He was. Let's turn the clock back to two thousand years ago and imagine that Jesus Himself was knocking at your door. Would you open it up and gladly welcome Him in? Or would you feel a little apprehensive?

The fact is, we should be living our lives in such a way that Jesus Christ Himself could come walking into our homes at any moment and we would welcome Him without embarrassment. The Bible says that Christ should be able to settle down and be at home in our hearts. That is an interesting statement to make to Christians. But those were Paul's words to the church of Ephesus. He said, "I pray that Christ will be more and more at home in your hearts. ... " The phrase Paul used doesn't just mean that Christ would simply live in their hearts. The reality is that He lives in the heart of every believer. The point Paul was making was that Christ should feel *at home* in their hearts.

Is Jesus at home in your heart right now? Is He comfortable? Is He at ease?

Tuesday

A TIME TO SIT

And she had a sister called Mary, who also sat at Jesus' feet and heard His word.
But Martha was distracted with much serving. ... (Luke 10:39–40)

When the Lord walked this earth, He had no place to call home (Matthew 8:20). But there was something He liked about a home in Bethany where a man named Lazarus lived with his two sisters, Mary and Martha. Maybe Martha was a great cook. Maybe they were wonderful hosts.

Mary and Martha were quite different from each other. Mary was more the quiet, contemplative type. Martha was more the grab-the-bull-by-the-horns, assertive type.

One day, Jesus came to their home. Martha thought it would be a good idea to make Him a meal. She went into the kitchen and started working. Meanwhile, Mary thought it would be a great opportunity to sit at Jesus' feet and hear what He had to say. As Mary was sitting there, taking it all in, Martha was working frantically in the kitchen, growing more frustrated because Mary was not helping her. Finally, she could not contain herself any longer. She came out of the kitchen, and looking down at Mary and Jesus, said, "Lord, do You not care that my sister has left me to serve alone? Therefore tell her to help me" (Luke 10:40).

Jesus responded, "Martha, Martha, you are worried and troubled about many things. But one thing is needed, and Mary has chosen that good part, which will not be taken away from her" (verses 41–42).

Sometimes we can do the same thing. We can get so worked up. Like Martha, we sometimes offer activity instead of adoration, work instead of worship, and perspiration instead of inspiration. There is a time to sit and there is a time to move.

WHEN GOD SEEMS LATE

*Then he told them plainly, "Lazarus is dead. And for your sake, I am glad
I wasn't there, because this will give you another opportunity to believe in me. "*
(John 11:14—15 NLT)

Sometimes God will not come through as quickly as we
want Him to. Mary and Martha, two friends of Jesus,
faced this dilemma. Their brother Lazarus was sick.
It was a serious illness. So they sent word to Jesus.

I think they probably believed that Jesus would make a
beeline to Bethany to get Lazarus off his sickbed. But Jesus
intentionally delayed His arrival. Mary and Martha were
thinking of what was temporarily good. But Jesus was thinking
of what was eternally good. This delay was for their sake. It was
for them to learn a lesson.

Meanwhile, Mary and Martha had probably been saying,
"Jesus will be here. He will drop whatever He is doing and be
here." But He didn't show up on the day they wanted Him to.
And He didn't come the next day or the day after that. Lazarus
had now passed from sickness to death. In their minds, all
hope was gone. By the time Jesus arrived in Bethany, Lazarus
had been in the tomb for four days.

Here was the problem: Mary and Martha wanted a healing.
But Jesus wanted a resurrection. He brought Lazarus back to
life, and as a result, many believed in Jesus. Mary and Martha's
faith was strengthened, as well as that of the disciples.

Like Mary and Martha, we will say, "God, if you loved me,
you would do this. You would take care of that." But God says,
"Because I love you, I am not going to give you these things."
God wants to do something greater in your life. Will you
let Him?

Thursday

LETTING GOD CHOOSE

Now glory be to God! By his mighty power at work within us, he is able to accomplish infinitely more than we would ever dare to ask or hope. (Ephesians 3:20 NLT)

When my oldest son was a little boy, I would take him to Toys "R" Us. We would look around, and I would tell him to pick out something for himself. He would look at the Star Wars figures. I would look at the X-wing fighter with the remote control, thinking that I would like to get it for him. The truth was that I wanted to play with it too. He would pick out his little figure. Then I would say, "I was thinking of getting you something better than that." He always went along with my idea.

After awhile, he started learning something about Dad, which was that Dad liked to get presents for his kids. He came to realize that it was better to say, "I don't know what to get, Dad. You choose it for me." He came to realize that my choices were often better than what he chose for himself.

Have you ever said to the Lord, "Here is the way I think You ought to work. But not my will, but Yours, be done"? Some might say, "I am not saying that to God. If I say that, He will make me do something I don't want to." I believe a person who thinks that way has a warped concept of God, a misconception that His will is always going to be something undesirable.

God may be saying no to something you have asked Him for because He wants to give you something far better than what you could ask or think. Don't be afraid to let your Father choose for you.

LEARNING TO YIELD

For our present troubles are quite small and won't last very long.
Yet they produce for us an immeasurably great glory
that will last forever! (2 Corinthians 4:17 NLT)

I read a story about a communication that took place some time ago between a U.S. naval ship and Canadian authorities off the coast of Newfoundland. The Canadians warned the Americans, "Please divert your course 15 degrees to the south to avoid a collision."

The Americans responded, "Recommend you divert your course 15 degrees to the north to avoid a collision."

The Canadians said, "Negative. You will have to divert your course 15 degrees to the south to avoid a collision."

The Americans: "This is the captain of a U.S. Navy Ship. I say again, divert your course."

"No, I say again, you divert your course."

"This is the aircraft carrier USS Lincoln, the second largest ship in the United States Atlantic fleet. We are accompanied by three destroyers, three cruisers, numerous support vessels. I demand that you change your course 15 degrees north. I say again, that is 15 degrees north or counter measures will be undertaken to assure the safety of our ship."

After brief moment of silence, the Canadians responded: "This is a lighthouse. It is your call."

Sometimes we don't like what God wants us to do, and we want Him to change course when, in reality, it is us who should change.

We need to understand that God's plans are better than ours. Having said that, it does not mean that they are always the easiest plans or even the most appealing at the moment. There are times when we are going through life that we might not like the plan of God. But God's plans are always better for us in the long run.

Weekend

HALF-HEARTED COMMITMENT

So Abram departed as the Lord had instructed him, and Lot went with him.
Abram was seventy-five years old when he left Haran. (Genesis 12:4 NLT)

At first glance, you might think that Abraham and his nephew Lot both were spiritual men. But a closer examination reveals that this was not the case. You see, Abraham lived for God. Lot, on the other hand, lived for himself. Abraham walked in the Spirit. Lot walked in the flesh. Abraham lived by faith. Lot lived by sight. And most significantly, Abraham walked with God, and Lot walked with Abraham.

Unfortunately, because of Lot's half-hearted commitment to the Lord, he was becoming a spiritual drain on Abraham. The relationship they had was pulling Abraham down. That is why, earlier in Genesis, God said to Abraham, "Leave your country, your relatives, and your father's house, and go to the land that I will show you" (Genesis 12:1 NLT).

But Abraham was reluctant to part ways with Lot. Then, when a famine came, Abraham actually went down to Egypt. It was a definite step backward. But Abraham eventually came to his senses and realized he was in a backslidden state. He decided to return to God and to the place where He had called him.

Sadly for Abraham, he reaped in the years ahead the results of that wrong choice. It was in Egypt that a woman named Hagar became Sarah's servant. Abraham ended up having a child with Hagar. The child's name was Ishmael, and conflicts between his descendents and the descendents of Isaac continue to this very day.

Have ungodly influences been wearing you down lately? Has a certain relationship or pursuit become a spiritual drain in your life? Have you been compromising? Then make a change. It isn't too late.

Monday

AGAINST ALL ODDS

And Jehoshaphat feared, and set himself to seek the Lord, and proclaimed a fast throughout all Judah. So Judah gathered together to ask help from the Lord; and from all the cities of Judah they came to seek the Lord. (2 Chronicles 20:3–4)

Jehoshaphat, King of Judah, faced a dilemma. His enemies greatly outnumbered him. To make matters worse, his enemies had joined forces with the other enemies of Israel and were coming to destroy him. One day, someone came to King Jehoshaphat and warned him that a gigantic army was headed his way, bent on his destruction. It was hopeless. There was no way that he could meet this army with what he had. He was going to be destroyed. What did Jehoshaphat do? The Bible says that he "set himself to seek the Lord." He prayed, "O our God, will You not judge them? For we have no power against this great multitude that is coming against us; nor do we know what to do, but our eyes are upon You" (2 Chronicles 20:12).

The Lord told Jehoshaphat, "Do not be afraid nor dismayed because of this great multitude, for the battle is not yours, but God's. ... Position yourselves, stand still and see the salvation of the Lord, who is with you" (2 Chronicles 20:15–17).

Jehoshaphat and his army went out to meet their enemies, but they put the worship team out front. The Bible says that when they began to sing and praise the Lord, the enemy started fighting among themselves and destroyed each other.

Maybe you are facing what seems like an impossible situation right now. You may not be able to see a way out. But God can. Call on Him. Then stand still and see what He will do.

Tuesday

KEEP MOVING!

Now the Holy Spirit tells us clearly that in the last times some will turn away from what we believe; they will follow lying spirits and teachings that come from demons. (1 Timothy 4:1 NLT)

It is clear that we are living in the last days. All around us, the signs that Jesus and the prophets told us to look for are taking place before our very eyes. The devil and his demons are doing their dirty work, and this should not surprise us. The Bible warns that in the last days, things will go from bad to worse. One of the signs will be an abandonment of the faith, or an apostasy. Some will fall away and will follow deceiving spirits and things taught by demons.

Could you or I ever become one of these spiritual casualties? Could you or I ever fall away from the Lord? Without question, the potential and even the propensity for sin lies within us. I have the potential to fall. You have the same.

That is why we must give careful attention to likely pitfalls for believers that are given to us in Scripture. There are things we must be alert to as we live in the last days. As the Apostle Paul wrote, "The night is almost gone; the day of salvation will soon be here. So don't live in darkness. Get rid of your evil deeds. Shed them like dirty clothes. Clothe yourselves with the armor of right living, as those who live in the light" (Romans 13:12 NLT).

Your relationship with Jesus Christ needs constant maintenance and cultivation. The day that you stop growing spiritually is the day you will start to become weak and vulnerable to the devil's attacks. The best way to not go backward is to keep moving forward.

No Other Gods

Therefore, my beloved, flee from idolatry. (1 Corinthians 10:14)

When God gave the Ten Commandments, He began by saying that we should have no other gods before Him.

Idols can be a lot of things. Essentially, an idol could be defined as anyone or anything that takes the place of God in our lives. An idol is any object, idea, philosophy, habit, occupation, sport, or whatever has one's primary concern and loyalty, or that to any degree, decreases one's trust and loyalty to God.

Alan Redpath defined idolatry this way: "Our god is the person we think is the most precious, for whom we would make the greatest sacrifice, who moves our hearts with the warmest love. He or it is the person who, if we lost him, would leave us desolate."

This definition really opens up the possibilities doesn't it? A lot of things could qualify as idols in our lives. It is a true but terrifying fact that a person can attend church every Sunday and still be an idolater.

Is there one thing in your life that, if God asked you for it, you would say, "Absolutely not"? Is there one thing, that if the Lord required it of you, you would say, "Anything but this"? If so, then maybe that thing, that pursuit, or that passion is an idol in your life.

Is there an idol in your heart today? Is there someone or something more precious to you than God Himself? Any person or pursuit that takes the place of God in your life will not satisfy. Let Him be your Lord. Let Him be your God. He will satisfy you.

Thursday

THE MASTER ARSONIST

God wants you to be holy, so you should keep clear of all sexual sin.
(1 Thessalonians 4:3 NLT)

When wildfires swept through Southern California in the fall of 1993, I noticed a photograph in the newspaper of an entire neighborhood that had been leveled by the fires. All that was left were the foundations. In the midst of all the burned, charred, rubble stood one house that remained completely untouched, even by smoke. This gleaming white house stood in stark contrast to all of the ruin around it.

When asked why his house was left standing when all the others fell, the homeowner explained how he had taken great care to make his house flame-retardant. This included double-paned windows, thick stucco walls, sealed eaves, concrete tile, and abundant insulation. Firefighters said, "It made it clear to us that this would be a place to make a stand." This man went the extra mile, and as a result, his house survived when the fires came.

Today, our country is being devastated by the wildfires of immorality. Satan, a master arsonist, is causing massive devastation. It destroys homes. It devastates families. And if we aren't careful, we could become its next victims.

The writer of Proverbs asked, "Can a man scoop fire into his lap and not be burned?" (6:27 NLT). The answer is no. Fire can burn out of control so easily.

If we as believers allow temptation to infiltrate our lives and allow our sinful natures to prevail, we could fall, as surely as a fire spreads by putting gasoline on it. But if we take practical steps to guard ourselves and to stay close to the Lord, then we don't have to fall. Let's go the extra mile to protect our homes and our lives against the wildfires of immorality.

EASY PREY

Be careful! Watch out for attacks from the Devil, your great enemy. He prowls around like a roaring lion, looking for some victim to devour. (1 Peter 5:8 NLT)

One has to go no further than the Psalms to see the intimacy of David's relationship with God. David loved God in a dear and tender way. Yet we know that he fell into sin.

If you were to ask the average person what he or she remembers from the life of David, the name Goliath would most likely come up. Another name probably would be mentioned as well: Bathsheba. Goliath and Bathsheba represented David's greatest victory and his greatest defeat. Satan was not able to defeat David on the battlefield, so he brought him down in the bedroom.

At this particular time in David's life as the King of Israel, we don't read about him worshiping. David had gotten away from that intimacy with God, and thus was more vulnerable. He lowered his guard.

One evening, David laid eyes on Bathsheba, and David sinned. Eventually, he confessed his sin and was forgiven. But he also reaped what he sowed. The very sins that he committed were repeated in the lives of his own children. The moment David stopped lowering his guard, he become an easy target for the devil.

The devil continues to look for easy targets. He knows that it's easier to hit something stationary than something that is on the move. Those who are moving forward in Christ, who are growing in their love for the Lord, are not nearly as easy to hit as a person who has begun to relax his grip on the Lord. That is the one whom the devil will set his sights on. That is the one who will become his next casualty.

Weekend

WHAT'S ON YOUR MIND?

"So commit yourselves completely to these words of mine. Tie them to your hands
as a reminder, and wear them on your forehead. Teach them to your children.
Talk about them when you are at home and when you are away on a journey,
when you are lying down and when you are getting up again."
(Deuteronomy 11:18–19 NLT)

Sometimes people ask me to sign their Bibles, which is not something I like to do, because I didn't write it. But when someone insists, I usually write this inscription in his or her Bible: "Sin will keep you from this book and this book will keep you from sin."

I have found that sin will always keep you away from the Bible, because the devil wants to keep you out of God's Word. He doesn't care if you read magazines. He doesn't care if you watch television. He doesn't care if you read the latest novel on the bestseller list. He doesn't care if you watch movies. But the minute you pick up the Bible and crack it open, you had better believe that he will try to distract you with everything he has. He doesn't want you to read it.

On the other hand, if you follow what the Bible teaches, it will keep you from sin. That is why we need to know the Bible. That is why we need to study it. While it is a great idea to carry a Bible in your briefcase, pocket, or purse, the best place to carry it is in your heart. Know it well. Fill the memory banks God has given you with Scripture, because the devil will attack you in the realm of your mind. The best defense is a mind that is filled with God's Word.

Monday

GIVING GOD A MAKEOVER

And do not become idolaters as were some of them. As it is written, "The people sat down to eat and drink, and rose up to play." (1 Corinthians 10:7)

At first glance, the sins that brought the children of Israel down in the wilderness don't seem to have any rhyme or reason. But a closer examination reveals that the root problem was a lack of relationship with the true and living God. Thus, when Moses was temporarily taken out of the scene when he went to meet with God on Mt. Sinai, the people wanted something to take his place. It was only a matter of time until they were bowing before a golden calf.

When you get down to it, Moses was their first idol, and the golden calf was their second. Moses was like God to them, so when Moses was gone, they created a god of their own making.

We do the same when we start remaking God in our own image. When we give God a 21st-century makeover, when we make God politically correct, when we start changing His Word to fit the perverted morals of our time, this becomes idolatry. We are remaking God because we are not comfortable with what He says. We don't like His standards. Thus, if we can remake God in our image, we can live the way that we want to and do as we please.

We want a celestial salad bar where we can casually stroll up, choose the attributes of God that most appeal to us, and leave the rest behind. It's religion á la carte. When we mold God and His Word into our image, it is as much an act of idolatry as it was when the children of Israel worshiped the golden calf.

Tuesday

The Dangerous Question

Therefore, whether you eat or drink, or whatever you do,
do all to the glory of God. (1 Corinthians 10:31)

What does it mean to test God? It is the mentality that asks the question, "As a Christian, how much can I get away with and still be saved? How far can I go and still be a child of God?" In other words, "How far to the edge can I get without falling off?" It is a dangerous question to ask

The church at Corinth had developed a similar problem. It was located in the midst of a metropolitan city, with visitors coming from all around the world. The city of Corinth was entrenched in sin. The problem with the believers there was that they thought they could commit certain sins and it would be acceptable to God. Paul had to set the record straight. He wrote to the Corinthian believers, "All things are lawful for me, but not all things are helpful; all things are lawful for me, but not all things edify" (1 Corinthians 10:23).

Let's not push the limits and see how much we can get away with as believers. Let's go the other direction. Instead, we should be asking, "How much more can I know this One who died for me and forgave me and has done so much on my behalf? How can I become more like Him? How can I make an impact in my world for Him?"

Let's not take for granted all that God has done for us in our lives. May we never see how far we can go and be guilty of testing the Lord. Rather, let's stay as close to Him as we possibly can.

CONDITIONAL OBEDIENCE

*"Yet they did not obey or incline their ear, but followed the counsels and
the dictates of their evil hearts, and went backward and not forward."*
(Jeremiah 7:24)

My dog practices selective listening. When he doesn't like what I am saying, he acts as though he doesn't understand me. If he is in my room at bedtime and I tell him to leave, he looks at me as if to say, "What?" It's as though his hearing is gone. On the other hand, he can be asleep behind closed doors, and if I go downstairs, open the cupboard, and pull out his leash, he suddenly has supersonic hearing. He is right there at my side. When he likes what I want him to do, my dog hears and obeys me. But when he doesn't like what I want him to do, my dog doesn't hear and doesn't obey.

We can be the same with God. When God tells us to do something we like, we say, "Yes, Lord!" But when He tells us to stop doing something, we say, "God, I think you're cutting out on me. I'm not hearing you clearly."

Jesus said, "You are My friends if you do whatever I command you" (John 15:14). He didn't say, "You are My friends if you do the things that you personally agree with." God has told us in His Word how we are to live. It is not for us to pick and choose sections of the Bible we like and toss the rest aside.

If God tells you to do something, He says it for good reason, and you need to obey Him. If God says not to do something, He also says it for good reason. Even if you don't understand it, obey Him.

Thursday

WHAT'S INSIDE?

"My righteousness I hold fast, and will not let it go; my heart shall not reproach me as long as I live." (Job 27:6)

I heard the story of a pastor who boarded a bus one Monday morning, paid his fare, and took his seat. A few minutes later, he realized that the driver had given him too much change. Some people might have put it in their pocket and said, "Lord, thank you for your provision." But this pastor knew that would be wrong. At the next stop, he walked to the front of the bus with the extra change and said to the driver, "Excuse me, sir, you gave me too much change, and I wanted to return it to you, because obviously you made a mistake."

The driver said, "Pastor, I didn't make a mistake. I was at your church last night and heard you preach on honesty. I wanted to see if you practiced what you preached." Fortunately, he did.

People are watching you as a Christian. They are scrutinizing your every move. You should know they are not hoping you will be a godly witness. They are hoping you will slip up so they will have something on which to conveniently hang their doubts and unbelief.

Humorist Will Rogers said, "So live that you would not mind selling your pet parrot to the town gossip." That is the idea of integrity: having nothing in our lives to be ashamed of. This personal integrity is something we are developing on a daily basis with every thought we think and every action we take. We are either building up character or tearing it down.

What kind of character do you have? Who are you in private? For all practical purposes, that is the real you.

THE SPIRITUAL BATTLEFIELD

"Therefore let him who thinks he stands take heed lest he fall."
(1 Corinthians 10:12)

Someone once asked the great evangelist Charles Finney, "Do you really believe in a literal devil?"

Finney responded, "You try opposing him for awhile, and you see if he is literal or not." If you want to find out if there is a literal devil, then start walking with Jesus Christ and seeking to be in the will of God. You will find just how real he is.

I think that many people, after they have decided to follow Christ, are surprised to find that the Christian life is not a playground, but a battleground. It is not a life of ease, but one of conflict, warfare, and opposition. Our choice is simple: will we be victorious or will we be victims on the spiritual battlefield?

It has been said that you can tell a lot about a man by who his enemies are. The same is true for us. We are no longer opposing God, but we now have a new, very powerful foe, and he is described in the Bible as the devil. The devil, of course, is not happy with the fact that he has lost one of his own. He is angry that you have surrendered your life to Jesus Christ. Now you have become a potential threat to his kingdom as well.

The closer you stay to the Lord, the safer you are, because you stand in the work that Jesus did on the Cross. Don't try to engage the devil in your own ability, because he can chew you up and spit you out. But if you stand in the Lord and in His power and stay as close to Him as you can, then you will be safe.

Weekend

Power with a Purpose

"But when the Holy Spirit has come upon you, you will receive power and will tell people about me everywhere—in Jerusalem, throughout Judea, in Samaria, and to the ends of the earth." (Acts 1:8 NLT)

What comes to mind when you hear the word *dynamite*? I automatically think of something explosive. And when something is described as *dynamic*, I know it is something unusual or special, something that stands out. Jesus told the disciples they would receive power when the Holy Spirit came upon them. The word that Jesus used for power is from the Greek word *dunamis*, the same word from which we get our words *dynamite* and *dynamic*.

Have you ever seen a fire hose on the loose? It can knock people and things over. It can be very destructive. But if you get hold of it and aim it in the right direction, you can do a lot of good. Power is exciting if it used for something productive. In the same way, God has given us the power of the Holy Spirit for a purpose. God's power is practical. He did not give us the Holy Spirit so that we would behave strangely. He gave us the Holy Spirit to be His witnesses and to effectively share our faith. It is power with a purpose.

When the Holy Spirit came upon those first-century believers on the Day of Pentecost, the Bible says that about 3,000 people made commitments to Jesus Christ (see Acts 2:41). Peter made an important statement about the Holy Spirit back then: the power they had received was not only available to them, but would be available to future generations of believers as well (see Acts 2:39). This means that the same power is available to us to change our world.

Monday

SOWING AND REAPING

For he who sows to his flesh will of the flesh reap corruption, but he who sows to the Spirit will of the Spirit reap everlasting life. (Galatians 6:8)

A successful building contractor called in one of his employees, a skilled carpenter, and told him that he was putting him in charge of the next house the company was building. He instructed the carpenter to order all of the materials and oversee the entire process from the ground up. The carpenter excitedly accepted his assignment. It was his first opportunity to actually oversee an entire building project. He studied the blueprints and checked every measurement. Then he thought, "If I am really in charge, why can't I cut a few corners, use less expensive materials, and put the extra money in my pocket? Who would know the difference? After we paint the place, no one would be able to tell."

The carpenter set about with his scheme. He used second-grade lumber and ordered inexpensive concrete for the foundation. He put in cheap wiring. He cut every corner he possibly could, but reported the use of higher-quality building materials.

When the home was completed, he asked his boss to come and see it. His boss looked it over and said, "This is incredible. You did a fantastic job. You have been such a good and faithful worker and have been so honest all of these years that I am showing my gratitude by giving you this house."

We will reap what we sow. Just as we can't plant weeds and reap flowers, we can't sin and reap righteousness. There are reactions to our actions. Think about it: every day, we are either sowing to the Spirit or we are sowing to the flesh. What kind of seeds will you sow today?

Tuesday

TEMPORARY PLEASURES

"Yes, a person is a fool to store up earthly wealth but not have a rich relationship with God." (Luke 12:21 NLT)

There is a story in the Bible about a man named Esau who gave up everything for a little temporal pleasure. As the firstborn, Esau had been given the family birthright, which meant that one day he would be the spiritual leader of his family and would be in the ancestral line of the Messiah. But Esau didn't seem to care much about that. One day, his brother Jacob came along and proposed a trade: Esau's birthright for some stew Jacob was cooking. It sounded like a good deal to Esau at the time. Later he realized how cheaply he had sold out. But it was too late.

Esau had no regard for spiritual things, and there are a lot of people like that today. They could care less about God until they are in a bind or until some tragedy hits. Then suddenly, miraculously, they have time for God. Then when the crisis is past, they return to their old ways.

Jesus spoke about a farmer whose crop had produced generously. The farmer decided to tear down his barns and build larger ones to store everything. That way, he could say to himself, " 'My friend, you have enough stored away for years to come. Now take it easy! Eat, drink, and be merry!' " (Luke 12:19 NLT).

But God said, " 'You fool! You will die this very night. Then who will get it all?' " (verse 20 NLT).

Are things on this earth more important to you than treasures in heaven? Everything you may hold dear will be left behind one day. And the only thing that will matter is what is waiting in heaven for you.

Wednesday

THE PERIL OF PRAYERLESSNESS

If you need wisdom—if you want to know what God wants you to do—ask him,
and he will gladly tell you. He will not resent your asking. (James 1:5 NLT)

The Bible's first recorded prayer of Jacob's is found in
Genesis 32:9–16. Up to this point, seven chapters
of Genesis have been devoted Jacob's life, with no
mention of prayer on his part. It makes me wonder if Jacob had
ever prayed up to this point. It is possible, but the Bible doesn't
specifically mention it. It may have been Jacob's very lack of
prayer and lack of dependence on God that made him feel as
though he had to manipulate his circumstances.

It was commendable that Jacob was reaching out to God, and
there are even some good things about his prayer. He acknowledged the God of Abraham and Isaac as the true God. He
confessed his own unworthiness. He brought his petition to
the Lord. But it would have been better if he had said, "Lord,
what should I do now?" Instead, he prayed and made his plans.
In other words, he decided what he was going to do and then
asked God to bless it.

Is that not like us? We make our plan and then asked God
to bless it. But that is not really praying about a matter. Instead,
we should pray along the lines of, "Lord give me wisdom from
your Word and from godly people who will guide me biblically.
Help me do the right thing." But Jacob did not do that. He
wanted what was right, but he went about it in the wrong way.

God helps those who *can't* help themselves. This is what Jacob
needed to realize. Let's learn to seek out God's will rather than
bypass it.

Thursday
GOD'S WAY

To the faithful you show yourself faithful; to those with integrity you show integrity. To the pure you show yourself pure, but to the wicked you show yourself hostile. (Psalm 18:25–26 NLT)

I t is interesting how God came to different people in the Bible. To Abraham, God came as a traveler. Abraham was outside his tent when three messengers arrived. Two were angels, while one was God himself. We know that Jesus said, "Your ancestor Abraham rejoiced as he looked forward to my coming. He saw it and was glad" (John 8:56 NLT). Why did the Lord come to Abraham as a sojourner? That is what Abraham was.

The night before Israel began their siege of Jericho, God came to Joshua, the commander of Israel's armies, as Commander of the Lord's army.

When God came to Jacob, He came as a wrestler, and Jacob wrestled with Him. Why? Jacob was always fighting, conniving, resisting, and wrestling to get what he wanted. Maybe you can relate to Jacob. Maybe there is something you want from God, even a good thing, like the salvation of a husband or wife. Maybe you are tired of being single and want to get married. Or maybe you want to serve God in a ministry. Don't resort to conniving, because you may get what you want, but at a great cost. Jacob got what he wanted and paid dearly for it. I believe that if he had waited on God, he would have received what he needed and what God had promised.

God wants to do His will in our lives in His way and in His time. If you need something from God, be patient and wait on Him. God will meet you wherever you are to lift you to where He wants you to be.

REVIVE US AGAIN!

Will You not revive us again, that Your people may rejoice in You? (Psalm 85:6)

Has it ever seemed to you that you are out there all alone as a Christian? Sometimes it feels like you are the only one who is serving the Lord or speaking up for Him at your workplace or school. You know others who are Christians, but they are afraid to stand up and be counted as such.

As dark as things are, remember this. Isaiah 59:19 says, "When the enemy comes in like a flood, the Spirit of the Lord will raise up a standard against him." So here is the good news: when things are really wicked, when things are really dark, you can anticipate that God will do something.

That is why, as I look at the way things are going, I am praying and hoping for a work of God in our generation. When you look back at the great revivals in history, biblical and otherwise, you find five traits that are true of every revival:

1. All revivals began during a time of national depression and deep moral distress.

2. Revivals usually began with an individual, someone whom God would work on or work through. It may have been someone who would pray or someone who would preach.

3. Every revival was built on the Word of God being preached and taught boldly and obeyed.

4. Every revival brought about an awareness of sin and the need to repent of it.

5. Every revival brought about a change in the moral climate; something happened in the culture as a result.

When God is forgotten, a moral breakdown soon will follow. But when we are really doing what God wants us to do, it will have an impact on our culture.

Weekend

IN SEARCH OF
ORDINARY PEOPLE

"People judge by outward appearance, but the Lord looks at a person's thoughts and intentions." (1 Samuel 16:7 NLT)

God uses ordinary people to do extraordinary things. Many times when we're looking for some great superstar to come on the scene, God is developing someone in obscurity whom we haven't ever heard of. We will say, "What if so-and-so became a Christian? Wouldn't that be wonderful?" And while we're wondering if so-and-so will ever come around, God is grooming someone unknown to us.

Think of the time when a giant Philistine was taunting the armies of Israel. Everyone was paralyzed with fear. So whom did God select? He chose a shepherd boy who had been sent by his father to take food to his brothers on the front lines. He went out to face the giant with a few stones and a sling, and more importantly, faith in God. That was the person God used.

At another time in Israel's history when they were immobilized by fear because of their enemies, God found this guy threshing wheat. His name was Gideon, and he was convinced that God had called up the wrong guy. But God selected him because he didn't trust in his own ability. Gideon had to trust in God.

If you have faith in God, if you believe that God can use you, if you are willing to take a step of faith here and there, then God can do incredible things through you. One thing I have said many times over the years is that God is not looking for ability but availability. He can give you ability in time. But God looking for someone to say, "I would like to make a difference where I am. Lord, I am available." You just watch what God will do.

SALT AND LIGHT

*"You are the salt of the earth. But what good is salt if it has lost its flavor?
... You are the light of the world—like a city on a mountain, glowing
in the night for all to see." (Matthew 5:13–14)*

I think that we Christians are sometimes tempted to isolate ourselves. We want to submerge ourselves in a Christian subculture of our own making and not get too involved in the world.

But Jesus said, "You are the salt of the earth." When He made that statement to His disciples so long ago, they understand the significance of what He was saying. It can be lost on us today because we don't know it what it means. In those days, salt was considered to be very valuable. In fact, the Romans considered salt more important than the sun itself. Roman soldiers would even be paid with salt. So when Jesus said, "You are the salt of the earth," He was saying in a sense, "You're valuable. You're important. You're significant. You can make a difference."

Stop and think about salt. It really can do a lot. A little salt on a bland piece of meat can make all the difference. Have you ever had someone put salt in your water when you weren't looking? You immediately noticed the change. A little pinch of salt can alter the flavor of something, just as one Christian in a situation can effect change.

Have you ever been in a dark room and someone turned on a flashlight? The light wasn't hard to find, was it? In the same way, one believer who lets his or her light shine can really make a difference.

God has singled you out to make a difference—a strategic difference.

Tuesday

BY THE BROOK

*The ravens brought him bread and meat in the morning, and bread
and meat in the evening; and he drank from the brook. (1 Kings 17:6)*

When the Bible says that ravens brought Elijah food,
it doesn't mean they took his order, flew through
the local fast food restaurant, and then delivered his
meal. Ravens are scavengers. They brought little bits of meat
and bread to Elijah. What's more, the water in the brook from
which he drank would have been somewhat polluted. It was not
an easy situation.

How easily Elijah could have said, "Well, Lord, I don't
really want to be in this crummy little place. I kind of like
being in front of people. I like the limelight." But the Lord
was preparing Elijah for something beyond his wildest dreams.
Not long after this, Elijah would be standing on Mt. Carmel
in that great showdown with the false prophets (see 1 Kings
18:20–39).

Sometimes we don't like where God has put us. We say,
"Lord, I don't like this situation. I don't like where I am. I
want to do something great for You. I want to make a difference in my world." Maybe the Lord wants you to be effective
right where you are. Maybe He wants you to take advantage of
the opportunities in front of you and be faithful in the little
things. Who knows what God has in store for you?

If God has you by some muddy little brook, so to speak,
just hang in there. Be faithful, do what He has already told you,
and wait on Him and on His timing. God will do something
wonderful for you or with you. Just be available and open to do
what He would have you to do.

Wednesday

BETWEEN TWO WORLDS

And I, brethren, could not speak to you as to spiritual people
but as to carnal, as to babes in Christ. (1 Corinthians 3:1)

The Bible mentions a category of Christians who are described as carnal. These are people in an arrested state of spiritual development. They have never really grown up. They're caught between two worlds: they have too much of the Lord to be happy in the world, but too much of the world to be happy in the Lord. They're the most miserable people around.

Many of us realize that this world doesn't have the answers and can't be trusted. But at the same time, we don't trust God either. We haven't made a stand. But it's time to say, "I believe in Jesus Christ." It's time to stand for our principles and not just blend into the woodwork. So often in our attempts to gain credibility, we lose our integrity. In our attempts to relate to people, we lose any power we will have in relating to them, because we have compromised our principles.

The Bible gives us many examples of people who stood up for what was right at the risk of losing something important, even their lives. One such person was Daniel, who held position of great influence in Nebuchadnezzar's court. Even so, he would not compromise his principles.

Maybe you're afraid to stand up for Jesus Christ. You're afraid that it could hurt your career, or a relationship or something else. But there comes a moment when we have to stand for what we know is true. You may be criticized, and might even lose something important to you. But whatever you lose, God will make it up to you. He will bless you for standing for what is right.

Thursday

MAKE YOUR CHOICE

And Elijah came to all the people, and said, "How long will you falter between two opinions? If the Lord is God, follow Him. ... " (1 Kings 18:21)

Have you ever had one of those indecisive days? I am usually decisive. But I get in those moods where I just can't decide. I can be at the window of a take-out place and suddenly be stricken with indecision. That's not so tragic at a take-out window. But when people are indecisive with God, it is a serious problem.

That's how it was with Israel in Elijah's day. For 85 years, the nation had gone back and forth between false gods and the true God. Not wanting to be responsible or live under absolutes, they would follow some other god. Then they would reap the results of following that god and would scurry back to the Lord and say they were sorry until their problems went away. Then they would go back like wayward children and do the same thing again. Every time they were on the brink of destruction, God would be merciful and forgive them. One day, Elijah basically said to them, "Enough is enough. Make a choice. Which side are you on?"

Moses posed a similar question to Israel when they fell before the golden calf. He said, "Whoever is on the Lord's side—come to me!" (Exodus 32:26). His successor Joshua challenged Israel to "Choose for yourselves this day whom you will serve . . ." (Joshua 24:15). And in Matthew 12:30 Jesus said, "He who is not with Me is against Me, and he who does not gather with Me scatters abroad." Jesus demands a response. He demands us to decide which side we're on. Choose this day whom you will serve.

Lukewarm People

"I know all the things you do, that you are neither hot nor cold. I wish you were one or the other! But since you are like lukewarm water, I will spit you out of my mouth!" (Revelation 3:15–16 NLT).

Milk is great cold. There's nothing quite like a cold glass of milk with couple of cookies. Milk is also good hot. With a little Ovaltine®, it's great. But lukewarm milk? The thought of it is sickening. It just doesn't cut it.

In Revelation 3, Jesus spoke of lukewarm individuals. He said, "I know all the things you do, that you are neither hot nor cold. I wish you were one or the other!" (verse 15 NLT). It's interesting that Jesus said He would prefer either hot or cold. You would think He would have said, "I would rather you be hot. But if lukewarm is all I can get, it's better than nothing." You would think that lukewarm would be more acceptable to Him, because it is somewhat close to hot. But Jesus was saying, "I don't want lukewarm. I don't want half-hearted commitments. I want you to decide. I want you in or I would rather you were out."

Here's why. If you're hot, you're in. If you're on fire, if you're walking with God, then you're where God wants you to be. But if you're cold, hopefully you will at least realize you're cold and one day realize your need for Christ and come to Him. But the lukewarm person is in the worst state of all because he is self-deceived. The lukewarm person says, "I go to church. I read the Bible sometimes. I kind of believe in God—when it's convenient." That is the worst state of all. What is your spiritual temperature today?

Weekend

HIS REPRESENTATIVE

"If they persecuted Me, they will also persecute you. ..." (John 15:20)

I t is hard for a lot of Christians to understand how suddenly their friends and family can turn against them. People they have been close to for years suddenly become hostile, simply because they have said they were now following Jesus Christ.

I am amazed at how parents have turned against children. I've heard teens and young adults tell me how they were strung out on drugs or living sexually permissive lives or getting in trouble with the law all the time. Then they found Christ and their lives changed. They began living moral lives. Their parents were angry with them for coming to faith when, in fact, they should have been elated by the change.

Sometimes even parents won't understand what the Lord is doing in your life. Sometimes your children won't understand. Sometimes your husband or wife won't understand. Sometimes your friends and coworkers won't understand.

Remember when Saul, later to become the apostle Paul, was striking out against Christians? One day on the Damascus Road, he met none other than Jesus Christ himself who said, "Saul, Saul, why are you persecuting Me?" (Acts 9:4). Saul thought his fight was with the Christians. But it wasn't. It was with Christ himself.

People take their hostilities out on you because you are God's representative. I have spoken with people who discover I'm a pastor and suddenly begin dumping everything they have against God on me. I have come to realize this happens because I am a representative of God, just as all believers are. It is a great honor to be His representative. But with that honor comes responsibility. Be careful. Don't keep someone away from Christ by misrepresenting Him.

THE FAITHFUL FOLLOWER

*"But whoever denies Me before men, him I will also deny before
My Father who is in heaven." (Matthew 10:33)*

Near the end of his life, the apostle Paul wrote to the young pastor, Timothy, "I have fought the good fight, I have finished the race, I have kept the faith" (2 Timothy 4:7). A few sentences later, he referred to a man named Demas who had deserted him, "having loved this present world, and has departed for Thessalonica ... " (2 Timothy 4:10). When it got too hard for Demas, he quit. He didn't want to be a follower of Jesus if it required anything of him, if it cost him anything, and certainly if it meant he would suffer persecution.

Jesus spoke of the same dilemma in the Parable of the Sower, in which He compared the Word of God entering the hearts of men and women to a farmer who scatters seed. Jesus explained, "He who received the seed on stony places, this is he who hears the word and immediately receives it with joy; yet he has no root in himself, but endures only for a while. For when tribulation or persecution arises because of the word, immediately he stumbles" (Matthew 13:20-21).

There are some who will abandon their Christian faith when trouble comes or persecution arises. They give up. They deny the Lord. One way people do this is by simply saying, "I don't know Him." But another way is to not confess your faith in Jesus Christ or to not speak up for Him when the opportunity arises. Do people know you're a Christian? Do your coworkers know you're a Christian? Do your family members know that you are a follower of Jesus Christ? Are you speaking up for Him? I hope so.

Tuesday

REMEMBERING TO SAY "THANK YOU"

*"Oh, that men would give thanks to the Lord for His goodness,
and for His wonderful works to the children of men!" (Psalm 107:8)*

In the Old Testament we find an interesting story of how King Jehoshaphat took an uncommon approach when his enemies waged war against him. Instead of sending in his army first, he sent in the choir and musicians. Imagine the scene: "All right, guys, here's the plan today. An army is out there, armed to the teeth. So, we are sending in the choir and the musicians." If I had been a choir member or musician, I might have wondered whether the king liked our music. But God had directed Jehoshaphat in this unusual battle tactic. We read that Jehoshaphat appointed people to sing to the Lord, praise the beauty of holiness, and go out in front of the army saying, "Praise the Lord, for His mercy endures forever" (2 Chronicles 20:21). So that is exactly what they did. The Bible tells us that when they began to sing and praise, God sent an ambush against the enemy, and they were destroyed. God's people were able to go into this situation giving thanks, because He was in control.

In approaching God to ask for new blessings, we should never forget to thank Him for the blessings He has already given. Have you recently come to God for help and He came through for you? Did you come back to say "thank you"? If we would stop and think how many of the prayers we have offered to God have been answered and how seldom we come back to God to thank Him, it just might amaze us. We should be just as deliberate in giving thanks to God as we are in asking for His help.

Wednesday

INGRATITUDE

Although they knew God, they did not glorify Him as God, nor were thankful, but became futile in their thoughts, and their foolish hearts were darkened.
(Romans 1:21)

A man who was nailing down a loose shingle on a roof lost his footing and began to slip. Working three stories above ground, he was terrified at the thought of falling to his death. He started shouting, "God, help me! I am falling! God, do something!" Just as he came to the edge of the roof, his belt loop caught on a nail and stopped him long enough to grab hold again. He shouted, "It's OK, God! I got caught on a nail."

That is how we can be. We cry out to God. He answers our prayers. Then we say, "It's OK, God . . . everything seemed to work out." But do we ever stop and think that God might have worked through certain circumstances to come to our rescue? My point is, we need to put as much zeal in thanking God for what He has done as we put into pleading with God when we are in need.

I heard about a hospital chaplain who kept a record of some 2,000 patients whom he had visited, all who seemed to be in a dying condition and showed signs of repentance. Among those restored to health, he felt that only two showed a marked change in their spiritual lives after their recovery. In other words, when these people thought they would die, they repented. But when they recovered, they forgot about God.

What would you think of a person who always wanted things from you, but never offered a word of thanks in return? We can be that way with God, can't we? Let's remember to thank Him.

Thursday

WHEN PRAISE BECOMES
A SACRIFICE

Therefore by Him let us continually offer the sacrifice of praise to God,
that is, the fruit of our lips, giving thanks to His name. (Hebrews 13:15)

There are times when it is a sacrifice to offer praise to
God, quite frankly, because we don't really want to.
There are times when we are down or depressed or
things aren't going that well. We don't really feel like praising
the Lord. Yet the Bible is filled with admonition after admonition to give glory and praise and thanks to God. Psalm 106:1
says, "Praise the Lord! Oh, give thanks to the Lord, for He is
good! For His mercy endures forever."

Notice that the Bible does not say, "Give thanks to the Lord
when you feel good." Rather, it says, "Give thanks to the Lord,
for He is good!" I don't praise God because I feel like it. I
praise God because He is worthy, regardless of what I am going
through. Praise can be a sacrifice sometimes. I have found
that when, out of obedience, I begin to praise the Lord, the
emotion will begin to engage with my act of obedience in time.
The point is, I should do it because God tells me to.

In the Gospel of Luke, we find the story of ten men who
were miraculously touched by Jesus. Because these men had
leprosy, they were the outcasts of their society. Yet Jesus went
out of His way to touch them and heal them of this dread
disease. Only one, a Samaritan, returned and gave thanks and
praise to God. Jesus then asked a provocative question: "Were
there not any found who returned to give glory to God except
this foreigner?" (Luke 17:18). In many ways, I think He is still
asking this question today.

Not Ashamed

For I am not ashamed of the gospel of Christ, for it is the power of
God to salvation for everyone who believes, for the Jew first
and also for the Greek. (Romans 1:16)

W e are living in a time in which people stand up for a variety of causes. People stand up for everything imaginable, and in some cases, they are even willing to lay down their lives for what they believe. Although we may not agree with what they are saying in some cases, we have to admire their courage for believing in something so strongly that they are willing to risk their lives for it.

Isn't it time that we, as Christians, stand up for what we believe? Romans 10:9 says that "if you confess with your mouth the Lord Jesus and believe in your heart that God has raised Him from the dead, you will be saved." What does it mean to confess the Lord Jesus? The very word "confess" gives us a clue. It is a word that means, "to be in agreement with." When I am confessing Jesus Christ, I am not merely acknowledging that He existed, nor am I just acknowledging that He is God. When I confess Jesus Christ before others, I am saying that I agree with Him. It is not enough to simply acknowledge that He has power and that He is moving in the lives of certain people. There must be a personal acknowledgement in which I have received Him as my own Savior and Lord.

In a day when so many are standing up for so many causes, it seems to me there are so many in the church who are not standing up for anything. Let's be willing to stand up and confess Jesus Christ before others.

Weekend

MAKE THE RIGHT CHOICE

"I have set before you life and death, blessing and cursing; therefore choose life, that both you and your descendants may live." (Deuteronomy 30:19)

W hen I first became a Christian, I decided that I would somehow find a way to live in two worlds. I was planning to hang out with my old friends and still be a Christian. For a time, I was sort of in a suspended state of animation. I wasn't comfortable with my old buddies, but I wasn't quite comfortable with the Christians either. So I decided to be Mr. Solo Christian. I even said to my friends, "Don't worry about me. You're thinking I will become a fanatic and carry a Bible and say, 'Praise the Lord.' It will never happen. I'm going to be cool about this. I won't embarrass you, but I'm going to believe in God now."

However, as God became more real to me and I began to follow Him more closely, He changed my life and my outlook, and my priorities began to change.

There are people who will discourage you from growing spiritually. They will say, "I think it's good you are a Christian. I go to church too: at Christmas and Easter, and for weddings. But you're getting a little too fanatical. You actually brought a Bible to work the other day. We were so embarrassed. You're no fun anymore. We're glad you have made changes in your life, but don't become too extreme." There are people like this who will discourage you.

When this happens, you have the choice to either do what God wants you to do or to go with the flow. Are you going to let people hold you back? Are you going to let people discourage you from wholehearted commitment to Jesus Christ?

Monday

AFTER THE DOVE

"The thief does not come except to steal, and to kill, and to destroy.
I have come that they may have life, and that they may
have it more abundantly." (John 10:10 NLT)

Often after great victories, the greatest challenges and temptations of the Christian life will come. I have found that after great blessings in my life, after God works in a powerful way, the devil will be there to challenge it.

Think about it. After God had powerfully worked through Elijah on Mount Carmel, the prophet became so discouraged that he wanted to die. After Jesus was transfigured, He came down from the mountain to find a demon-possessed person waiting for them. After Jesus was baptized in the Jordan River and the Holy Spirit came upon Him in the form of a dove and God said, "This is my beloved Son, and I am fully pleased with him" (Matthew 3:17 NLT). Then He was led into the wilderness to be tempted by the devil. After the dove came the devil.

The devil will always be there to challenge whatever God has done. It may come after church, after God has blessed you and spoken to you. You leave the parking lot and get hit with a heavy-duty temptation. You wonder how that could happen. But that is just the devil's way. He wants to make your life miserable. Most importantly, he wants to steal anything that God has done in your life.

The devil is watching us and he's looking for vulnerabilities. That is why we need to pray for any person whom we know that God is using. And that is why we need to brace ourselves. The more you step out to be used by the Lord, the more you can expect opposition from the devil.

Tuesday

GETTING TO THE ROOT

We use God's mighty weapons, not mere worldly weapons, to knock down the Devil's strongholds. (2 Corinthians 10:4 NLT)

So often when something is going wrong in our country, we want to organize a boycott or want to protest. But did you know that as believers, we have something more powerful than boycotts? It is called prayer, and the Bible tells us to devote ourselves to it (see Colossians 4:2). We need to pray for our country. We need to pray for people that need to hear the gospel. And we need to share the gospel. We need to share the good news of Jesus Christ with that woman who wants to abort her child. We need to share the gospel message with that man or woman who is trapped in the homosexual lifestyle. We need to share Christ with the gang members. We need to share Him with those in our society who are hurting. As people learn there is another kingdom, it will change the way they live in this one. Far too often, we Christians have been preoccupied with the symptoms in our society and haven't touched the root of the problem. The root is sin. The solution is the gospel.

So let's get the solution to the root. Our country needs to turn back to God. We keep thinking that a president will solve all of our problems. Or Congress will solve them. Or some program will solve them. But they won't be solved through any efforts of our own doing. We need to turn back to God. Let's tell others about Christ and not be so preoccupied with what they are doing because of their sin. Let's try to reach people where they are really hurting. And, let's always be sure we are praying.

SIMPLE THINGS

Because the foolishness of God is wiser than men, and the weakness of God is stronger than men. (1 Corinthians 1:25)

Have you ever wished you could do a miracle for friends or family members who weren't believers? You think, "If this happened, then they would believe." We think we need something dramatic or earthshaking. But so many times, God works in simple ways to reach people.

For example, I read about a hardened atheist who had a young daughter. He didn't want her to believe in God. So one day, he wrote down the words "God is nowhere" on a piece of paper and told his little girl to read them aloud. She picked up the piece of paper. She was just learning to read, so she sounded out her words and said, "God is .,. let's see, N-O-W-H-E-R-E. Oh, I understand, Daddy. God is now here." The atheist was so touched by that simple little event that he became a believer in Jesus Christ.

I'm reminded of a couple that attended one of our Harvest Crusades in Southern California. As they were walking down the street, they spotted a crumpled but colorful piece of paper on the ground. When they picked it up and smoothed it out, they discovered a Harvest Crusade flyer. They read it, and then prayed and received Christ. They also went to the crusade and walked forward at the invitation. What a simple thing God used: a little crumpled flyer that contained a gospel message.

So often we think we need something dramatic to reach nonbelievers. We need the greatest argument to reach them. And so often, God does His work in unexpected ways. God can use such simple things and speak in such simple ways. You just never know.

Thursday

HEARING GOD

"Your word is a lamp to my feet and a light to my path." (Psalm 119:105)

There are a lot of people today who say they hear the voice of God telling them to do thus and so. But what we must remember is that God will never contradict His Word. He will always lead us according to what the Bible says.

Some people come up with some lame concepts, such as "We're not married, but God has told us it's okay to have sex." I could assure them that God didn't say that, because in His Word He says, "You shall not commit adultery" (Exodus 20:14). God will not contradict His Word.

Let's say you were hoping for a letter from someone. You stand at the window, waiting for what seems like an eternity for the mail carrier to come by. Finally, he drives up and you bolt over to your mailbox. You're looking for that letter. Maybe it's from someone you're in love with. Maybe it's an answer to a job application. Maybe it's something you ordered in the mail. Maybe you've won the sweepstakes.

But imagine this. What if you had a handwritten note sent from God to you? Would you carry it around in your pocket for a couple of weeks and open it when you got around to it? I doubt it. You probably would tear it open as you're thinking, "Wow, God spoke to me! What does He have to say?"

The Bible is a written letter from God. A lot of us carry it. We have it in different colors and sizes. We have it in different translations. But we never read it. Yet it's a letter from God to us. If want God to speak to you, then open up His Word.

Friday

THE VOICE OF CIRCUMSTANCE

So Gideon said to God, "If You will save Israel by my hand as You have said—
look, I shall put a fleece of wool on the threshing floor; if there is dew on the fleece
only, and it is dry on all the ground, then I shall know that You will save Israel
by my hand, as You have said." (Judges 6:36–37)

Not only does God speak to us through His Word and not only will He never contradict His Word, but God also speaks through circumstances. Although I'm not one to base major life decisions on circumstances alone, clearly there have been times when I have sensed that something was the will of God and then things would fall into place circumstantially. At other times, circumstances have made it obvious that God was saying no.

A classic example of God speaking through circumstances was when God spoke to Gideon, who laid his fleece out on the ground, asking God to confirm His Word. Certainly Jonah got the right message when God brought his journey to an abrupt halt, and he found himself in the belly of a very large fish.

Of course, as a part of this process, God speaks to us through people. For example, there have been times when I have been listening to a someone preach or have been talking with a friend, and suddenly what he is saying addresses the situation I'm going through, even though he is completely unaware of my circumstances. It makes me realize that it is God himself speaking to me through those individuals.

Maybe God has spoken to you through a pastor or a Christian friend. Or perhaps He has been speaking to you through circumstances. Listen carefully, and remember that He will never contradict His Word.

Weekend

THE VOICE OF PEACE

For you shall go out with joy, and be led out with peace ... (Isaiah 55:12)

Not only does God speak to us through His Word, and not only does He speak to us through people and circumstances, but God also speaks to us through His peace. Colossians says, "Let the peace of God rule in your hearts, to which also you were called in one body; and be thankful" (verse 15). Another way to translate that verse is, "Let God's peace act as an umpire in your lives, settling with finality all matters that arise."

God's peace can act as an umpire in your life. He can settle with finality what you should do. Here's how it works. Maybe you think that something is the will of God. Circumstantially, things have fallen into place. You begin to proceed, but then you have a complete lack of peace. Something inside of you is saying, "Don't do it."

The Old Testament tells the story of a clever group of individuals known as Gibeonites, who lived in Canaan. God had instructed Joshua not to make any deals with the inhabitants of the land. So the Gibeonites put on old shoes and clothes and pretended as though they had come from a distant country. They told Joshua they had come to enter into an agreement with him. But Joshua unknowingly struck a deal with his enemies because he failed to consult the Lord.

Things can look good outwardly. Everything can seem right. Be careful. Learn to listen to that still small, voice. Learn to pay attention to that peace, or lack of it, in your life because that is one of the ways God will lead you. When you're in the will of God, you will have His peace.

Monday

WHEN TO RUN

"Run from anything that stimulates youthful lust. Follow anything that makes you want to do right. ... " (2 Timothy 2:22 NLT)

Some years ago, there was a story in the news about a man who had a tree fall on his leg. With no one around to come to his rescue, he took out a pocketknife and proceeded to amputate his leg. Then he made his way up the road and someone picked him up and raced him to help. Amazingly, this man who had a severed leg still had enough presence of mind to tell the driver of the vehicle not to go too fast. He said, "I didn't come this far to die on the road. Take it easy."

I remember reading that story and thinking, "He did what? How could this guy cut off his leg? I would have laid under the tree and just waited for help." But the doctors who treated him later said that if he wouldn't have taken such a drastic measure, he would have died. He did it to save his life.

Sometimes we must take radical, drastic steps to remove ourselves from whatever it is that is hurting us spiritually. That may mean immediate change. It may mean physically getting up and saying, "I'm out of here."

You might be at that party. In that movie. In that relationship. In that car. Wherever it is, you realize you shouldn't be there. God is convicting you. He is saying, "What are you doing here?" Don't be foolish. Just get up and go. That's not always possible, but many times it is.

Is there a relationship or a situation in which you don't belong? Has God been speaking to you about it? You'll be glad you took the time to listen.

Tuesday

SEIZE TODAY

*"For the eyes of the Lord run to and fro throughout the whole earth,
to show Himself strong on behalf of those whose heart is loyal to Him."*
(2 Chronicles 16:9)

What kind of people does God want to use? We find the same pattern throughout Scripture: the people God used were faithful in what He had placed before them. The people that God used for big things were people who were faithful in the little things. Perhaps you have considered dedicating your life to Christian service one day, maybe even in another country. That is a good and noble aspiration. But how about just serving the Lord where you are right now? How about seizing the opportunities around you today?

When God used David to defeat Goliath, he was on an errand for his father, taking food to his brothers on the front lines. But as he was faithful in a little way, God gave him more. We know that when God called Gideon to lead Israel, he was threshing wheat. When Elijah called Elisha into the Lord's service, he was plowing a field. When Jesus called Peter and John to become fishers of men, they were mending their nets. Not one of them was sitting around thinking, "I wonder if God will ever do anything in my life?" They were busy with the work at hand.

While we're looking for distant opportunities, we might miss the ones that are right in front of us. Are you serving the Lord right now with what He has called you to do? Be faithful in that. Do it well. Do it as unto the Lord. It may seem like your efforts go unnoticed, but there is someone who sees. And He will one day reward you openly.

DIVINE DISCIPLINE

God blesses the people who patiently endure testing. Afterward they will receive the crown of life that God has promised to those who love him. (James 1:12)

W hy does God bring tests into our lives? Is it because He wants to give us a hard time or embarrass us? No. It is because God wants us to learn. He wants us to mature spiritually. God wants us to learn to trust Him even when we don't understand Him. He wants us to be patient with Him even when He doesn't work according to our schedules.

The Bible says, "For whom the Lord loves He chastens . . ." (Hebrews 12:6). Although God will discipline you when necessary, the word *chasten* also means "to train." God wants to teach you. He wants you to grow. He loves you so much that He will bring a series of tests and lessons into your life to whip you into shape. Those very tests, those very difficulties, and those very obstacles all can be indications of God's love for you.

When you start to cross the line and do something you shouldn't, God's Holy Spirit will be there to convict you. When you try to do something that you know is wrong and God puts an obstacle in your path, it is because He loves you.

The times you should be concerned are when you can do things that you know are wrong and feel no remorse. But when you know something is wrong and struggle with it, that is a sign you are a child of God and He loves you enough to show you when you are going astray. Instead of seeing God's chastening as an intrusion in your life, welcome it. And be thankful He is looking out for you.

Thursday

THE TRAP OF TEMPTATION

"Therefore submit to God. Resist the devil and he will flee from you."
(James 4:7)

R ight after I became a Christian, other believers warned me, "Greg, watch out. There is a devil who will tempt you."

I said, "Right. A devil." I thought of the red figure with the pitchfork and horns.

They said, "No, the devil is real. He is a real spirit power and he will tempt you."

I said, "Get out of town. He is not going to tempt me."

I was in high school at the time, and there was a certain girl in my art class whom I sort of had a crush on. I hadn't mustered up the courage to walk up and talk to her. I was sitting in class one day as a brand-new Christian, and suddenly she walked up to me and said, "Hi. What's your name?" We had been in the same class for months, and she had never even acknowledged my existence.

I told her my name. She said, "You know, you're kind of cute. I'm going up to the mountains this weekend. Why don't you just come up with me? Let's get to know each other better."

I thought, "This is it. This is what they told me about. It's temptation!" I declined her invitation and realized there had to be something to what had just happened. I thought, "I'm not an idiot. No girl has ever come up to me and said this before. This is a set-up."

That experience made me want to follow the Lord even more, because I saw the reality of the spiritual world beginning to unfold. Remember, the devil wants to keep you from coming to Christ. And once you have come to Christ, he wants to keep you from moving forward.

Spiritual Casualties

*"Now the Holy Spirit tells us clearly that in the last times some will turn away
from what we believe; they will follow lying spirits and teachings
that come from demons." (1 Timothy 4:1 NLT)*

I t is clear that we are living in the last days. All around
us, we see signs being fulfilled before our very eyes that
Jesus and the prophets told us to look for. The Bible warns
that in the last days things would go from bad to worse (see 2
Timothy 3:1–13). The Scripture also warns that one of the
signs of the last days will be a falling away from the faith, or
an apostasy.

The question is, could you or I ever become one of those
spiritual casualties? Could you or I ever fall away from the
Lord? Without question, the potential, even the inclination,
to sin is clearly within us. I have the potential to fall. You have
it as well.

This is why we must give careful attention to the potential
pitfalls that Scripture describes. We must be aware of certain
things as we are living in the last days. As the apostle Paul wrote
in Romans 13, "The night is almost gone; the day of salvation
will soon be here. So don't live in darkness. Get rid of your
evil deeds. Shed them like dirty clothes. Clothe yourselves
with the armor of right living, as those who live in the light"
(verse 12 NLT).

This is not a time to be playing games with God and living
in half-hearted commitment to Him. The only way to survive
as a Christian and even flourish in these last days is to be
completely committed to Jesus Christ. Otherwise, we will be
easy targets for the tactics, strategies, and flaming arrows of
the devil.

Weekend

LIVING VICTORIOUSLY

*When the enemy comes in like a flood, the Spirit of the Lord will lift up
a standard against him. (Isaiah 59:19)*

I remember reading a story about one of the battles between
General Lee and General Grant during the Civil War.
General Lee was, of course, the head of the Confederate
forces and was known for his brilliant tactics in doing a lot with
a little. He did not have the organization of the Union army or
the manpower, but he was able to move in an effective way and
foil his enemies on a number of occasions. His exploits had
become so legendary that the Union soldiers were terrified of
him. One night, some Union soldiers were standing around
the campfire talking about General Lee. They said, "What if
General Lee does this? What are we going to do?"

General Grant was standing a few feet away. He walked over
and said to the soldiers, "The way you boys are talking, you
would think that General Lee is going to do a somersault and
land in the middle of our camp. Stop talking about what he's
going to do, and let him worry about what we're going to do."

Sometimes I see the same thing happening in the church:
*Oh, the devil is doing this. The devil is doing that. Did you hear about this
wicked thing that happened?* I think we should stop focusing so
much on what the devil is doing and stop worrying so much
about what he will do and instead let him worry about what we
Christians will do.

Rather than trembling in fear about what the devil is doing,
we can rejoice in the power that God has given us to live victo-
riously and effectively for Him.

Monday

THE LITTLE THINGS

Don't you realize that whatever you choose to obey becomes your master?
You can choose sin, which leads to death, or you can choose to obey
God and receive his approval. (Romans 6:16 NLT)

When I was a kid, I collected snakes. I thought they were just great, and I had them in all shapes and sizes. I met a man who collected venomous snakes and had worked in some type of zoo. I really admired him. He had been bitten by a tiger snake, which is the most venomous snake on earth, even worse than a cobra. This man survived the snakebite because he had been taking serum and had developed an immunity to the tiger snake's venom. As a result, this man basically thought he was indestructible, that no snake would ever take him down. He actually had cobras that had not been defanged slithering around loose in his house. One day in his home, he was bitten by a cobra and didn't realize it until later when his leg began to swell. He was rushed to the hospital and died. This man thought that because he had survived the tiger snake's bite, he didn't need to worry about cobras. That became his downfall.

Many times it is the little things that bring us down. Some Christians think, "I can handle this. I'm strong. I'll never fall." But we need to be careful. When we feel the most secure in ourselves, when we think our spiritual lives are the strongest, our doctrine is the most sound, and our morals are the purest, we should be the most on guard and the most dependent on the Lord. Sometimes the weakest Christian is not in as much danger as the strongest one, because our strongest virtues can become our greatest vulnerabilities.

Tuesday

CROSS-BEARING

When He had called the people to Himself, with His disciples also, He said to them, "Whoever desires to come after Me, let him deny himself, and take up his cross, and follow Me." (Mark 8:34)

Sometimes we say, "We all have our crosses to bear. My cross is my supervisor at work," or "My cross is this health problem," or "My cross is this relative." But I think we have lost the meaning of the cross. If you were living in first-century Jerusalem and saw someone surrounded by Roman guards and carrying a cross down the street, there would be no question in your mind regarding where that person was going. You would know he was about to be taken outside of the city, laid on the cross, and crucified. Someone carrying a cross was someone who was about to die. So when Jesus said, "Whoever desires to come after Me, let him deny himself, and take up his cross, and follow Me," His disciples would have understood what He meant.

Taking up the cross speaks of dying to ourselves and wanting God's will more than our own. It does not mean that your life is ruined when you decide to walk with God. What it does mean is that now you will have life and have it more abundantly as Jesus promised, because you want God's will more than your own. Jesus said, "Whoever desires to save his life will lose it, but whoever loses his life for My sake and the gospel's will save it" (Mark 8:35).

Are you taking up the cross and following Jesus? Bearing the cross will affect and influence every aspect of your life. The result will be life as it was meant to be lived: in the perfect will of God.

REMEMBER THE GIVER

"For unto us a Child is born, unto us a Son is given. ... " (Isaiah 9:6)

When people give Christmas gifts to each other, they usually think a great deal about it beforehand. A gift tells us quite a bit about the giver, doesn't it? You can estimate, more or less, what people think of you by the gifts they give you. On the other hand, we can all probably remember Christmases from childhood when we sometimes failed to fully appreciate what we had been given.

It seems to me that presenting gifts to one another is a very right and very good thing for us to do. I believe that in doing so, humanity is unconsciously helping to underscore the greatest and most important thing for us to realize about this day.

At Christmas, we must never forget that God the Father is the giver. Of course, it is natural and right that we should think about the child in Bethlehem, our blessed Lord, lying as a helpless baby in a manger. But let's never forget this: God is the giver. It was the Father who sent His Son into the world. It was the Father's purpose. It is God who "so loved the world that He gave His only begotten Son ... " (John 3:16). It is God who "sent forth His son, born of a woman, born under the law, to redeem those who were under the law ..." (Galatians 4:4).

There is no greater insult to a giver than when someone is more interested in the gift than in the giver. Let's never forget, therefore, that the Son of God was sent by the Father and that He was sent to bring us to the Father, the great and eternal Giver.

Thursday

No Greater Gift

Every good gift and every perfect gift is from above, and comes down from the Father of lights, with whom there is no variation or shadow of turning. (James 1:17)

Some of the most precious gifts tend not to attract our attention at first. We take a hurried glance and see nothing of significance. But if we go back and take another look, we begin to discover the glory and the wonder of that gift.

So it was with the helpless baby in the manger: He was the only begotten Son of God. Words cannot describe it, as Paul wrote in 2 Corinthians, "Thanks be to God for His indescribable gift!" (9:15). Even God couldn't give a greater gift than He has given. He gave His dearly beloved Son. He has given the One who was with Him from all eternity and sent Him into the world.

Our Lord Himself spoke of such a sacrificial act in His parable about the vineyard owner. The owner, who had unworthy servants looking after his property, sent his representatives and servants to the vineyard. One after the other was maltreated, even killed. Then the owner thought, "If I send my son, they won't do this to him. Surely they will respect my son. There is nothing beyond this. It is the last act."

Hebrews 1:1 says that God sent many servants into the world and to the nation of Israel. God has endowed and endued the world with many outstanding men and women. But God has surpassed them all with the gift of His Son.

This is what should fill our minds and hearts with astonishment at Christmas: that God has done something that even He Himself cannot exceed. He gave His only Son, His eternal Son, and sent Him into the world.

A DIVINE DEPARTURE

But when the fullness of the time had come, God sent forth His Son, born of a woman, born under the law, to redeem those who were under the law, that we might receive the adoption as sons. (Galatians 4:4–5)

When we think of Christmas, we think of the arrival of Jesus: "For unto us a Child is born, unto us a Son is given" (Isaiah 9:6). In reality, it was also a departure. For us, a Child was born. But for God the Father, a Son was given.

In heaven, the time had come for the departure of God's Son. We even have a record in Hebrews 10 of Jesus' farewell words to the Father. He said, " 'Sacrifice and offering You did not desire, but a body You have prepared for Me. In burnt offerings and sacrifices for sin You had no pleasure. Then I said, "Behold, I have come—in the volume of the book it is written of Me—to do Your will, O God" ' " (Hebrews 10:5–7).

Jesus literally went from the throne of heaven to a feeding trough. He went from the presence of angels to a stable of animals. He who was larger than the universe became an embryo. Scripture sums it up well: "Though He was rich, yet for your sakes He became poor . . ." (2 Corinthians 8:9).

No one who has ever lived has even remotely affected human history the way Jesus Christ has. He has been opposed, censored, banned, and criticized by every generation since His birth. Yet His influence continues unabated. There has never been anyone like Jesus, because Jesus was not just a good man. He was the God-man who came and walked this earth. And that is what we celebrate at Christmas.

Weekend

A Lesson from Mary

Now in the sixth month the angel Gabriel was sent by God to a city of Galilee named Nazareth, to a virgin betrothed to a man whose name was Joseph, of the house of David. The virgin's name was Mary. (Luke 1:26–27)

It is difficult for us to understand, two thousand years later, the significance of the angel Gabriel's appearance to Mary in Nazareth. After all, he could have found the future mother of the Messiah in Rome, the capital of the greatest power on earth at the time. He could have found her in Athens, the cultural center of the world, or at Jerusalem, the spiritual center of the world. But God chose Nazareth, an obscure but extremely wicked city that was notorious for its sin. Upon hearing that Jesus was from there, Nathanael said, "Can anything good come out of Nazareth?" (John 1:46).

What is amazing about Mary is that she lived a godly life in a godless place, and she did so as a very young teenager. Commentators believe she may have been as young as 12, but not much older than 14. Here she was, a nobody living in a nothing town in the middle of nowhere—precisely the kind of person that God goes out of His way to call. He chose an unknown girl in a relatively unknown city to bring about the most-known event in human history, an event so significant that we actually divide human time by it.

Maybe you are trying to live out your faith in a godless place today, maybe at work or school or among unbelieving family members. You're wondering if it can be done. It can. Mary stands as an example for us, proving that it is possible to live a godly life in an ungodly world.

Monday

MAKING ROOM FOR JESUS

And she brought forth her firstborn Son, and wrapped Him in swaddling cloths, and laid Him in a manger, because there was no room for them in the inn.
(Luke 2:7)

Imagine for a moment that it's your birthday and your friends and family have decided to throw you party. It isn't just any party. It's a mega party. Everyone that you know is there. There are gifts galore and the largest cake you have ever seen. Your name is strung in lights outside the house. Pictures of you are on display. Songs with your name in them are playing in the background.

But there is just one small problem with your birthday party. Someone forgot to invite you. At first, you think it is an oversight. You know they want you to be there. But when you arrive at the party, the music is so loud and everyone is so preoccupied that no one opens the door, even though you are pounding on it. Then you actually see some people notice you and say something to each other. But they go back to their conversation without stopping to let you in. What you don't realize is they have decided to just ignore you, assuming that you eventually will get tired of knocking and will go away.

I think Christmas has become like this for many people today. They string their lights. They decorate their trees. They listen to Christmas carols. They run around buying things for everyone they know. But how many people actually take time for Jesus? We often forget to make room in our schedules for Him.

This Christmas, will you make room for the things of God? Even Christians can become so busy that we forget about Jesus. Is there room in your life for Him?

Tuesday

GOD WITH US

"And she will bring forth a Son, and you shall call His name Jesus,
for He will save His people from their sins." (Matthew 1:21)

When an angel of the Lord appeared to Joseph in a dream, he was not only telling him that Mary had not been unfaithful as he had thought, but that she was the virgin spoken of by the prophet Isaiah: "The Lord Himself will give you a sign: 'Behold, the virgin shall conceive and bear a Son, and shall call His name Immanuel" (7:14). That prophecy, given 750 years before, would be fulfilled in Mary. The child she is carrying is Immanuel: God with us. What a staggering thought that must have been for Joseph. And what a staggering thought it is for us. It is really the essence of Christianity.

If you took the Christian faith and compared it to all other religious worldviews, this would be the clear distinction: Christianity is "God with us." Christianity does not require that we try to somehow earn God's approval. The Christian faith teaches that it is God with us, living inside of us, helping us to be the men and women He has called to be. Christianity says that we are never alone again. Jesus echoed this same thought when He said, "Lo, I am with you always, even to the end of the age" (Matthew 28:20). And in Hebrews 13, God said, " 'I will never leave you or forsake you' " (v. 5).

Maybe you need to be reminded of this right now. Maybe you are feeling alone. God is with you. Maybe someone close to you has let you down or disappointed you. God is with you. The great message of Christmas that we must always remember is this: "Immanuel: God with us."

MISSING THE POINT

And the light shines in the darkness, and the darkness did not comprehend it.
(John 1:5)

I read a newspaper article about a man who was having a little trouble with Christmas and was shooting off some steam. For this man, however, it resulted in a trip to jail. It all started when he went to put up Christmas lights outside, only to discover they were wadded up in a giant ball. Upset with his wife for balling up the lights, he was trying to untangle them when his daughter returned home in her car. She backed over the lights he had just managed to untangle. Needing to vent his frustration, he went into his backyard, pulled out his 45-caliber pistol, and began firing shots into the ground. Meanwhile, his family was decorating their Christmas tree. The police were called, who then came and arrested him for reckless endangerment. He told the officers that he had attended some anger management classes a few months before and thought that discharging his gun would help him discharge his anger.

This is a classic example of someone who was missing the whole point of Christmas. Certainly this time of year can be like that for many people. You can go to endless parties and malls, listen to countless Christmas songs, and can give gifts to everyone imaginable. Yet the One whose very birth, life, death, and resurrection we should be celebrating can be completely forgotten. Many of us become so preoccupied that we forget about the Lord.

They missed Christmas the first time around too. When Jesus was born in Bethlehem, by and large, most people did not grasp the significance of what had happened. They were too busy and preoccupied with other things.

Don't miss Christmas this year. Make room for Jesus.

Thursday

THE TROUBLE WITH HEROD

When Herod the king heard this, he was troubled, and all Jerusalem with him.
(Matthew 2:3)

The wise men who came from the East were men of great importance, VIPs. If they came to our country today, they would arrive with an entourage amid high levels of security. These were important people who came to Jerusalem and announced that it had been revealed to them that one had been born King of the Jews.

This was the wrong thing to say to a guy like King Herod. History tells us, as well as Scripture, that Herod was a paranoid tyrant. He always was worried about someone taking over his throne. In fact, he liked to refer to himself as the king of the Jews. To hear another described this way by foreign dignitaries was troubling.

The word, "troubled," used in Matthew 5:3 means, "agitated, stirred up, shaken up." Herod was shaken. Whenever Herod was stressed out, everyone was stressed out, because when Herod sensed there was a rival to his throne, he would start having people killed. By bitter experience, people knew that if Herod suspected a threat to his power, heads would roll. Literally. Herod viewed the dignitaries' announcement as a threat to his kingdom. So he sent word to have this so-called King of the Jews killed.

There are a lot of people like Herod today. They will not allow anyone or anything to interfere with their career, their lifestyle, or their plans. They see Jesus as a threat to all of that. They don't mind celebrating the birth of Jesus, as long as He stays in the manger as a baby. There are OK with God, as long as He stays out their lives. But like Herod, they miss what they have been searching for all along.

A DIFFERENT KIND
OF MESSIAH

He came to His own, and His own did not receive Him. (John 1:11)

When King Herod heard that one had been born King of the Jews, he summoned the chief priests and scribes to inquire where the Christ was to be born (see Matthew 2:4). They told him, "In Bethlehem of Judea, for thus it is written by the prophet ...' " (Matthew 2:5–6).

Not only did these religious leaders know the answer, but it appears as though they knew it right away. "The Messiah? Bethlehem is where He will be born." Then why weren't they looking for Him? Doesn't it seem a little unusual that foreign dignitaries had come from the East, claiming to have been led to that very area by some star, and were looking for one who is called the King of the Jews? Certainly that must have piqued their curiosity a little bit. Yet these theological experts could not even bother to walk a few miles to Bethlehem to find out whether the Messiah had indeed been born.

They knew the Word of God, yet they did nothing in response. They were too busy with themselves to be concerned about Jesus. In fact, when His public ministry began, they were Jesus' principal adversaries. They were looking for a different kind of a Messiah. They were looking for someone who would support their religious system and their chosen way of living, someone who would cater to their whims and conform to their wishes.

A lot of people today want Jesus, but they want Him on their own terms. They want the kind of Jesus who will not challenge them. These religious leaders were like that. They knew Scripture—they could quote it verbatim. Yet they did nothing to meet the living Savior.

Weekend

GIFTS FOR GOD

"For we have seen His star in the East and have come to worship Him."
(Matthew 2:2)

Christmas is a time of giving, and I've found it to be true that it is more blessed to give than to receive. If you are like me, you can't wait to give your gifts. When you get something for someone, you want to see the joy he or she has in receiving it.

The wise men brought gifts to Jesus: gold, frankincense, and myrrh. What kind of gifts are these for a child? Myrrh, after all, is an embalming element. Why give an embalming element to a baby? I believe these wise men had insight into who Jesus was. They gave Him gold because they recognized it was a proper gift for a king. They gave him frankincense because that is what a high priest used when he went into the temple to represent the people before God. They gave Him myrrh because they recognized that this king would die for the world.

What can we give to God during this holiday season? What do you give to God, who has everything? What does God want from us? He wants our lives. The greatest gift you can give to God this year is yourself. The greatest gift you can give to God is to enter into a brand-new year of opportunities and say, "Lord, I give You my life. I give You my talents. I give You my abilities. I give You my dreams. I give You my future. I give You my weaknesses. I offer myself to You. Here is my gift to You."

Let's be like these wise men and worship Him and give to Him. You will be glad you did, because you can never outgive God.

Monday

GIVING CHEERFULLY

"Don't give reluctantly or in response to pressure. For God loves the person who gives cheerfully." (2 Corinthians 9:7 NLT)

I don't know about you, but when Christmas rolls around, it seems there is always someone for whom I feel obligated to buy a gift. Although I don't really enjoy the process, I do it out of duty. On the other hand, it is exciting to buy a gift for someone you really love, isn't it? You look forward to it.

This is how God wants us to give to Him—not out of duty that says, "Oh, I had better give to God and help Him out." Or, "I guess I should help in the Sunday School. After all, God needs my help with those kids." Or, "I ought to go tell someone about Jesus, because God needs my help in getting the gospel out." If this is how we feel, then we should keep our money, keep our time, and keep our service, because God doesn't want them. Our hearts and our attitudes matter more to Him than our "gifts."

If you give your money, time, or anything out of duty, constraint, or an expectation of receiving something in return, then your motive is wrong and it won't count for anything before God. Your heart needs to be right first. Giving is a voluntary action. You don't have to do it if you don't want to.

Maybe you feel as though you don't have much to offer. God can do a lot with a little. Just take what you have, present it to Him, and say, "Lord, it isn't much, but here it is. It's yours." Then watch what God can do and how He can bless the life that has been dedicated to Him with a willing heart.

Tuesday

GIVING OUR BEST

"What can I offer the Lord for all he has done for me?" (Psalm 116:12 NLT)

A farmer who was known for his frugality owned a cow that gave birth to two calves. He said to his wife, "I am going to dedicate one of these calves to the Lord." Knowing his miserly ways, she was very surprised and asked which one he was planning to give to the Lord. "I haven't decided yet, but I'll let you know," he said. A few days went by, and again she asked which calf he was giving to the Lord. "I'm still thinking about it," he told her. Then one day, one of the calves got sick. It grew worse and worse, until one night the farmer walked up on the porch with the calf draped over his arms. He said to his wife, "Honey, I have bad news. The Lord's calf just died."

Many times we tend to give God that which we don't really want ourselves. Think about a typical day. What place do we give to the things of God? Maybe we utter a quick prayer as we roll out of bed or offer some hurried words of thanks over breakfast? Then we rush off to our responsibilities. At the end of the day, we say, "Oh, right. I'll give God these last four minutes as I'm dozing off."

If God is important, then why do we give Him our leftovers? God doesn't want our leftovers. In Malachi 1:7, God said to Israel, " 'You have despised my name by offering defiled sacrifices on my altar. Then you ask, "How have we defiled the sacrifices?" You defile them by saying the altar of the Lord deserves no respect.' "(verses 7–8 NLT).

God gave us His best. Let's give Him ours.

Wednesday

THE SMART THING TO DO

> *Do you not know that to whom you present yourselves slaves to obey,*
> *you are that one's slaves whom you obey, whether of sin leading to death,*
> *or of obedience leading to righteousness? (Romans 6:16)*

Whose slave are you? Maybe you believe that you are your own person, the master of your own destiny. But in reality, each of us yields or gives ourselves to someone or something. We are all slaves of someone or something.

I want to be a slave of God. The apostle Paul wrote to believers, "But now having been set free from sin, and having become slaves of God, you have your fruit to holiness, and the end, everlasting life" (Romans 6:22). This word "slave" was translated from a Greek word that would have been readily understood in that culture. It referred to a slave who had been bought off the auction block and was then granted freedom. In other words, the master would purchase that slave and then set him or her free. Slaves who were so thankful to their masters for such a compassionate gesture and wanted to voluntarily serve them would be designated as a "bondslave," meaning a slave by choice. The grateful slave was not a slave for pay or a slave out of fear, but a slave by choice—a loving servant. That is what Paul said he was, and that is also what we ought to be.

Whose slave are you? You're either a slave of God or you're a slave of sin. The choice is up to you. You can either yield to sin and pay the price and live a miserable life, or you can yield to God, giving Him your gifts, time, and future, and live life to its fullest. It's the smart thing to do.

Thursday

CONFORMED OR TRANSFORMED?

Don't copy the behavior and customs of this world, but let God transform you into a new person by changing the way you think. Then you will know what God wants you to do. ... (Romans 12:2 NLT)

A flock of wild geese was flying south for the winter when one goose looked down and noticed a group of domestic geese by a little pond near a farm. He noticed they had plenty of grain to eat. Life seemed relatively nice for them. So, he flew down and hung out with these geese until spring and enjoyed the food that was there. He decided that he would rejoin his flight of geese when they went north again. When spring came, he heard them overhead and flew up to join them, but he had grown a bit fat from all of the seed. Flying was difficult, so he decided to spend one more season on the farm and then rejoin the geese on their next winter migration. When the geese flew south the following fall, the goose flapped his wings a little, but he just kept eating his grain. He had simply lost interest.

That is what happens in the subtle process of the world influencing our lives. It is not necessarily dramatic, nor does it usually happen overnight. It is gradual, causing erosion in our lives as we begin to lower our standards. Soon, the things of God become less appealing, and the things of this world become more appealing. After awhile, we have no interest in the things of God.

We have a choice: either we will be conformed to this world, or we will be transformed by the renewing of our minds. It is one or the other. The only question is, which way will you go?

DESTRUCTION IN DISGUISE

Don't just pretend that you love others. Really love them. Hate what is wrong.
Stand on the side of the good. (Romans 12:9 NLT)

One of the first things I remember taking place when I committed my life to Jesus Christ was the erosion of bitterness and anger and the growth of a love I had not known before. Years of bitterness and anger that had been building up just began to dissolve. If we claim to be followers of Christ and harbor bitterness or hatred in our hearts toward someone, there is something very wrong. John was very distinct when he wrote, "If someone says, 'I love God,' but hates a Christian brother or sister, that person is a liar; for if we don't love people we can see, how can we love God, whom we have not seen?" (I John 4:20 NLT). John was saying, that if we have hatred in our hearts toward fellow members of the body of Christ, fellow Christians, there is something wrong in our spiritual lives.

Maybe someone has wronged or hurt you. Yet you are to love. You are to forgive. You are not to avenge yourself. Here is why: that bitterness and hatred will do more harm to you than the person to whom you are directing it. It will eat you up inside. It will destroy your life. It will hinder your time of prayer with God. It will hinder your worship. It will, for all practical purposes, act as an obstacle in the relationship God wants to have with you.

There is no room for hatred in the heart of a child of God. There is no room for bitterness. There is no room for prejudice. God wants our love to be honest, and He wants it to be without hypocrisy.

Weekend

NOT FINISHED YET

"For I know the plans I have for you," says the Lord. "They are plans for good and not for disaster, to give you a future and a hope." (Jeremiah 29:11 NLT)

I am an artist, and one thing I know that will often bother artists is when someone offers criticism on a work that is still in progress: "What is this? Well, I don't like the way it looks." But the critic doesn't see what the artist sees.

That is how we can be with God sometimes. "Hey, Lord, what are You doing here? What's the plan here? What do You have in mind here?" A literal translation of the phrase, "to give you a future and a hope," in Jeremiah 29:11 would be, "to give you an expected end." God has a plan in mind. You are a work in progress. While you see only the beginning and the present, God sees the end from the beginning. You see only what is happening now, but God sees what He will do in the future.

There is a great promise in Romans 8:28 that we should never forget, especially when we are going through difficulties: "And we know that God causes everything to work together for the good of those who love God and are called according to his purpose for them" (NLT). When life seems hard and it seems as though things are falling apart, here is God's personal pledge and promise to you: "All things are working together for good." He is control of all circumstances that surround the life of the Christian. As I have said many times, the word "oops" is not in God's vocabulary. So rejoice. God doesn't make mistakes. He doesn't forget about what He is doing. And He doesn't forget about you.

ABOUT
THE AUTHOR

The senior pastor of Harvest Christian Fellowship in Riverside, California, **Greg Laurie** began his pastoral ministry at age 19 by leading a Bible study of 30 people, which God has since transformed into a congregation that is among the eight largest churches in America. In 1990, Laurie began holding public evangelistic events called Harvest Crusades. Since then, nearly three million people have attended Harvest Crusades across the United States and in Australia. Laurie is the featured speaker on the nationally syndicated radio program, *A New Beginning*, heard coast-to-coast and overseas. He is also the featured host of the television program, *Harvest: Greg Laurie*, seen internationally. He is the author of a number of books, including the Gold Medallion Award winner, *The Upside-Down Church*. Laurie also has authored the study notes for two Bibles in the New Living Translation. He and his wife Cathe have two children and live in Southern California.